THE COMING REVOLUTION

THE
COMING
REVOLUTION

Signs from America's Past That
Signal Our Nation's Future

DR. RICHARD G. LEE

THOMAS NELSON
Since 1798

NASHVILLE   DALLAS   MEXICO CITY   RIO DE JANEIRO

Published in Nashville, Tennessee, by Thomas Nelson. Thomas Nelson is a registered trademark of Thomas Nelson, Inc.

Thomas Nelson, Inc., titles may be purchased in bulk for educational, business, fund-raising, or sales promotional use. For information, please e-mail SpecialMarkets@ThomasNelson.com.

Unless otherwise noted, Scripture quotations are taken from the King James Version.

Scripture quotations marked NKJV are from the New King James Version®. © 1982 by Thomas Nelson, Inc. Used by permission. All rights reserved.

Library of Congress Cataloging-in-Publication Data

Lee, Richard, 1946–
  The coming revolution : signs from America's past that signal our nation's future / Richard G. Lee.
     p. cm.
  Includes bibliographical references (p. 213–24) and index.
  ISBN 978-0-8499-4829-9 (hardcover)
  1. Christianity and politics—United States. I. Title.
  BR515.L43 2012
  261.70973—dc23   2011036213

Printed in the United States of America

12 13 14 15 16 QG 5 4 3 2 1

To my fellow countrymen,
past and present, who have
sacrificed so much for liberty,
justice, and the American way.

CONTENTS

ACKNOWLEDGMENTS

My deepest gratitude to the following individuals at Thomas Nelson Publishers who, through their time and many talents, helped to bring this book to print: Vice President and Publisher Matt Baugher, along with Paula Major, Emily Sweeney, Stephanie Newton, and Julie Faires; and Jack and Marsha Countryman, dearest friends, who have played such a vital role in all of my recent writings concerning God and country.

And finally to my longtime friend and scholar, Dr. Jim Nelson Black, who helped to bring my many thoughts together into this one volume.

As in most everything that has worth, it takes a great team working together, and this book is no exception. So to each of these team members and many more, I express a special thanks.

INTRODUCTION

W ho could have anticipated, even a year or two ago, that the
backlash against increasing government control we are seeing in Washington and in state capitals all around the country would
be happening now? The truth is, traditional conservatives and people
of faith have been speaking out about the direction of government
and the need for accountability for years. There have been books and
broadcasts of all kinds warning about the risks—I have produced a
number of them myself—but it wasn't until there was a critical mass
of concerned men and women willing to stand up and speak out that
such a moment could actually happen.

Led by their own deeply held convictions and the promptings of
their faith, men and women with highly visible public platforms helped
spread the word, and that vital spark has helped to set a whole range of
events in motion. The Restoring Honor rally on the Washington Mall
on August 28, 2010, was a striking example of that emerging spirit, but
it was just one event. There will be many others, so long as the need is
there and the will of the people remains as strong as it is today.

Surprisingly similar to those who birthed another Revolution on these shores 236 years ago, ordinary citizens are the real voices of this anti-big-government revolution. All they really want is to get back to the kind of government the Founders gave us in the first place. There are no signs of violence at the moment, and that is because most Americans are still optimistic that their voices are being heard by our newly elected officials. They believe the results of the 2010 midterm elections will help to restore power to the citizenry. The new conservative majority in the U.S. House of Representatives is moving toward less government spending and reduced regulations for the moment, but if something should happen to derail that progress or if enough people feel they are being disenfranchised by our political leaders, then anything could happen.

Many of the identical social and religious provocations that spurred the American colonists to revolt in the eighteenth century are present again today, inspiring a new generation of patriots to seek what the Founders called "a new birth of freedom." To appreciate where we are and where all these things can lead, I believe we will need a better understanding of our history and of why the founding documents were written as they were, granting unprecedented freedoms to the people and establishing the rule of law. If we understand the environment of the revolutionary era as well as the political conditions we are facing today, we will have a much better idea of how things will likely play out in the future, and that will be an important part of this book.

A NEW SENSE OF URGENCY

Revolutions don't just happen. They happen because of widespread frustration and a history of disappointments, insults, and provocations of many kinds that eventually compel people to respond. Whether they happen in politics or some other area of society, revolutions are always volatile phenomena. They generally come only after years of agitation, but they are never about just one thing. They result from a long list of offenses, both perceived and real, that set off a natural chain reaction that quickly becomes irreversible. And in the right environment, the situation can be explosive.

As Malcolm Gladwell pointed out in his 2000 bestseller, *The Tipping Point: How Little Things Can Make a Big Difference*, revolutionary change often comes suddenly and dramatically. When a large enough group of people reach a high enough level of frustration, they take action first by speaking out more and more forcefully. But if their concerns are ignored or rebuffed, and if there is no sign that things are getting better, there can be a sudden and momentous change of direction. It doesn't take much imagination to see that this is precisely what's going on in America today.

I am convinced we are on the threshold of a revolution of some kind. I don't believe it will be a violent revolution—it doesn't need to be. We have many other alternatives, and no one is suggesting that direct action will be needed. Thanks to the success and endurance of the Tea Party movement, we're seeing reasonable and measured resistance to the expansion of big government in this country, and it is peaceful resistance. Thousands of ordinary Americans are joining forces to challenge the direction our leaders have been taking us. For the most part these are all ordinary citizens, men and women from all walks of life, and people who have never been politically engaged in this way before. But through their combined efforts, they are speaking out with a new sense of urgency, determined to bring an end to what millions now perceive as arrogant and predatory behavior by Washington bureaucrats and other elected and unelected officials who wield too much power.

There is no mistaking the emotion or the intensity of those who are speaking out. The conservative news media have been talking about it for years now. But for the hundreds of thousands of men and women who came to Washington at their own expense to participate in Glenn Beck's Restoring Honor rally in August 2010, as well as for the millions who watched those events on TV or on the Internet, that was a monumental occasion. As a participant myself—and as a representative of the newest generation of what the Founders called the Black Robe Regiment—I can vouch for the powerful emotions we all felt.

That event was a way of making our grievances known in a respectful and honorable way. We came because we were upset with Washington, but we also realized that the surge of individuals' involvement in social and political issues today is of revolutionary proportions because a dramatic restoration of our constitutional values needs to happen. Those who came on that beautiful August day were of one mind: they all wanted to make a difference. They had seen what the Obama administration's idea of hope and change was all about, and they'd had enough.

EVIDENCE OF FAITH

The American people don't need to be reminded that this is not the first time a large-scale popular rebellion has taken place in this country. The first Revolution was preceded and inspired, I believe, by the Great Awakening—a powerful and seminal event. As I have reexamined and written about conditions during the nation's founding era over the past several years—and especially since completing my Foundation House studies at Oxford University, focusing on the relationship between the American Revolution and the Great Awakening—I have come to believe that we are in the early stages of another awakening, perhaps of even greater magnitude.

The Christian faith of the founding generation inspired their love of liberty and emboldened them to demand freedom from British rule, and the greatest expression of that love of liberty was visible in the Great Awakening from the 1730s to 1750s. The sparks of the American Revolution were fanned into flame by pastors and teachers—the Black Robe Regiment—who taught the people the biblical basis of personal liberty and obedience to the call of conscience. Today we're seeing a new wave of pastors and teachers who are speaking out about these issues, warning about the abuse of power by our public officials and stressing the importance of "restoring honor" in all areas of life.

What we are seeing is nothing less than a new American revolution: not with muskets and cannonballs this time but with ideas. It is a revolution of conscience, of morality, and of honor, dedicated to responsible social, moral, and political reforms. I confess I don't care too much for the word "change" these days, but vast numbers of men and women are standing up and speaking out, demanding change from the socialistic direction our political, judicial, and intellectual leaders have been taking us, and back to the values of the Founders.

By any measure, this is a time of monumental change. Washington's idea of change has failed, and that is why so many people are reacting as they are. We are witnessing a rebirth of the American Spirit and a recommitment to our cherished American ideals. And just as in that earlier Revolution, this one involves an amazing outpouring of religious commitment as well. We see it in the tea parties taking place from coast to coast, and we see it in the explosion of conservative book sales, the tsunami of grassroots activism, and the sudden appearance of a new generation of political leaders who are motivated by their Christian faith and who are having a tremendous impact in the voting booths.

GETTING OUR PRIORITIES RIGHT

This book is a response to the growing demand for information, insight, and inspiration. In it I will examine the connections between our Christian faith and responsible political action, focusing on the importance of personal liberty and showing how revolutions past, present, and future may be connected. In the final sections of the book, I will also take a brief look at the darker side of revolution, which emerged nearly a century ago in a formerly Christian nation, the Soviet Union, and which continues to threaten democratic institutions to this day.

It is my hope that a renewed appraisal and understanding of our nation's core values will motivate many people to take positive action in their homes, communities, workplaces, and especially the voting booths. The information contained in this book may be taken in a prophetic or predictive context, based on lessons learned from social conditions today as well as the events of the Great Awakening and the American Revolution. I conclude the book with a discussion of some of the ways every citizen can become involved now to help shape the future.

I am convinced that every one of the problems confronting this nation today can be solved through concerned citizen action. Lawlessness, economic insolvency, and government interference in people's lives can be stopped. Sound political action that arises from sound moral judgment and individual initiative can help turn the tide and restore order in all these areas. We have to make personal commitments to be involved for any of these things to happen, and most of all, we need to have our priorities right.

One of the most important things we can do is to follow through as the Founders did, not merely by changing our representatives in the state and national legislatures but by holding all our leaders accountable for their actions and insisting they serve as our representatives, not as irresponsible and unresponsive dictators. And, not least, we need to make sure our own houses are in order, that we have a resilient faith and express our reverence for the One who is the true Author of Liberty.

During the fall of 2011 we witnessed a very different expression of dissent, the so-called *Occupy Wall Street* demonstrations in the streets of New York and other American cities. While the protesters claimed to represent 99 percent of real America, researchers described them as "an unrepresentative segment of the electorate that believes in radical redistribution of wealth, civil disobedience and, in some instances, violence." Writing for the *Wall Street Journal*, former Clinton pollster Douglas Schoen said that more than half of the OWS crowds are serial protesters. Approximately 98 percent of those interviewed said they support civil disobedience, and 31 percent support the use of violence to achieve their goals. Some of those questioned by reporters could not explain coherently the issues they were protesting, and many admitted they were being paid by left-wing groups and labor unions.[1] These are not the voices of hope and change but of anarchy, dissipation, and despair. Groups such as OWS are likely to become more numerous in the days ahead as socialistic-minded elites become more and more fearful of the growing strength and number of outspoken conservatives who are beginning to rise up and be heard. The revolution that I see coming is a good and needful one, one of faith and virtue, of responsibility and positive action, and a radical return to the values and beliefs that made America great.

As I have spoken about these ideas from coast to coast, I have discovered that many people sense the hand of divine Providence moving in America today. Consequently we cannot help feeling we are engaged in something beyond the merely temporal and transitory concerns of the day. It is not just that we may be in the early stages of a popular rebellion but that we are part of a bold new awakening. The signs are all around us, and if we can grasp and reconsider the unique and extraordinary events that shaped our nation during its illustrious history, it ought to be possible to understand how many of those same factors that energized those events will prepare and propel us toward the Coming Revolution.

History does repeat itself, so with a better grasp of our history—focusing on the unique relationship between faith and freedom—we can gain a new understanding of the political, social, and religious events that are likely to occur in this country within the next few years. And that's a substantial part of what I feel compelled to say in these pages. It is my hope and prayer that many may be awakened, empowered by the Holy Spirit, and prepared for the events that will be taking place in our nation in the coming days.

—Richard G. Lee

One

PORTRAIT OF A NATION

What is the source of America's greatness? By any standard this country has a remarkable story to tell, with its dramatic history and an enviable record of achievements in almost any area you can think of. America is the world's longest surviving democratic republic, operating under the same Constitution and laws for the past 236 years. The nation enjoys the greatest level of personal liberty, the highest standard of living, the largest economy, the most dynamic commercial and industrial sectors, and the most consequential foreign policy of any nation—all of it defended by the best-trained and most technologically sophisticated military in human history.

But America is not merely the world's richest and most powerful nation. It is also the most benevolent, rushing to the four corners of the earth to bring relief to nations stricken by wars, famines, and disasters of every kind. Public and private charities, relief organizations, and international aid societies are constantly on the move, reaching out to "the least of these" wherever there is pain and suffering. They do it without pay and often without credit of any kind because they understand that the blessings of prosperity have made this nation a beacon of hope to the rest of the world.

On average, the American people give more than $300 billion each year to charitable causes. According to the most recent report from Giving USA, Americans donated more than $303 billion in 2009, $315 billion in 2008, and $295 billion in 2007. These donations are distributed among approximately 1.2 million IRS-registered charities and 350,000 religious congregations. This is in addition to the $25 billion the U.S. government spends each year in foreign aid to countries around the globe. Germany's foreign aid, by comparison, ranks second with contributions of about $13 billion.

Americans give the largest percentage of their charitable donations to religious organizations, at approximately $101 billion, followed by educational organizations at $40 billion, charitable foundations at $31 billion, human services organizations at $27 billion, and health organizations at $22.5 billion. Especially interesting is the fact that 65 percent of U.S. households with annual incomes less than $100,000 donate to charity.[1] Wealthy Americans may give more, but middle-class Americans give a larger percentage of their income. In addition to the financial gifts, America also leads the world in volunteerism, donating time and service to charitable and faith-based organizations. And that's a custom as old as the nation itself.

In the 1830s, the French statesman Alexis de Tocqueville visited America and was impressed by many things, but the one thing that really surprised him was the great number of "voluntary associations" in this country. In his classic work, *Democracy in America*, he writes:

> Americans of all ages, all stations in life, and all types of disposition are forever forming associations. There are not only commercial and industrial associations in which all take part, but others of a thousand different types—religious, moral, serious, futile, very general and very limited, immensely large and very minute. Americans combine to give fêtes, found seminaries, build churches, distribute

books, and send missionaries to the antipodes. Hospitals, prisons, and schools take shape in that way. Finally, if they want to proclaim a truth or propagate some feeling by the encouragement of a great example, they form an association.[2]

This spirit of generosity and commitment to worthy causes was unique in that day, he felt, and was matched only by the industry and imagination of the American businessman. When he looked at all the incredible achievements this country had racked up in less than a century, he marveled at the wealth of the American Spirit:

> The Americans arrived but yesterday in the land where they live, and they have already turned the whole order of nature upside down to their profit. They have joined the Hudson to the Mississippi and linked the Atlantic with the Gulf of Mexico across a continent of more than 500 leagues separating the two seas. The longest railways yet constructed are in the United States.[3]

Entrepreneurship and vision were the hallmarks of American business then just as they are today, but what Tocqueville found most compelling was the fact that everywhere he looked the citizens were working together, building things, giving freely of their time and labor. "I am even more struck," he writes, "by the innumerable multitude of little undertakings than by the extraordinary size of some of their industrial enterprises."[4]

Most of what this nation has achieved over the past three centuries is due, I believe, to the faith and character of the American people. These qualities are under great stress today, that's true, but where would the world be if it weren't for the resolute faith and indomitable spirit of America's pioneers? If you ask the average person to name our greatest achievements, many would no doubt point to education. As early as the mid-1600s, public education was already widespread in New England. Thomas Jefferson was among the first to formulate plans for universal public education, and by the end of the nineteenth century that goal had been accomplished.

America is also home to some of the world's leading universities—the whole world sends its sons and daughters to this country for the advanced studies that will allow them to succeed in whatever professions they may choose. The context and character of secondary and higher education have changed dramatically over the past half century—not for the better, unfortunately—but it's true nevertheless that the emphasis on education is among our most noteworthy achievements.

Visitors like Tocqueville, as mentioned above, have been impressed by such things as the vast network of railroads spanning the continent, but from the earliest days of the republic, we have profited from the contributions of individual inventors and innovators, such as Benjamin Franklin, who gave us the lightning rod, the Franklin stove, bifocal reading glasses, improved printing presses, and countless other inventions. The Wright brothers were among the first to discover the basic principles of lift and thrust in fixed-wing aircraft, which opened the door to modern aviation. Eli Whitney invented the cotton gin, which transformed the processing of cotton fiber and revolutionized the textile industry.

Thomas Edison, "the genius of Menlo Park," was granted more than one thousand patents during his life for his inventions with electricity, including the incandescent lightbulb, the telephone, the telegraph, and the motion picture camera. And there was Henry Ford, whose goal was not simply to build a better car, but to build an automobile that every family could afford. He built the first Model-T Ford in 1908—the Tin Lizzie—and shortly thereafter developed the concept of the assembly line, which revolutionized manufacturing the world over. George Eastman, who invented and popularized the Kodak camera, gave us the first portable and affordable cameras that anyone could operate. Such inventions have literally changed the world.

At the same time, American scientists and engineers have pioneered some of the most formidable advances in civil engineering, such as the construction of the Hoover Dam during the midst of the

Great Depression. It was a monumental undertaking, and it continues to provide electricity and water today for more than eight million people in the states of California, Nevada, and Arizona. Any list of American achievements in science would have to include the great strides this country has made in medicine and medical technology, improving the lives of billions around the world.

Advances in medical practice and emergency treatment save lives every day through fast-response trauma teams and state-of-the-art surgical procedures. Modern medicines have extended life-expectancy by decades while advances in audiology, dentistry, and optometry have improved the quality of life for millions more. America is still the only country to put a man on the moon or to send an unmanned rover vehicle to the planet Mars, some forty million miles from Earth. And I should also mention the successes of Hollywood, the cinema, documentary filmmakers, radio, television, and the broadcast media in all their various forms. No other medium has done more to inform, educate, and entertain us than the arts of broadcast and film.

Along with all of this, the telephone may be the real success story of our time. Telephone technology has come a long way since the days of Alexander Graham Bell and Thomas Edison, giving us the Internet, high-speed local- and wide-area networks, cellular telephones, the iPhone and iPad, and countless other modern inventions. America leads the world in the development, distribution, and commercial success of all these modern marvels, and has unleashed a new era of mass communications.

No one disputes the importance of these things, but few realize that none of them would have happened if it weren't for the even greater achievements in political discourse: specifically, the Declaration of Independence and the Constitution of the United States, including the Bill of Rights. These two documents, which for the first time in history laid out the principles of limited government and natural rights in a precise, ordered, and prescriptive manner, are America's gift to the world. The War of Independence that led to the establishment of this new nation was not simply a blow for personal freedom; it was above all a statement of the value the American people place on liberty and freedom of conscience for all people. And it was a statement of our willingness to defend those liberties at home and abroad.

AMERICA'S GREATEST ACHIEVEMENT

As we consider these various achievements, it's important to recognize that the true source of America's greatness is not merely the inventions and creature comforts we've accumulated over the years but the wisdom and vision that made them possible. That legacy comes to us from men such as John Adams, Thomas Jefferson, James Madison, Benjamin Franklin, and George Washington, through the values and beliefs they enshrined in our founding documents. Among the greatest gifts one generation could ever give to another are freedom of worship, freedom of speech, freedom of the press, freedom of association, and the right to a fair and just hearing. These were all gifts from the Founders.

It is important to understand, furthermore, that these liberties are the outward expressions of our Judeo-Christian heritage. When the Pilgrims left the safety and comfort of their homes in Europe to cross an angry sea and plant the first colonies in the New World, they were guided by their strong Christian faith. The principles they lived by have been the cornerstone of America's success for the past 250 years and are still the moral compass we follow today. Despite the claims so often repeated these days that the Founders were simply Deists who believed in a watchmaker God who left the creation to fend for itself, we now know that fifty-two of fifty-six Founding Fathers were devout believers in Jesus Christ.

I have written about this in previous works and won't recite all the evidence here, but even the man whom most people agree was the least religious of the Founders, Benjamin Franklin, knew that no great nation would ever rise upon these shores without the aid and intervention of a great and wise God. In one of the most surprising speeches of the revolutionary era, the sage of Philadelphia reminded his colleagues in the Continental Congress that, "Except the LORD build the house, they labour in vain that build it" (Psalm 127:1). He then petitioned that body, which had been hopelessly mired in debate, to begin each day's deliberations with prayer. The delegates were humbled by his words because they knew he was right. They paused then for a time of prayer, and they vowed to pray every day in the same manner until they had resolved their differences. The document they produced has guided this nation ever since, and it was even hailed by an English prime minister, William Gladstone, who said, "The American Constitution is, so far as I can see, the most wonderful work ever struck off at a given time by the brain and purpose of man."[5]

The story of America's greatness is not only about glory and triumph. Some of the nation's greatest achievements were only made possible by the adversity our ancestors endured. Between 20,000 and 25,000 Americans lost their lives in the American Revolution, and nearly the same number were seriously wounded. Despite the risks, they were willing to sacrifice their lives for the great prize of independence and individual liberty. More than 600,000 Americans died in the Civil War, but that struggle preserved the nation and transformed our understanding of human and civil rights. Add to that the more than 115,000 Americans who died in the First World War and the 292,000 in the Second, and you have a glimpse of the enormous price our predecessors paid to keep this country free.

More than any other nation, including all the great empires of the past, America has spread the dream of liberty around the world and helped to bring a higher standard of living to untold millions. And like those ancient empires, which were the standard-bearers of culture and learning for a time, today America has been entrusted with transmitting the blessings of freedom. More than mere business connections or scientific expertise, what America has to share with other nations is our appreciation of the values of integrity, self-discipline, and self-determination passed down to us by the Founders. Whether it's in regard to politics or economics or industry or any of the modern disciplines, we will find that in every area America's greatness is founded upon the moral and religious values of those pioneers.

As the scholar and historian Russell Kirk has written, "Every people, no matter how savage or how civilized, have some form of religion: that is, some form of belief in a great supernatural power that influences human destiny."[6] Culture, Kirk said famously, comes from the cult. That is, the distinctive qualities and customs of every culture arise from the religious beliefs of its people. The Communists attempted to deny the existence of God and made atheism the only acceptable form of belief. But as the Soviet Union's collapse in 1989–1990 made clear, the empire had failed to stamp out religious faith completely, and today Christianity is thriving once again in the former Soviet bloc. The Communists discovered that no nation can survive for long without a foundation of sound moral principles.

Concern for the well-being of others is one of the key traits of good character. Unfortunately, we see less and less of that these days. And when we see rising crime rates, evidence of corruption in business and government, the breakdown of the family, the increase in out-of-wedlock childbirths, the ongoing tragedy of abortion, and a rising climate of immorality and vulgarity in the popular culture, we have to wonder if our great moral heritage can survive. Author and attorney Charles Colson has written that, "A nation or a culture cannot endure for long unless it is undergirded by common values such as valor, public-spiritedness, respect for others and for the law; it cannot stand unless it is populated by people who will act on motives superior to their own immediate interest."[7]

The American ideals of freedom and individual rights, charity, duty, honesty, and love for others are, above all, religious beliefs. Even though America is less visibly a religious nation today than it was a century ago, it is the depth and strength of the foundations laid down by our Christian forebears that have allowed us to thrive in the twentieth and twenty-first centuries. And, even with all our struggles and doubts, we are still living on the dividends of that investment.

America's success in almost any area is a tribute to the beliefs that shaped the American character. "These beliefs," writes Russell Kirk, "are the fatherhood of God, the brotherhood of man, and the dignity of man. From these beliefs have developed Christian convictions as to how we should conduct our lives, how we should treat our fellow human beings, and what makes life worth living."[8] Even though we may be troubled by growing hostility toward our Christian faith and the increasing coarseness of American culture, we can be certain that God will not give up on this country so long as a faithful remnant continues to seek His favor and proclaim these truths.

THREATS FROM WITHIN

The problem is that we have already come a long way down the road of dissolution, and it will take more than a little effort to recover our losses. According to the most recent Census Bureau reports, the number of people between the ages of twenty-five and thirty-four who have never married is now greater than those who have married. This has never happened before in our history—or in world history for that matter. Married adults now make up just 52 percent of the population, which is the lowest level since records have been kept.[9]

This has a direct impact, of course, on the illegitimacy rate, which is now almost 41 percent overall, and 72 percent among African Americans.[10] No wonder so many young people find themselves trapped in chaotic and empty lives. The link between illegitimacy and poverty is well documented, and the link between poverty and crime is undeniable. Senator Daniel Patrick Moynihan was among the first to warn the nation what was in store for this country if the breakdown of the traditional family persisted. In a stern warning penned in 1965, he said,

> From the wild Irish slums of the nineteenth-century Eastern seaboard
> to the riot-torn suburbs of Los Angeles, there is one unmistakable
> lesson in American history: A community that allows a large number

of young men to grow up in broken families, dominated by women, never acquiring a stable relationship to male authority, never acquiring any rational expectations about the future—that community asks for and gets chaos . . . [In such a society] crime, violence, unrest, unrestrained lashing out at the whole social structure—these are not only to be expected, they are virtually inevitable.[11]

A complex society such as ours is made up of a whole range of unspoken commitments. We agree to respect one another's privacy, property, and personal dignity. We agree to abide by a code of ethics, legal and moral restraints. We agree to care for our loved ones and family, and to be responsible members of our community. We also agree to pay our taxes, participate in free elections, and contribute to the common defense. But what happens when those commitments no longer matter? What happens when young men and women give up on marriage and responsible family formation? What happens when a generation of young Americans, or more than one, is abandoned to the wasteland of idleness, drugs, and premarital sex?

When a culture is vital and thriving, we take our roles as citizens seriously. We agree to support causes that are worthy and to avoid behaviors that are destructive. These commitments are part of the common code of decency passed down from one generation to the next. Although there are individuals in the media, the popular culture, and the halls of academia who insist these old-fashioned ideas no longer matter, we need to remember what the Soviets learned after seventy years of communism: no nation can survive for long without a body of sound moral principles.

In a small but important little book called *The Broken Hearth: Reversing the Moral Collapse of the American Family*, former secretary of education William Bennett makes the case that the American family is the most important incubator of the values that allow individuals and their communities to prosper. Healthy families instill values and beliefs that are essential for happiness and success. Among these are the habits of trust, altruism, personal responsibility, and mutual obligation. Unfortunately the well-being of the American family has been subverted in recent years by a sustained assault on marriage and family, and the evidence of that is not a pretty sight. Bennett writes:

> Since 1960, the divorce rate has more than doubled, out-of-wedlock births have skyrocketed from one in twenty to one in three, the percentage of single-parent families has more than tripled, the number of couples cohabiting has increased more than elevenfold, the fertility rate has decreased by almost half. In record numbers, we have seen fathers deserting their wives and children—and being permitted to do so without reproach or penalty of any kind. We have seen stay-at-home mothers mocked.[12]

Throughout most of human history marriage has been regarded as a sacred covenant, yet today we are told that marriage and family life are a burden, outdated customs with little or no importance. Unfortunately it is not just the rock stars and teen idols who are propagating this nonsense, Bennett writes, but "feminists, academic analysts with an agenda, and libertines masquerading as liberationists."[13] There are celebrities and popular television personalities who would have us believe that "sin is in" and faith in God is a dangerous myth. Those assumptions are not only false but dangerous to our entire way of life. As Bennett concludes, "There is a natural order that we may build on and improve but that we attempt to do away with at peril of the very fabric of our lives, our happiness, our true and solid contentment. Too many of us have attempted to do just that and have reaped a whirlwind."[14]

You don't have to spend a lot of time browsing the morning's headlines to recognize the levels of controversy and chaos that pervade American society these days. The nation is socially, politically, and morally divided on so many issues; immersed in disputes of one kind or another; and wrangling over questions unimaginable just a few years ago. It often seems as if everything is now up for grabs.

The Pledge of Allegiance, which every American ought to be able to recite with pride, has become a topic of debate in many places, and concepts such as American exceptionalism and manifest destiny are either forgotten or ignored by the mainstream culture. Simply flying the American flag is considered controversial in some places, and posting the Ten Commandments in schools or public buildings is out of the question. All of this compels me to ask, are we still "one nation under God"? Is this once-proud nation of immigrants from every corner of the globe still, in fact, "indivisible"? The red and blue maps emblazoned across the front pages of newspapers and websites after every election tell pretty much the same story. The social consensus is fragmented. We are a nation of red and blue states, red and blue counties, and even red and blue neighborhoods. Our political and cultural differences are magnified by the media to such an extent that we often wonder if the republic can survive.

Not long ago we learned that Washington lawmakers were working behind closed doors, plotting and planning through the night to pass a massive health-care bill and other legislation they knew the American people had overwhelmingly rejected. The results of the 2010 elections were a partial response to that, but we still have many areas of concern. With shocking regularity, the courts have been handing down edicts, overruling the voters on important social issues, defying both common sense and traditional moral values. At the same time, the mass media are continually bombarding us with coarse and violent images that stagger the imagination.

TRUE STRENGTH OF CHARACTER

It would be easy to lose hope in this environment, but sometimes in the midst of all the noise and confusion we hear about an act of kindness that gives us renewed hope that the American Spirit is not dead just yet. We want to believe that, deep down, there is still something good and decent about the American people, and I don't think that is a false hope. The courage and resolve that made this the greatest, freest, and most prosperous nation on earth refuse to fade away, and every once in a while we witness a spark of humanity that reminds us of that fact. We are still a God-fearing people. And despite the bickering and name-calling, there is still a strong sense that we're in this thing together.

That is how many of us felt when we first heard the story of Captain Chesley "Sully" Sullenberger, who was the pilot on U.S. Airways Flight 1549 from New York to Charlotte on January 15, 2009. Shortly after takeoff that afternoon, Captain Sullenberger radioed the tower that his plane had hit a large flock of birds, and at least one engine was on fire. They talked about landing the Airbus A320 at another airport but soon realized that was going to be impossible. Sully knew they would never make it, so he decided to ditch the plane in the only place where his passengers might actually survive: Manhattan's Hudson River.

Hundreds of men and women standing on the embankment, driving their cars on the parkway that runs alongside the river, and sitting in the skyscrapers nearby watched in amazement as Sully maneuvered his plane toward the middle of the river and then splashed down with the fuselage and both wings resting safely on top of the water. Coast Guard and Port Authority boats, as well as a couple of sightseeing boats, quickly encircled the aircraft to pick up the stranded passengers and crew.

Then after two quick tours of the cabin to make sure no one was left onboard, Captain Sullenberger grabbed the pilot's log from the cockpit and joined the others. He was the last man out, and moments later, as the rescue boats were making their way to shore, the plane began listing to one side and then slipped farther into the water.

When reporters looked into everything that happened that day, they discovered that life had prepared Sully Sullenberger for that moment. He had learned to fly airplanes as a teenager, attended and graduated from the Air Force Academy near the end of the Vietnam War, and flown fighter jets in the military. He had become an expert on aviation safety and had spoken to professional groups about maintenance and safety procedures. Later when he was interviewed on national television about the events of that day, Sullenberger said, "One way of looking at this might be that for forty-two years I've been making small, regular deposits in this bank of experience: education and training. And on January 15 the balance was sufficient so that I could make a very large withdrawal."[15]

That's a nice way of putting it, but it isn't the whole story. Captain Sullenberger's first concern was the safety of the people on that plane, and this was what motivated his heroic actions. Certainly education and training can help prepare a person for making critical decisions, but other things are needed as well—things such as faith, courage, determination, and love for others. Captain Sully's words inspired a lot of people and reminded us what really matters, but they also reminded us of all the brave men and women who serve this country in times of crisis.

Who will ever forget the example of the New York firefighters who raced into the World Trade Center in the aftermath of the 9/11 terrorist attacks, knowing they might never return? The towers were weakened—smoke and debris were everywhere—it was just a matter of time until they began to collapse. But people were dying in those buildings, and there was no time to waste. Without hesitation the firefighters climbed the stairs, hundreds of them, with no thought for their own safety, guiding thousands toward the exits, bringing hope and relief and renewed determination to men and women who might otherwise have been stranded in those doomed towers.

Those public servants weren't in it for the money. Not one of them was looking for glory. They could have refused to go up, but they accepted the risks and went in because they believed in something greater and more enduring than their own personal safety—the call of duty, the love of others, and the pledge that each of them had made to defend, protect, and serve. Like thousands of police officers and firefighters all across this country who risk their lives each day, the New

York firefighters embodied the finest traditions of honor and bravery. And a grateful nation will never forget what they did.

It's important to remember that spirit of caring and compassion when we are constantly bombarded by bad news. The shooting of Arizona congresswoman Gabrielle Giffords by an irate gunman on January 10, 2011, was yet another reminder that there is still a lot of senseless violence in our streets. But even in that case, where more than a dozen people were wounded or murdered by a deranged psychopath, it was the courage and heroic actions of ordinary Americans who risked their lives to subdue the shooter and render aid to the injured that will be remembered long afterward.

Later that day during a live TV interview with NBC's Brian Williams, one of the heroes made the comment that those of us living in the age of 9/11 can no longer just stand by and watch when something bad is happening. We have to be prepared to jump in and resist evil, to take a stand even when it means almost certain peril. I thought that was a perceptive observation. Unfortunately, it is a lesson that can only be learned through adversity.

We've all heard stories of cowards who stand by and watch when innocent people are being victimized or people who refuse to get involved because it is inconvenient or dangerous. But I think there is less of that today than there was a decade ago. One of the best examples of that sort of bravery is the story of the five young men who rushed the cockpit of United Flight 93 to stop a fourth group of 9/11 terrorists from crashing that plane into the White House or the Capitol building. During cell phone conversations with wives and friends back home, the young men learned that two planes had already struck the twin towers in New York and a third had hit the Pentagon. Then, when they realized their own plane was being hijacked, those five brave men— Todd Beamer, Jeremy Glick, Mark Bingham, Tom Burnett, and Lou Nacke—decided to take action. It was an all-or-nothing gamble, and they knew it could ultimately cost them their own lives, but they were determined to stop the terrorists in their tracks.

Most of us remember the rest of the story: there was a violent struggle in the cockpit; the plane spiraled out of control, then crashed in a field in Shanksville, Pennsylvania, approximately 125 miles from Washington, DC. Although America still grieves the loss of the passengers and crew of United 93 and the heroes who refused to let an even greater disaster take place on their watch, their actions gave the nation a new sense of hope at a very difficult time. Since that day the heroes have been memorialized for their bravery. Books and articles have been written about them, and Todd Beamer's call to action, "Let's roll!" has become a rallying cry that will be remembered forever.

Just thinking about that amazing act of self-sacrifice reminds us once again of the inner core of goodness that still survives, as strong as ever, in so many Americans. Hearing about such acts of valor brings things back into focus. It is as if we have to experience such horrors before we understand what really matters. And when there is so much disappointment and self-doubt all around us, it helps to know there are still people who care enough to risk everything for others.

BEYOND THE CALL OF DUTY

Jesus said, "Greater love hath no man than this, that a man lay down his life for his friends" (John 15:13), and that is the story of another American hero, Marine Corporal Jason Dunham, who served in Iraq during Operation Iraqi Freedom. In the spring of 2004, Jason was a team leader with the 3rd Battalion, 7th Marines. While on patrol in the village of Husaybah, Iraq, his team spotted a suspicious-looking individual in a white SUV. As they approached the vehicle, the man jumped out and began threatening the marines. During the brief struggle that ensued, Jason realized the man was going to throw an armed grenade. As soon as he saw it, the corporal yelled to his men to take cover. Then, in a flash, he knocked the grenade from the man's hand, took off his Kevlar helmet and covered the grenade, then threw himself on top of it.

Wall Street Journal reporter Michael Phillips, who was embedded with Jason's battalion at the time, was so moved by the young man's act of bravery that he told the story in his book, *The Gift of Valor*. Corporal Dunham had less than five seconds to make that fateful decision, Phillips wrote, but he didn't hesitate to sacrifice himself for others. If he hadn't reacted so quickly, the carnage would have been much worse, but Jason Dunham willingly gave his own life to save his fellow marines.[16]

Corporal Dunham survived in a coma long enough to be evacuated to Bethesda Naval Hospital in Maryland. The magnitude of his wounds was just too great, but his mother and father were at his bedside when Jason died eight days later. They were heartbroken, but they nevertheless understood the courage and commitment that had motivated their son's actions.

On January 11, 2007, President George W. Bush presented the Medal of Honor to the Dunham family in a ceremony at the White House. Afterward, Jason's father said he wanted everyone to understand that while he was proud of his son's act of bravery, these are the types of heroic actions our young service men and women are prepared to perform every day. They are all heroes, he said.[17] And we can't help but ask, as many others have asked before, where do we find such brave men and women?

The answer, I believe, is that we find them among people who understand the true meaning of duty, honor, country, and all those fine virtues the mainstream culture loves to ridicule and disdain. We find them among people who have seen the arrogance and selfishness of those who refuse to risk anything for anyone else and have rejected that kind of thinking. Even if we sometimes feel that decency and concern for others are disappearing from our culture, it's encouraging to discover it is still there, and there are still men and women willing to go beyond the call of duty.

If we want to see our communities restored, mothers and fathers will need to instill self-discipline and good judgment in their children, teaching them by example. Our churches will need to teach the precepts of faith, hope, and love; and the schools ought to be teaching our children the importance of personal responsibility and self-respect. But for these lessons to be understood and applied, there has to be something even more essential: there has to be an awareness that we are not alone. We are part of a family, a community, and a nation; and the privilege of citizenship in this great nation means that we have a number of important rights and responsibilities.

The Founders believed education was an essential component of citizenship, as was instruction in moral and religious values. The Northwest Ordinance of 1787 expressed it this way: "Religion, morality, and knowledge, being necessary to good government and the happiness of mankind, schools and the means of education shall forever be encouraged."[18] Schools, they said, were entrusted with the task of helping to mold the character of young people, and the Christian faith was a vital part of that.

Benjamin Rush, a signer of the Declaration of Independence and delegate to the Continental Congress, offered this counsel:

> Let the children who are sent to those schools be taught to read and write and above all, let both sexes be carefully instructed in the principles and obligations of the Christian religion. This is the most essential part of education. The great enemy of the salvation of man, in my opinion, never invented a more effectual means of extirpating Christianity from the world than by persuading mankind that it was improper to read the Bible at schools.[19]

The constitution of the commonwealth of Massachusetts at that time went even further, stating that, "It is the right, as well as the duty, of all men in society, publicly, and at stated seasons, to worship the Supreme Being, the Great Creator and Preserver of the Universe. . . ."[20] It may be surprising to some people to realize that this was the common view of practically all Americans during the founding era, and for more than a hundred years afterward. But no one expressed the views of the citizens of New England better than our second president, John Adams, who said,

> [I]t is religion and morality alone which can establish the principles upon which freedom can securely stand. . . . We have no government armed with power capable of contending with human passions unbridled by morality and religion. . . . Our constitution was made only for a moral and religious people. It is wholly inadequate to the government of any other.[21]

There is no way to explain away such statements. The United States of America was founded on Christian principles because the Founders were building a nation and laying the foundations for an empire. They understood that good citizenship demands good character. They were well educated, steeped in the history of great nations of the past, and they knew that no nation can survive unless the citizens are infused with the principles of sound moral judgment from their earliest years. The president of the Continental Congress, Elias Boudinot, explained why this was so important: "Good government generally begins in the family," he said, "and if the moral character of a people once degenerate, their political character must soon follow."[22]

Men and women with shabby morals and weak character cannot be expected to sustain a great nation. They can't vote wisely, lead productive lives, or educate their own children. The Founders understood that character and virtue grow out of the spiritual truths we learn in our earliest years, but that view is no longer taught in the nation's public schools and universities. Over the past century, our leading educational institutions have made Christianity virtually unmentionable—not just prayer in the schools but any mention of Jesus Christ or the beliefs of at least 80 percent of the American people.

Even though all of our first universities—including Harvard, Yale, Princeton, Dartmouth, Brown, and Columbia—were founded as Christian institutions with seminaries to train clergy and educate future leaders of the republic, today's educators no longer tolerate those beliefs. Instead of sound moral instruction, students on thousands of campuses all across the country are being exposed to a steady drumbeat of anti-Americanism, race and gender hostility, and a preoccupation with social and sexual experimentation. Classes and entire academic departments are devoted to "oppression studies," "women's studies," "queer studies," and other forms of politically correct programming.

At many schools, incoming freshmen are required to attend mandatory sensitivity training sessions and seminars on race and gender. Dorm counselors are expected to hold encounter sessions in which new students are indoctrinated into the pro-homosexual campus culture through role-playing and other types of psychological manipulation. The campus code words *diversity* and *tolerance*, which are so pervasive, are simply a mask for the anti-American, hypersexualized, pro-homosexual, and anti-Christian bias that is now the norm in the vast majority of our colleges.

With all this happening on high school and college campuses, how can we expect our young people to develop the character and commitment to duty that will make them good citizens? American sociologist Paul Hollander has described the modern university as "the reservoir of the adversary culture."[23] Rather than teaching our bright young men and women to respect their country and its heritage of freedom and self-reliance, professors and administrators have created an environment that is openly hostile to the beliefs and aspirations of the Founders.

Silly ideas we laughed at back in the 1960s are now the reigning dogma on many of America's most prestigious campuses. Students are taught that all values and beliefs are relative, that truth is in the eye of the beholder, that conventional religion is a myth, and only science and mathematics are to be trusted. Subjects such as history and literature have become vehicles for indoctrinating students in the doctrines of multiculturalism and diversity. Our children are taught by their sociology professors that the American way of life is no better than that of the most backward tribes. And for purveyors of the environmental movement, our way of life is a threat to global ecology. Some members of that movement claim that human beings are the problem, so the number of people on the planet needs to be dramatically reduced to save the earth.[24]

Concepts such as civic virtue, character building, and moral restraint, on the other hand, are scorned by faculty members while the false doctrines our parents rejected, including communism and Marxism, are applauded. I am told by university associates that the surest path to tenure for young professors these days is to espouse a Marxist interpretation of their academic discipline. And the surest way to be denied tenure or fired is to let it be known that you have a Christian worldview.

The greatest evils are no longer sloth, gluttony, envy, and pride, but capitalism and Christianity, which are openly mocked in some places. As one recent study puts it, "Since the social revolution of the sixties, the agenda of the Left has been to transform the United States into a socialist utopia; consequently, the issue of greatest concern on America's most distinguished university campuses is no longer traditional learning but a new form of social and sexual indoctrination."[25]

ASSESSING THE DAMAGE

"Professing to be wise, they became fools, and changed the glory of the incorruptible God into an image made like corruptible man . . ." (Romans 1:22–23 NKJV). So wrote the apostle Paul, proving that, ages before today's radical professors came onto the scene, such behaviors were well known. Sadly, the results were much the same then as now, and we can see the impact of declining standards in a long list of reports detailing the poor performance of American students on standardized tests.

On the 2005 National Assessment of Educational Progress (NAEP) science test, for example, 46 percent of American twelfth-grade students scored "below basic." On the math portion of the exam, 39 percent scored "below basic"—which tells us that nearly half of all high school seniors cannot answer even the most basic algebra and geometry questions. Researchers found that very few students were excelling. In science, just 29 percent of twelfth-grade students scored at the "proficient" level, and just 3 percent scored "advanced." Math scores were equally disappointing, with 35 percent of U.S. students in the "proficient" group, and a shocking 5 percent at the "advanced" level.[26]

Performance of American students compared to students in other countries is even more disturbing. The percentage of American college students earning degrees in science, technology, engineering, and mathematics lags well behind the percentage of students from China, India, Japan, Russia, Mexico, and the Middle East. According to research from the Heritage Foundation, the 2007 Trends in International Mathematics and Science Study (TIMSS) report reveals that students in other countries (especially the Asian countries) consistently outperform U.S. students in science and math.[27]

Results from the 2009 Program for International Student Assessment (PISA) exam, which is administered every three years to students from sixty-five countries, reveal that American teenagers rank well below their peers in the top thirty industrialized countries, and they continue to score well below average in critical subject areas. While students from Singapore and China scored consistently at the highest levels in all categories, American fifteen-year-old students scored seventeenth in reading, twenty-third in science, and thirty-first in math. They came in twenty-third or twenty-fourth in most subjects, and even lower in subjects in which they were expected to excel.[28]

For years the evidence of deteriorating educational standards has been most pronounced in the upper grades, with twelfth-grade students scoring generally worse than students in the lower grades. But according to results of the 2009 National Assessment of Educational

Progress (NAEP) assessments, just 34 percent of fourth graders, 30 percent of eighth graders, and 21 percent of twelfth graders are performing at or above the "proficient" level. Furthermore, just 1 or 2 percent at each grade level scored at the "advanced" level, and relatively large numbers of students didn't even attain the most basic level.[29]

Even the current secretary of education, Arne Duncan, had to admit that current levels of educational attainment are a threat to America's future success. At the first public unveiling of the latest results, Duncan said, "The results released today show that our nation's students aren't learning at a rate that will maintain America's role as an international leader in the sciences." He added that, "When only 1 or 2 percent of children score at the advanced levels on NAEP, the next generation will not be ready to be world-class inventors, doctors, and engineers."[30]

In a stunning comment on the state of public education in this country, the National Commission on Excellence in Education said that, "If an unfriendly foreign power had attempted to impose on America the mediocre educational performance that exists today, we might well have viewed it as an act of war. As it stands, we have allowed this to happen to ourselves . . . we have, in effect, been committing an act of unthinking, unilateral, educational disarmament."[31]

You would think such findings would prompt massive changes in public and higher education, but the authors of the summary report for the 1990 National Assessment of Educational Progress were obliged to admit that "large proportions, perhaps more than half, of our elementary, middle, and high-school students are unable to demonstrate competency in challenging subject matter in English, mathematics, science, history, and geography. Further, even fewer appear to be able to use their minds well." Comments like these, reported by author and educational sociologist Charles J. Sykes, provide a staggering array of anecdotal and statistical information confirming the risks to children in America's public schools. His book, *Dumbing Down Our Kids*, ought to be required reading for every parent and educator.[32]

Combining the candor of such statements with the fact that the professional "educrats," the major teachers' unions, and many of our universities are mainly concerned with the social and sexual indoctrination of America's young people, you realize we have a big problem. Fortunately not everyone is happy with this situation, and as more and more evidence of the damage being done to the next generation of Americans comes to light, more and more of our citizens are rising to the challenge.

For many of the educational programmers, money is a major motivating factor; but many of those at the forefront of the radical transformation of American values in the schools and colleges are losing supporters and funding. Some of those giant endowments are shrinking. Furthermore the results of the 2010 midterm elections suggest that large numbers of people in this country are giving up on the progressive agenda, and this means many more parents and public officials will be looking for answers concerning what's been going on in the schools.

CHANGING DIRECTIONS

A Rasmussen Reports national telephone survey taken in December 2010 revealed that Americans are deeply troubled by the way things have been going in this country. Leading up to the presidential inauguration in January 2009, the number of voters who felt the country was heading in the right direction was below 20 percent. Confidence rose briefly to 40 percent in early May, but it began falling after that. While approximately half of black voters still believed the country was heading in the right direction, 74 percent of whites and 76 percent of all other voters were pessimistic about the course the country was on.[33]

Subsequently the Rasmussen Poll for June 18, 2011, found just 21 percent of American voters strongly approve of the way President Obama is performing as president. Meanwhile 41 percent said they strongly disapprove, giving the president an approval index rating of −20. In his book *In Search of Self-Government*, published in late 2010, Scott Rasmussen offered the perceptive observation that "the gap between Americans who want to govern themselves and politicians who want to rule over them may be as big today as the gap between the colonies and England during the 18th century."[34]

The concerns that led to the American Revolution were taxation without representation and the imposition of unjust laws by the British Parliament. Among them was the act of Parliament closing the Port of Boston to normal commerce, the appointment of British aristocrats to oversee colonial governments, the protection of English criminals from the judgment of colonial courts, the quartering of British troops in American homes without payment of rent or lodging expenses, and the interference in religious customs with punitive policies and statutes that favored Canada and the growing wave of Catholic immigrants to that country. Furthermore the colonists were not allowed to elect their own representatives to the English House of Commons, and they had no standing in the House of Lords. Ultimately it was these "Intolerable Acts" that propelled the American patriots toward revolution. Because they had no say in their own government and were subject to the whims of autocratic English governors, the colonists concluded that England had no legitimate claim on America.

We are not seeing signs of an insurrection on that scale in this country so far, but a lot of people are on edge because of the incompetent handling of the economy, the bailouts of corrupt financial institutions, the government takeover of automobile and insurance companies, the passage of universal health care, and the threats of increased taxation. There have been no violent demonstrations or marches on the White House—most people believe the 2010 midterm elections sent a message to Congress and are still optimistic that our voices are being heard.

We are by nature a peaceful people who are accustomed to an orderly and natural transition of power. We are hopeful that the presidential election in 2012 will help reduce the interference of the federal government in business and our private lives. But if something should happen to derail those hopes or if enough people begin to feel they are being cheated and disenfranchised by the administration or its allies on Wall Street and in the federal courts, then who knows what could happen? It doesn't have to result in a massive demonstration of discontent, and I doubt that it will. It is possible to deal with all these issues politically and diplomatically. But if for some reason the American people come to believe they are being cheated out of their constitutional right to determine how they are governed, then it is possible things could take a very different turn.

All conservative voters really want is to get back to the type of government the Founders gave us in the first place. It is very important that we have a better understanding of our history and why the founding documents were written as they were. We need to understand how revolutionary those documents were and still are, granting unprecedented freedoms to the people and establishing the foundations of the rule of law. If we understand the environment of the revolutionary era as well as the environment we are dealing with today, then we will have a much better grasp of how things will play out from here on.

But let me be clear about this: I believe we are on the threshold of a revolution—a peaceful revolution, to be sure—but a genuine change in how We the People relate to our elected representatives from now on. We believe that substantial changes will have to be made, and the difficult task of undoing some of the laws enacted by the last Congress and safeguarding our sacred liberties will mean resisting the impulse to compromise while defending our time-tested conservative principles against the charges and countercharges our political opponents will make.

But we are trusting that the men and women we've sent to Washington as our representatives in the most recent housecleaning operation will be faithful to the challenges we have given them and do the right things. We are not being naive, thinking things will suddenly change in Washington without the need for voters to exercise due caution and vigilance, but we do believe salutary changes will come.

We are deeply concerned that a generation of young people has been taught that America is corrupt and our system of government is not worth saving. They have been taught this in our schools, and their heads have been filled with politically correct nonsense. The generation coming up may not even be equipped to take the reins of government when its time comes. That is why we will have to start making changes from the top down.

We used to think reform would come from the bottom up, but that is not going to happen. Changes will need to be made in the centers of power, from the administration in Washington and all the various agencies of government to the state and local levels. At the same time, we will need to lobby for reforms in both public and higher education if we expect to see real, long lasting change.

ACCEPTING THE CHALLENGE

We are going through difficult times in America today, but it is not the worst we have endured. The country is in the midst of an economic downturn, and most people are not living as well as they did a decade ago. Nevertheless, sometimes it takes a little stress to make people stop and think about what they've been doing. I believe these may turn out to be some of the best times we have ever seen if we are able to recapture a vision of who we are and what this nation was meant to be.

As a Christian minister, I tend to believe that God may have allowed these tough times to come about so that the men and women of this nation will wake up and reclaim their patrimony. We need to take a look around and remember the incredible privilege we have as Americans. The rally on the Washington Mall hosted by Glenn Beck back in August 2010 was dedicated to restoring honor, and that's really what it's all about. We have to rededicate ourselves to the essential virtues of honor, truth, integrity, and faithfulness if there is any hope of restoring our lost honor.

Duirng a speech I heard Ronald Reagan deliver in the late 1980s, he said, "Never has there been a time when people with so much to lose have done so little to keep it." I think that may have been the case in recent years, but it is not going to be the case much longer. We have lost more than enough ground, but I see the banners of a million dedicated patriots rising above the horizon, and bigger and better changes are on the way. Regardless of what happens in Washington this year or next, I believe there is hope. Throughout all the years, from the American Revolution through the Civil War and two world wars until this very day, the thing that has kept this nation going is hope, which comes from knowing who we are and whose we are. And that vision is still very much alive.

It is such an important message: yes, there is going to be a tomorrow, and we can make that tomorrow better. We have already begun to prove that by our actions at the polls. The citizens of Iowa proved it when they removed three liberal judges from the bench for ignoring the wishes of the people in order to push a far-left agenda. Voters crowding into town hall meetings all over the country are proving it by showing up and confronting unaccountable senators and congressmen. And all these changes are coming straight from the hearts of decent, hardworking Americans.

One of the tremendous things about this country is that we are a republic that can correct itself through informed citizen action without resorting to violence. President Obama made a dramatic promise of hope and change during his 2008 election campaign. That promise, along with the fact that he would become the first African American president, was apparently enough to persuade the voters to elect him to the nation's highest office. Mr. Obama knew that we have a constitutional system that allows us to make major changes of policy. We can change direction without a violent revolution, and his administration made some of the most dramatic changes in the history of the republic. But there is also a safety net, which is the will of the people.

The Founders designed a system in which those who are elected to public office may only make major decisions with the consent of the governed. And when a government strays too far to the left or the right, the people have the right and constitutional duty to hold those elected individuals accountable. They have the power to right the ship of state through citizen action and the choices they make at the ballot box.

Those who want to make the most radical changes in our form of government, to take the country in a new and untested direction, identify themselves today as "progressives." Underlying their platform and their belief system is the idea that there is some new territory, some golden new sunrise, or some shining utopia out there that guarantees equality and peace and plenty for all if we can just shake off the shackles of the past and strike out in a new direction. But what they are offering is not new at all: it is the oldest fabrication known to man.

The idea of a man-made utopia has been the promise of every totalitarian society since the collapse of the Roman republic. But it is a false vision, a mirage, a wisp of smoke, and we would be foolish indeed to abandon the achievements of the greatest republic in the history of mankind for a system that has been the source of some of the greatest miseries ever known. The progressive promise is in reality a hallucination.

The men and women who took control of the United States Congress in January 2009 were on a mission, and the legislation they passed is clear evidence of the direction in which they were headed. I have heard from some of our representatives in Washington that if many of the most liberal members of Congress had not been turned out by the voters in the 2010 election, the progressives were poised to go much, much further. Within a couple of years they would have been calling for a total revision of the United States Constitution. That's how radical the aims of some of our leaders have become.

But the 2010 election was a watershed. It was in effect a firewall against further encroachments and further legislative destruction from the Left. It was a good start, but it was just a start. Those who would like to undermine our form of government, our traditional values and beliefs, and our way of life haven't gone away. They're just waiting for an opportunity to strike again. That's one of the reasons why I've written this book, as a warning and a wake-up call to every citizen to stand up, speak up, and become engaged in the contest for America's future.

Make no mistake; we are in a contest to see what this nation will be for the next two hundred years. Will we uphold the values of the Founders, who were dedicated to life, liberty, and the pursuit of happiness? Will we defend the moral and ethical values our forefathers fought and died for? Or will we stand by silently, like the dazed and defeated citizens of a half-dozen fallen empires of the past, and watch this nation sink into the swamp of socialism, totalitarianism, and anarchy, ultimately leading to collapse? This is the choice we have to make, and it is one contest we can't afford to lose.

THE PROMISE OF AMERICA

Before we can take corrective action to restore the foundations of American culture and regain a vision of this country's high calling, it is imperative that we understand the premises upon which the nation was built. Unfortunately the authentic history of the founding era and the birth of the republic has been almost completely forgotten. A generation or two ago schoolchildren celebrated the arrival of the Pilgrims with plays and vignettes of the landing at Plymouth Rock or the first Thanksgiving, but even these were incomplete and not very faithful accounts of what really happened.

Even more troubling, many schools no longer teach very much about the colonial period at all, and what they do teach is so loaded with revisionist history that the miracle of America's founding is lost. This is tragic because we need to remember. If we truly understood what the first Americans endured to bring forth on this continent a new nation—as Abraham Lincoln phrased it—we could never again ignore their courage and determination, and no one would ever doubt that this is a Christian country. So to help us remember where they came from and what our forefathers accomplished, I would like to step back in time for a moment to see where it all started and how America came to be what it is today.

There is no way of knowing how many ancient explorers may have set foot on the continent of North America before Christopher Columbus came ashore at San Salvador—Spanish, French, Dutch, English, and Scandinavian sailors all claimed to have done so—but news of the Genoese navigator's discovery in 1492 spread quickly through the palaces and public houses of Europe, prompting wild speculation about what kinds of fantastic treasures were simply waiting to be discovered in the New World.[1]

English explorers and privateers had been scouting the coastline of North America for more than fifty years before the Cavaliers under John Smith arrived in 1607 in search of new territory for the British empire. Pirates and traders had come looking for new sources of gold and precious spices. Adventurers such as John Cabot and Francis Drake reached our northern coasts years before the first settlements were established at Roanoke and Jamestown, but without leaving any settlements of their own.

Queen Elizabeth I, who reigned from 1558 to 1603, was intrigued by the tales she heard from seafarers such as Francis Drake and adventurers such as Walter Raleigh and Richard Hakluyt, who spoke of vast new lands and wealth beyond the dreams of avarice. Tantalized by these reports, the queen gave official sanction for further exploration, along with authorization for English trading companies to issue land grants establishing colonies in the New World.

For the Puritan congregations of England, however, rumors of a new land where men could be free from persecution, political oppression, and bodily mutilation awakened a very different set of emotions. Religious conflict had been raging across Europe for centuries. As many as two thousand men and women were tortured, beheaded, or burned alive during the Inquisition, and thousands more suffered terrible wounds. At least thirty thousand Protestants were slaughtered during the St. Bartholomew's Day massacre in France in 1572. Those purges had taken place in continental Europe, but when the Protestant Reformation reached the British Isles in the mid-sixteenth century, English dissenters who followed the new teachings suddenly became an endangered species.

To put all this in perspective, what we know today as the Protestant Reformation began in the year 1517, when Martin Luther nailed his Ninety-Five Theses to the door of the castle church at Wittenberg in northeastern Germany. Luther, who was an ardent student of the Bible, realized that many common practices in the churches of that day were unbiblical and not in keeping with the teachings of Saint Paul. However, when he attempted to inform the bishops of his concerns during a trip to Rome, church officials ordered Luther to stop complaining. He was warned of serious consequences if he persisted, at which point he returned to Wittenberg deeply shaken.

After a long period of anguish and introspection, Luther realized he could not remain silent. Heresy had crept into the church over many centuries and needed to be stopped. The letters of Saint Paul taught that salvation comes by grace through faith, not by works, yet the church was saying that acts of devotion, including gifts of money, could purchase "indulgences" that ensured salvation and forgiveness of sins. And there were many other concerns.

The list of questions and complaints Luther nailed to the church door created an immediate sensation, but the cardinals and bishops in Rome were not amused. The charges and countercharges that followed exacted a tremendous toll on Luther and his followers, and they led to insurrections, open defiance, and several bloody confrontations with church authorities. When he was summoned to appear before a papal court at Worms in 1521, Luther refused to admit he had been wrong, at which point he was excommunicated and forced into hiding.

The eight months he spent in a secret apartment at Wartburg Castle were agonizing for Luther, but he used the time profitably, translating the New Testament into everyday German and writing dozens of pamphlets and tracts to explain key biblical teachings in a pure and simple way. When he eventually returned to Wittenberg, he was hailed as a hero and the leader of the reform movement. Over the next half century, the controversy he had ignited spread like wildfire across Europe and far beyond.

Congregations that adopted Luther's reforms in England were declared heretics by the archbishop of Canterbury. The English church was Catholic at that time, and dissenters were subjected to severe punishments. The word *Puritans* was originally a form of mockery, but the dissenters liked the name because the purity of the gospel was all they really wanted. Throughout the sixteenth and seventeenth centuries, those who refused to conform were declared outlaws and subjected to severe persecution. Hundreds were whipped, hung, burned, or branded with hot irons or had their ears cut off or their noses slit. Some were drawn and quartered. The lucky ones escaped and went into hiding, or were simply killed outright.

Protestant pastors in England, many of whom were graduates of the universities of Oxford and Cambridge, were stripped of their positions and livelihoods. Some were tried by the ecclesiastical courts and banished, and sometimes they faced much worse. As the persecutions became more and more intense, some of the reformed congregations, identified as "separatists," began looking for safer places across the English Channel in Europe where they could practice their beliefs without fear.

One of those congregations in the village of Scrooby in Nottinghamshire was led by a group of faithful Christian men; which included William Brewster, William Bradford, and John Carver; and two separatist pastors, Richard Clifton and John Robinson. Brewster, who had served as private secretary to a member of the royal court in London, learned from foreign travelers that Holland was the safest place in Europe for dissenters. When he shared the news with his congregation, a group of 125 separatists voted to sell their homes, farms, and all they had, and relocated to that country.

THE YEARS OF SEPARATION

The story of what happened during the difficult months and years that followed was recorded by William Bradford in his detailed history, *Of Plymouth Plantation (1620–1647)*. Although Bradford served as governor of Plymouth Colony for more than thirty years and is remembered as one of the guiding lights of the American founding, his book was generally unknown for nearly two centuries until it was republished in 1856. Since that time the book has been called the first great work of American literature and a classic of American history. Even so, it is seldom read today.

In his narrative Bradford describes how the separatists arranged for a ship to transport them to Holland under cover of darkness, only to be betrayed by the ship's captain. When they arrived to begin the voyage, the villagers were attacked by thugs who ransacked their baggage and clothing, taking all their valuables and leaving them destitute. Nevertheless, they didn't give up, and when they were able to reorganize and secure additional funds, they set out from a different port the following spring. This time William Brewster made a bargain with a trustworthy Dutch sea captain to take them to Holland.

Bradford then describes how the men boarded the ship at night, and how the women and children, who waited offshore in small boats, were chased by the authorities and attacked by gangs of cutthroats. Seeing the mayhem and fearing for his own safety, the Dutch captain set sail immediately, forcing the women and children to stay behind in England until the men could return weeks later to gather what was left of their families. Eventually, by the grace of God and their extraordinary perseverance, the separatists arrived in Holland in the year 1607 and were able to find lodgings in Amsterdam, where they remained for one year.[2]

The following year they relocated from Amsterdam to the village of Leiden, where they remained for eleven more years in relative peace and quiet. They had to learn a new language, find new occupations, and fit in with their Dutch neighbors without losing their own culture and traditions. By 1617, however, they could see that their children were becoming more Dutch than English and picking up bad habits from the locals, so they began making preparations for the even more ambitious journey to the New World.

Through the Brewster family's friendship with Sir Edwin Sandys, who was treasurer of the London Company, the congregation was granted patents to establish a new colony in "the northern parts of Virginia." King James I, who succeeded Elizabeth to the throne in 1603, was nominally protestant in his beliefs but was brutal in his attacks upon the Puritans. He had authorized publication of the King James Version of the Bible in 1611 as an act of compromise with Puritan dissenters—it was his most important contribution to the separatist movement and to religious liberty. But he had also declared the separatists to be outlaws and enemies of the Crown, and he said in one famous outburst, "I will make them conform themselves, or else I will harry them out of the land, or else do worse."[3]

The separatist congregation in Holland had prayed for years that they might be able to return to their homes in England in due time. But at age fifty-four and in his fifty-second year as king of Scotland and seventeenth year as king of England, James I showed no signs of relenting. It was common knowledge that the king was strongly influenced by his Catholic wife and many court favorites who despised the dissenters. This left only two options for the separatists: they could either stay where they were or risk the dangerous voyage to an untamed wilderness in North America.

When it came time to leave Holland, half of the English separatists decided to stay behind. The others arranged for passage to Southampton, England, on the ship *Speedwell*, where they joined another group of separatists who had chartered the 180-ton cargo vessel *Mayflower*. By the time they set sail on September 16, 1620, about half of the 102 passengers and crew aboard the *Mayflower* were from the original Scrooby congregation.

It was a long and difficult crossing—sixty-five days at sea before they came within sight of land on November 19. Four members of the party died during the journey, but two babies were born—the boy Oceanus Hopkins was born at sea, and another, Peregrine White, was born while the ship lay at anchor off Cape Cod. Strong winds and heavy seas prevented them from going ashore in Virginia as originally planned. The ship was forced back, then farther up the coast until they were finally able to anchor at the site of Provincetown, on the tip of Cape Cod.

Before going ashore, the men William Bradford identifies as the Pilgrim Fathers met in the captain's stateroom to draw up the legal covenant that became known as the Mayflower Compact, creating the first form of government in the new colony. The document reads in its entirety:

> In the name of God, Amen. We whose names are underwritten, the loyal subjects of our dread sovereign Lord King James, by the grace of God, of Great Britain, France, and Ireland king, defender of the faith, etc.
>
> Having undertaken, for the glory of God, and the advancement of the Christian faith, and honor of our king and country, a voyage to plant the first colony in the northern parts of Virginia, do by these presents solemnly and mutually in the presence of God, and one another, covenant and combine ourselves together into a civil body politick, for our better ordering, and preservation and furtherance of the ends aforesaid; and by virtue hereof, to enact, constitute, and frame such just and equal laws, ordinances, acts, constitutions, and offices, from time to time, as shall be thought most meet and convenient for the general good of the colony: unto which we promise all due submission and obedience.
>
> In witness whereof we have hereunder subscribed our names at Cape Cod, the 11th of November in the year of the reign of our sovereign Lord King James of England, France, and Ireland, the eighteenth and of Scotland the fifty-fourth. Anno Domine 1620.

The covenant was signed by forty-one members of the ship's company, including William Bradford, William Brewster, Myles Standish, and John Alden. It was originally drafted as a temporary measure to avoid dissension among the passengers and crew, some of whom were angry that the ship had landed at Provincetown instead of Virginia. The aim of the agreement was to establish the ground rules for what they called a "Civil Body Politick" until revised patents could be sent from England granting them official permission to settle at the new site.

The Mayflower Compact has since been called the birth certificate of America and America's first constitution. Our sixth president, John Quincy Adams, the son of John Adams and a descendant of John Alden, referred to the compact as the true foundation of the U.S. Constitution. William Bradford included a copy of it in his history. The document makes it perfectly clear that the Pilgrims had come to America "for the glory of God, and the advancement of the Christian faith," and not out of greed or imperialism or any of the reasons often given by the revisionists.

After all the hardships they had miraculously survived, the leaders of the expedition were anxious to find a safe landing place. They scouted the coastline for several days and ultimately decided on Plymouth Harbor on the western side of Cape Cod Bay. They made their historic landing at Plymouth Rock on December 21, and the settlers disembarked with all their remaining goods on December 26. It was only later that they discovered how the hand of Providence had protected them and delivered them safely to their present destination.

BY THE GRACE OF GOD, AMEN

If the *Mayflower* had actually landed in "the northern parts of Virginia" as originally planned, the passengers would have been exposed to even greater perils than those they survived in England. The coastal marshlands in the south were infested with plague and malaria, and the local Indian tribes were hostile to European settlers. Chances are they would not have survived. They did not realize it at the time, but God had sent strong winds to push the *Mayflower* farther north until they arrived at the one place where they would find safe harbor.

God's grace was upon them there as well. After they landed they learned that the Patuxet tribe that inhabited the area had been wiped out by disease. The first Native American the settlers met at Plymouth was the lone survivor of the Patuxets, Squanto. They were surprised to learn that Squanto had been captured by English traders and taken to England years earlier. He was exhibited as a curiosity for several years—the first "Red Indian" the English had ever seen—but he returned to his home just one year before the colonists arrived. While he was away learning the English language and customs, his tribe simply disappeared. Finding no trace of his own people, he went to the Wampanoag tribe and was adopted by its chief, Massasoit.

The Wampanoags were generally peaceful, and Squanto introduced the chief and tribal leaders to the settlers. These were the Indians with whom the Pilgrims celebrated their first Thanksgiving in America, in 1621. There were skirmishes at various times, and during the first tragic winter that William Bradford called "the starving time," Massasoit would not allow any of his tribesmen to offer the Pilgrims food, shelter, or assistance. It was a tragic and potentially crippling time, but eventually Squanto was able to show the men how to fish and hunt for the local game, and how to plant corn and other native crops. He also helped them find safe places to build homes and begin their new lives.

The colonists knew they would have to face many hardships, but the prospects for success were few, indeed, in the beginning. William Bradford describes the sorrows of that first winter:

> Being thus past the vast ocean, and a sea of troubles before in their
> preparation . . . they had now no friends to welcome them, nor inns
> to entertain or refresh their weather-beaten bodies, no houses or
> much less towns to repair to, to seek for succor. It is recorded in

scripture as a mercy to the apostle and his shipwrecked company, that the barbarians showed no small kindness in refreshing them, but these savage barbarians, when they met with them (as after will appear) were readier to fill their sides full of arrows than otherwise. And for the season it was winter, and they that know the winters of that country know them to be sharp and violent and subject to cruel and fierce storms, dangerous to travel to known places, much more to search an unknown coast.[4]

"What could now sustain them," Bradford asked, "but the Spirit of God and His grace?" But would anyone remember the sacrifices the Pilgrims made to find a new home for religious liberty? Would the men and women of our own time tell their children where the story of America really began? Bradford then goes on to ask, "May not and ought not the children of these fathers rightly say, 'Our fathers were Englishmen which came over this great ocean, and were ready to perish in this wilderness; but they cried unto the Lord, and He heard their voice and looked on their adversity'?"

Then, reciting from various passages from the Psalms, he writes:

Let them therefore praise the Lord, because He is good: and his mercies endure forever. Yea, let them which have been redeemed of the Lord, show how He hath delivered them from the hand of the oppressor. When they wandered in the desert wilderness out of the way, and found no city to dwell in, both hungry and thirsty, their soul was overwhelmed in them. Let them confess before the Lord His lovingkindness and His wonderful works before the sons of men.[5]

During that first cruel winter twenty-six men and eighteen women died. Only three of the married women survived. According to Edwin Gaustad's account, "It was a small and terribly depleted group that survived to give thanks for the first harvest in the fall of 1621."[6] Nevertheless the survivors began to adapt to their surroundings and settle into a practical routine, and over time they found ways to overcome the limitations of the harsh environment. Little by little the colony began to grow and prosper, and the rumors of its progress were being cautiously weighed by the Puritan congregations back in England who were growing more and more desperate under unrelenting persecution.

King Charles I, who succeeded James in 1625, made no pretense of compromise with the separatists. After marrying a Catholic Spanish princess, Charles was even more determined to stamp out Puritan influence on the Church of England than his predecessors had been. With the cooperation of Catholic-leaning bishop William Laud, who would be appointed archbishop of Canterbury in 1633, Charles made life hell for English Puritans.

In particular Laud exploited the Star Chamber system of the English courts with draconian efficiency. Prominent pastors and members of Parliament who favored the Puritan reforms to the Church of England were dragged before the court, where they were accused and humiliated. Trials before the Star Chamber were conducted in secrecy, like a kangaroo court. Prisoners were allowed to present no witnesses; they had no right of appeal and no opportunity to defend themselves since the outcomes were predetermined. In the hands of Laud and the privy counselors chosen by the royal court, the Star Chamber was the religious and political weapon par excellence. The practice was finally halted in 1641 as a result of the uprisings among Puritan supporters that would ultimately lead to the English Civil War in 1642.

Charles battled with Parliament throughout his reign, but he probably sealed his own fate when he disbanded Parliament in 1629 for a period of eleven years—a time known as the Eleven Years' Tyranny. Laud would remain his most trusted ally, always eager to please his monarch. But the more Laud tried to defy the Parliamentarian objections to rising taxation of the people and Catholic influence on the Church of England, the louder the protests of the Puritan separatists became. As journalist and historian Rod Gragg describes it:

[Bishop Laud] preferred unmarried ministers, like the Catholic priesthood, and the Puritans objected. He advocated Catholic-style prayers for the dead, and the Puritans called it unbiblical. He ordered church members to kneel for communion; and the Puritans said it was worshipping the elements rather than the Lord. He required bowing at the church altar, and the Puritans said it was misplaced devotion. He implemented a relaxed observance of the Sabbath, and the Puritans considered it irreverent. He called for more ceremony in worship services, and the Puritans saw it as prideful. He required ministers to wear the Catholic-style surplice or tunic, and the Puritans insisted it was man-centered adornment.[7]

Ultimately Laud would not win the debate. Supporters of the republican leader Oliver Cromwell, who sided with the Parliamentarians and defended the Puritan reforms, accused Laud of treason and confined him to the prison in the Tower of London. When he was put on trial for his crimes in 1644, Laud was found guilty and sentenced to death. He was executed in January 1645, and Charles I would meet a similar fate four years later when the new Parliament, led by Cromwell, convicted the king of treason and he was beheaded. Two years later, following the Battle of Worcester, the English Civil War came to an end.

A CITY UPON A HILL

Throughout the long years of controversy, the good reports coming from New England contrasted sharply with the troubles in Britain and convinced dozens of Puritan congregations to follow the example of the Scrooby separatists and relocate to the New World. A group of two hundred settlers arrived with grants at the new Massachusetts Bay Colony in 1630. They were followed by groups of seven hundred, eight hundred, then more than three thousand in a single year. The promise of religious liberty and the prospect of a healthy distance from the political oppression they had suffered at home were more than enough to persuade the faithful to abandon their native land for a new start in the American wilderness.

These travelers did not come, as the *Mayflower* Pilgrims had, in a leaky old cargo vessel. Instead, they journeyed in fleets—seventeen ships in one flotilla delivered more than a thousand souls. Between 1630 and 1640, more than twenty thousand English settlers crossed the Atlantic Ocean to North America. So many made the journey that it became known in England as the Great Migration. Never before had so many Englishmen left their native land in such a short span of time for such an arduous and uncertain adventure.

After 1630, most of the new arrivals settled in the Massachusetts Bay Colony, which was situated just a few miles north of the Plymouth Colony. While the original settlements remained reasonably small and close-knit, the Massachusetts Bay Colony grew rapidly, with a more diverse population. The foundations of the first city in New England were laid there in 1630, on the Sawmut Peninsula at the confluence of the Mystic and Charles Rivers. The town was named for the Port of Boston in Lincolnshire, England, from which many of the new immigrants had come.

A decade after their arrival, the population of Plymouth Colony was still only a few hundred, scattered among seven small villages. By 1660, the same year the English monarchy was restored under Charles II, there were just over two thousand in that colony, at which point the Plymouth colonists voted to join the larger and more prosperous Massachusetts Bay Colony. As the number of Puritan congregations continued to grow, both in America and Britain, there was mounting pressure on the English Church to disavow the anti-Puritan purges, but it was not until the Act of Toleration in 1689, under William and Mary, that the persecutions finally came to an end.

All of the men and women who had risked so much to come to the New World had to give up much, leaving homes and families and in many cases bringing nothing with them except the clothes on their backs. But John Winthrop, who served several terms as governor of the Massachusetts Bay Colony, wanted the Puritan congregations of New England to remember that they had all come to America to fulfill a sacred promise. In the Arbella Covenant, which was drafted in 1630, Winthrop wrote, "We must love one another with a pure heart, fervently," and "we must bear one another's burdens. . . ." Above all, he said, "we are a Company professing ourselves fellow members of Christ."[8] Regardless of their wealth or status in life, he said, they had all made a solemn pledge to live godly lives and abide by the teachings of Scripture. Winthrop said they must never forget their dependence upon the Lord who had brought them there. Then, reminding the people of what was really at stake, the Covenant states:

> Thus stands the cause between God and us: we are entered into covenant with Him for this work; we have taken out a commission, the Lord hath given us leave to draw our own articles, . . . if we shall neglect the observation of these articles . . . the Lord will surely break out in wrath against us. . . . Therefore, let us choose life, that we, and our seed may live; by obeying His voice and cleaving to Him, for He is our life and our prosperity.[9]

Echoing the words of Jesus in Matthew 5:14, Winthrop penned some of the most famous words of the colonial era: "We must consider that we shall be as a city upon a hill. The eyes of all people are upon us."[10] The settlers of Plymouth Colony were all separatists, and the world was truly watching them. Calvinist in their doctrinal stance and Congregationalist in their church polity, they had made a clean break with the Anglican communion. The men and women who built the Massachusetts Bay Colony, on the other hand, were devoutly Puritan but still considered themselves to be part of the Church of England. And none of them doubted the truth of Winthrop's words or the importance of the oath they had taken.

John Cotton, who was one of the best-known pastors in the town of Boston in those years, outlined the Puritans' complaints against the

Church of England. The national church, he said, was subject to rigid conformity according to the edicts of the bishops and the threats of English law. The Book of Common Prayer, he believed, violated the second commandment—which says, "Thou shalt not make unto thee any graven image . . ." (Exodus 20:4). The Anglican prayer book was a work of human invention, not of God, and ought to be abandoned. Cotton further held that the governance of the churches should be congregational in form, not Episcopal or Anglican because the congregants were the authentic source of authority in the churches, not the bishops or even the local pastors. The church, he said, is not a building but a gathering of believers. It is a fellowship of the redeemed—bound together in a covenant relationship—not subject to the arbitrary policies and judgments of any government or legislative body.

Some historians of the colonial period have suggested that New England church polity tended to be Presbyterian in form, with important decisions left in the hands of elected elders (presbyters) and deacons who spoke for the congregation. The New England churches insisted that the congregations should be free to select their own ministers and make their own rules of church governance. Whereas farther south in Virginia, colonies that grew out of the Jamestown Plantation founded in 1607 tended to favor the Episcopalian form of worship and were somewhat skeptical of their Puritan brethren in the north.

First at Massachusetts Bay, then in the Connecticut Colony and each of the subsequent towns and villages settled by the Puritans, there emerged a spirit of unity that became known as the New England Way, "molding itself with such firmness and care," as one writer describes it, "that it stamped upon that region a way of thinking and living that would endure far beyond the colonial period."[11]

A DECLARATION OF INDEPENDENCE

The Puritans had come to America for religious liberty and the opportunity to practice their beliefs as they saw fit. That is simply a fact that cannot be explained any other way. In our own time, many historians have often focused on the lack of tolerance and diversity in the Puritan settlements, which is a wholly unjustified approach. In the first place, it is unreasonable to judge the men of that time by twenty-first century standards: it was a very different world, and there were perfectly good reasons for maintaining uniformity. And second, what's missing in the revisionists' account is the fact that the Pilgrims never intended to establish a colony that was open to any and all persuasions. "The Puritans," reliable historians tell us, "came to create a pure church and to conduct a holy experiment free of opposition, distraction, and error. They were not hypocrites who demanded freedom of religion then denied that same freedom to others. Freedom of religion across the board was never the plan, never the commission or errand."[12]

Instead, the Pilgrims came to show that it was possible to establish a society and a church so faithful to the biblical model of purity that the churches they had left behind in England might be transformed by their example. If the Pilgrims saw themselves as "a city upon a hill," it was not because they lacked admirers but because they wanted to be examples of the life Christ and the apostles had ordained for the church. They meant to be "a light to the world," and this meant the community was expected to live faithfully, according to the precepts and biblical beliefs that bound them together.

Throughout the nation's formative years, the clearest statement of the values and beliefs of the American people was to be found in their sermons, and this would be the case well into the nineteenth century. Pastors and teachers in separatist churches gave voice to the hopes, fears, and aspirations of the people, and this was only possible because the colonists were in general agreement on such matters. For more than a century their understanding of the duty of citizens and believers in Jesus Christ was virtually unanimous. This uniformity of conviction made the meeting house the preeminent place for preserving civic and spiritual discipline, and the unity of purpose was communicated best by the sermons.

The spoken word has remained an essential component of American culture. As historian and former librarian of Congress Daniel J. Boorstin points out, "The public speech, whether sermon, commencement address, or whistle-stop campaign talk, is a public affirmation that the listeners share a common discourse and a common body of values. The spoken word is inevitably more topical than the printed word: it attempts to explain the connection between the shared community values and the predicament of man at a particular time and place. It is directed to people whom the speaker confronts, and to their current problems."[13]

The seventeenth century, Boorstin says, became known as the great age of the English sermon. Back in Great Britain, Anglican pastors such as John Donne and Jeremy Taylor were the best-known preachers of the day. They delivered homilies in what was known as the "metaphysical" or "high" style, drawing upon sophisticated allusions and philosophical turns of phrase. In the Plymouth Colony, on the other hand, the most compelling pastors were those like John Robinson, the original pastor of the Scrooby congregation, who preached in what the Puritans described as the "plain" style. Although Robinson did not make the journey to New England with his flock, his teachings had a profound influence on the character of the early church in America.

The characteristics of the plain style were laid out in a slim handbook called *The Art of Prophesying*, written by William Perkins, a Cambridge University lecturer and pastor in the late-sixteenth and early-seventeenth centuries. The book, which was published in Latin in 1592 and in English in 1606, was on nearly every list of essential books, and few pastoral studies in New England would have been without a copy. The basic style of the Puritan sermon, Perkins says, was that it ought to be straightforward, with natural and logical development of ideas. To be a "plain sermon," it didn't have to be simplistic or superficial but direct and free of the sort of elevated rhetoric favored by the Anglican divines.

The New England sermon was evangelical, to be sure, in the sense that it was meant to persuade the listeners and convince them of their need of saving grace. But it was above all practical, logical, and delivered in the common language of the day. Many of these sermons were more like a lawyer's brief than a work of art. Perkins proposed that each sermon should be composed of three main parts: "doctrines, reasons, and uses."[14] The doctrine came directly from the biblical text, which was where every Puritan sermon began. The reasons offered a brief discussion of the text, along with the meaning of the passage and its importance. The uses, then, were the practical application of the teaching to the lives of the members of the congregation.

In New England, Boorstin says, the sermon was far more than a literary form: it was an institution. "It was the ritual application of theology to community-building and to the tasks and trials of everyday life. It was not, as it was inevitably in England, a mere sectarian utterance of a part of the community. It was actually the orthodox manifesto and self-criticism of the community as a whole, a kind of reiterated *declaration of independence*, a continual rediscovery of purposes. The pulpit, and not the altar, held the place of honor in the New England meetinghouse. So too the sermon itself, the specific application of the Word of God, was the focus of the best minds of New England."[15]

RULES OF FAITH AND PRACTICE

Since the church played such a key role in the daily life of Puritan communities, the people would have expected there to be sermons presented at every important occasion. There were usually two of them on Sundays, along with a Weekday Lecture on Thursdays, sometimes called the Fifth-Day Lecture. Thursday Lectures were begun by John Cotton in 1633, and were continued weekly for two hundred years. These were combined with Market Day Lectures, where congregants came together to discuss social and political events of the day. This was the custom in Boston, and the other New England colonies followed their example. In the beginning, attendance at these services was required by law, and skipping them was punishable by a fine. This practice eventually faded away because of the sheer size of the community and the difficulty of enforcement. Still, faithful church attendance was a fact of life.

In addition to the routine church programs, there were sermons for all sorts of public occasions, including holidays, barn raisings, and harvest celebrations. There were also Election Day Sermons, in which the pastors reminded the citizens of their civic duties and the responsibility to choose wisely. Such sermons would have stressed the importance of selecting orderly and self-disciplined leaders, according to the admonitions found in passages such as Deuteronomy 1:15, 1 Peter 5:5, and 1 Timothy 3:2, which emphasized wisdom, accountability, and a godly concern for the well-being of the community. The Election Day Sermon was a New England institution throughout the American Revolution.

Another standard was the Artillery Sermon, given whenever there was need to raise a militia for protection from attacks by local tribes or to issue a call for the election of military officers—a custom that began in the year 1659. There were also, of course, sermons for days of fasting and prayer, of which there were many during the Pilgrims' first half century in America. Daniel Boorstin indicates there were at least ten Thanksgiving celebrations in the Massachusetts Bay Colony in 1639, and as many as fifty between 1675 and 1676. Some of them lasted anywhere from three days to a week.[16]

Attendance at these events was often compulsory, but the sermons were always greeted with enthusiasm. There were few books in the colonies in the early years, so the sermons given on special occasions offered the men and women of these communities a sense of participation in the events of the day. The sermon was, in that sense, the essential community forum as well as a constant reminder of their dependence upon a benevolent heavenly Father. Consequently many congregants would bring along notebooks in which to record whatever they heard. These notebooks would, in turn, become invaluable resources for later generations to recall the beliefs and customs of the colonial era.

Despite the vast distances separating them from the land of their birth, the citizens of New England were remarkably well informed. They were blessed with a well-developed attention span, and they were in no need of trivial amusements or seeker-sensitive entertainments to hold their interest. They were hungry for knowledge and, for the most part, they were perceptive in their grasp of ideas. "All these circumstances," writes Boorstin, "served to hold the early New England preacher to a high intellectual standard and encouraged him to make his performances merit their central place. The New England sermon, then, was the communal ceremony which brought a strong orthodoxy to bear on the minutiae of life."[17]

The men who were entrusted with preserving orthodoxy were uniformly men of the cloth. Richard Mather (1596–1669) and John Cotton (1584/85–1652) were the most gifted preachers in the Massachusetts Bay Colony. In matters of both church and state, they tended to be authoritarian, which helped preserve stability in the colony but led to divisions among the clergy. Thomas Hooker (1586–1647), who agreed with Cotton's theology in the broadest sense, nevertheless, disagreed with him on governance and elected to move his parish farther west, to the town of Hartford, where he and one hundred followers founded the Colony of Connecticut in 1635.

There were also Christian leaders who came to be classified as nonconformists. Among them, Roger Williams (1603–1683) rejected the authoritarian style that was common in the Plymouth Colony. After several disagreements, and after having been tried and convicted of nonconformism, he was exiled. Then, with the help of Indian tribes he had befriended, he established Providence Colony farther west on a small strip of land sandwiched between Plymouth and Connecticut known as Rhode Island.

Williams, who was leader of the Baptists in the colonies, was never comfortable with traditional Puritan customs, and his new colony attracted many nonconformists and others of a more democratic spirit. He maintained that his purpose was to preserve freedom of conscience, and to allow his followers to pursue godliness in their own ways.

THE NEW ENGLAND COLONIES[18]

Circa 1641

As previously mentioned, most of the pastors and teachers in the founding generation were Calvinist in their interpretations of Scripture. Not all were in complete accord with the five points of Calvinist theology, but the doctrine of salvation by grace through faith alone was universal. The five points of Calvinism, then and now, focus on (1) the total depravity of man, (2) unconditional election, (3) limited atonement, (4) irresistible grace, and (5) the perseverance of the saints. Each of these would require a more detailed analysis, which I won't attempt to offer here, but more importantly, all the Puritan churches would have stressed the importance of a personal salvation experience.

By the same token, colonial ministers held the view that Christians were expected, as Jesus instructed the church, to "render to Caesar the things that are Caesar's, and to God the things that are God's" (Mark 12:17). This meant the laws ought to be obeyed, and reasonable taxes and levies ought to be paid. But Christians also had a duty to hold their leaders accountable for their decisions, and property-owning "freemen" were obliged to participate in the life and governance of the commonwealth.

While they recognized that government was not the church, and that the governing authority must never interfere in the affairs of the churches, there was no question that they expected government leaders to be believers in Jesus Christ. While they did not set out to create a theocracy per se, they did believe church and state were mutually supportive institutions, due to their mutual commitment to order and civic discipline. In a healthy society, both church and state contribute to the common good.

In order to facilitate the administration of justice and public order in the colonies, the Puritans had been given the right to establish their own self-governing society with royal approval. Rather than being forced to answer to Parliament or to any particular instructions from the trading companies in England, the Puritan leaders were able to make their own rules and manage their own business with minimal interference from abroad. As the colonies grew in size and became more and more productive, however, this convenient relationship would change, as we shall see in subsequent chapters.

In the beginning the New England colonies were self-governing and faith-based. And like the settlers at Plymouth, the citizens of the Massachusetts Bay Colony based their government on the biblical model of a covenant relationship. Accordingly, free, nonindentured adult males, known as "freemen," were obliged by the terms of the covenant to submit to the authority of the General Court, which was the main governing body. Each local government followed the same basic model. The Salem Church Covenant of 1629 spelled out the terms of the agreement:

> We Covenant with the Lord and with one another and do bind ourselves in the presence of God, to walk together in all his ways, accordingly as he is pleased to reveal himself to us in his blessed word of truth. And do more explicitly, in the name and fear of God, profess and protest to walk as followeth through the power and goodness of the Lord Jesus Christ.[19]

It was a "Covenant with the Lord and with one another," based on the "blessed word of truth." The civil government was a representative democracy based on biblical models, but with leaders who exercised a great deal of discretion in how the laws were applied. The book of Acts describes how the early church selected its leaders, and the Puritans attempted to follow that model in both church and civil government. This gave the first Americans biblical grounds for resisting civil magistrates and authorities in England who attempted to undermine the civil order and moral balance of the community. The apostles had resisted the civil authorities by declaring, "We ought to obey God rather than men" (Acts 5:29), and the colonists declared, "No king but King Jesus." In time the American spirit of independence would lead to an escalation of the hostilities between the colonists and their rulers in London.

THE AMERICAN BIRTHRIGHT

The Massachusetts Body of Liberties (1641) was the first formal register of the legal statutes of New England, and it would eventually be a model for the patriots of 1776 as they sought to codify the distinctive elements of American law and government. The Body of Liberties spelled out America's birthright and included a "bill of rights" declaring the right (in John Locke's original phrasing) to life, liberty, and the pursuit of property. It guaranteed equality under the law, free and regular elections, protection from self-incrimination, and the right to trial by jury. It also placed restrictions on "taxation without representation."

The document began with a paraphrase of the English Magna Carta (1215) that restrained the authority of the monarch and asserted that even kings are subject to the authority of Almighty God. It then placed certain limitations on judicial proceedings and outlined the rights of freemen, women, children, foreigners, and even "the brute creature." The document described the organization of the churches as the "Liberties the Lord Jesus hath given to the Churches."[20]

Although public order was rigidly enforced, no one should assume the colonists were passive when it came to matters of controversy. Many disputes in early New England arose out of debates over what sort of men were best suited to serve as magistrates and governors, and how leaders ought to be selected. The political history of the Massachusetts Bay Colony, Daniel Boorstin suggests, could be written as a history of their disagreements over such questions. What was the proper relationship between magistrates and deputies? How many deputies were needed for each town? What restrictions could be imposed on judges and juries, and what were the justifiable grounds for corporal punishment? Many a sermon was devoted to such topics.[21]

By 1644, the colony had established a bicameral legislature with a governor, deputy governor, and other officials elected annually. John Cotton offered a somber warning concerning the limits of political power, however, saying, "Let all the world learn to give mortal men no greater power than they are content they shall use—for use it they will. And unless they be better taught of God, they will use it ever and anon. . . . And they that have liberty to speak great things, you will find it to be true, they will speak great blasphemies."[22] Because they understood the doctrine of original sin, the colonists had a profound respect for law and order; but they also understood the dangers of unlimited power.

As the population of the colonies continued to grow in the late seventeenth and early eighteenth centuries—and particularly as the generation of young people born on American soil came to maturity and moved into positions of leadership—the Puritanism of the founding generation began to lose some of its influence on everyday life. The powerful preaching of ministers such as Jonathan Edwards (1703–1758) and Samuel Hopkins (1721–1803) helped to preserve the main tenets of Puritan beliefs in the eighteenth century, but rapid growth also brought rapid change.

In the beginning Puritanism had a beneficial effect on the moral and intellectual life of the people. Although after about 1820, the religious beliefs of the founding generation were no longer as dominant as they had once been, Puritan ideals were still very much alive and could be seen in the community's emphasis on education, in the people's concern for the religious views of candidates for public office, and in the benefits derived from the "Protestant work ethic," which was without question a gift of the founding generation. But the Puritan spirit was particularly alive in the passion for liberty that was, and still is, the defining characteristic of the American people.

Many young people learned a trade through informal apprenticeships. The custom for centuries had been that each family would train its children to pursue the same professions their fathers had pursued. But during the eighteenth century, this custom began to change as well. Reading, writing, and ciphers, which were the principal focus of education in the colonies, were also the responsibility of the family, but the churches played an important role in educating the children, ensuring that each child was able to read the Bible for himself or herself.

When public schools were established, approximately forty years after the foundation of the colony, the General Court of Massachusetts Bay authorized public funding of schools. Plymouth Colony was the first to begin operating a publicly funded school in 1673. Ten years later there were five such schools in the colonies.

All the colonies in New England experienced dramatic growth in both population and wealth during the eighteenth century. The rough-cut colonial society that had fought and scratched to eke out a living in the midst of a vast and unforgiving wilderness was, at long last, acquiring an image of sophistication and polish. The town of Boston, which was New England's most important seaport, was rapidly becoming a cosmopolitan center. The census of 1765, which was the last one taken before the American Revolution, listed 1,676 houses and 2,069 families. This included 2,941 adult males and 3,612 adult females, along with 4,109 males and 4,010 females under the age of 16. The census also listed the number of blacks and mulattoes in Boston at 510 males and 301 females. There were 37 Indians, male and female, and 32 residents of French origin, which brought the total in Boston to 15,552 souls.[23] This is minuscule by today's standards, but there were approximately 250,000 settlers in New England by the year 1700. Before the first shots were fired at Lexington and Concord in 1775, the number had increased to 2,250,000. By 1800 the total was more than 5,300,000.

As the nation expanded, large numbers of non-English-speaking immigrants began streaming into the colonies as well. By 1775, there were more than 250,000 Germans, most of whom settled in the middle colonies and farther south. These newcomers were generally Lutheran or German Reformed although, like the Puritans, they were also Calvinist in their doctrinal views. And there was a substantial influx of Moravian, Mennonite, Amish, and other pietist denominations who were doctrinally Arminian.

Beginning in the 1730s, there was a continuous wave of immigrants from Scotland and Ireland, including entire communities of Scotch-Irish Presbyterians escaping from the political and religious persecutions in their home countries. By 1776, the number had grown to more than 250,000, and many of these individuals were native Gaelic speakers with little or no fluency in English. Many, in fact, could not read or write. This was especially the case with the eighteenth-century immigrants who came to this country as indentured servants, meaning they were obliged to work for a specified period of time (usually seven years) to repay the cost of their passage to America.

There was also a smaller percentage of criminals transported to America from the jails of England, most of whom were imprisoned for debts or certain other offenses. The Georgia Colony, which was chartered in 1732 by the English reformer James Oglethorpe, was the principal destination for debtors and other persons exiled by the English courts. The Colony of Carolina was chartered in 1663 but remained largely unsettled until about 1670. Then, in the third decade of the eighteenth century, Carolina was divided into two separate colonies, South Carolina in 1721 and North Carolina in 1729.

In 1686, the colonies were reorganized for a brief interval as the Dominion of New England. It included the colonies of Plymouth, Massachusetts Bay, Connecticut, Rhode Island, and New Hampshire. New York, West Jersey, and East Jersey, which had been part of the Dutch colony of New Netherland, became part of the Dominion in 1688; however, the merger didn't last long. After two years, Plymouth Colony withdrew from the Dominion, and the entire unification effort collapsed in the wake of the Glorious Revolution of 1688, which substantially altered colonial relations with England.[24]

The Plymouth Colony's return to self-rule was short-lived, however. A delegation led by Increase Mather, who was the son of Richard Mather and father of Cotton Mather, traveled to London to negotiate renewal of the colonial patents that had preceded the Dominion agreement. At that point a new charter was issued, making the Plymouth Colony a permanent part of the Massachusetts Bay Colony. The last official meeting of the Plymouth General Court took place in the summer of 1692.

AN ENDURING LEGACY

Looking back across this amazing panorama, it is remarkable that in the span of just seventy-two years, from the landing at Plymouth Rock to the emergence of Massachusetts as the most dominant social and political entity in the New World, a nation was born, built on endurance, an irresistible passion for liberty, and the covenants of the Christian faith. To claim that this country was a secular nation, that the Founders were ambivalent about religion, or that the Christian faith was not an essential part of their daily lives, one would either have to be ignorant of the facts or intentionally deceitful. Unfortunately, as I argued in the previous chapter, that actually may be the case for many Americans today.

There is no question that the spiritual heritage passed down to us from the colonial period has had a long-lasting impact on the nation, not simply because a band of religious extremists successfully crossed an ocean and erected the framework of a prosperous society in North America, but because the character, resilience, and moral fiber they exhibited has remained the hallmark of the American experience ever since.

In the year 1820, the great nineteenth-century statesman Daniel Webster expressed the hope that the American people might never forget "the religious character of our origin." In remarks celebrating the two-hundredth anniversary of the landing at Plymouth Rock, Webster said, "Our fathers were brought hither by their high veneration for the Christian religion. They journeyed by its light and labored in its hope. They sought to incorporate its principles with the elements of their society and to diffuse its influence through all their institutions, civil, political, or literary."[25]

No one hearing those words in 1820 would have been the least surprised by what Webster was saying. No one would have disagreed. It is only now, after a hundred and fifty years of material comfort and academic reprogramming, that the average American is predisposed to believe that the faith of our fathers had no lasting importance in the nation's founding. But nothing could be further from the truth.

During an address in New Hampshire honoring the *Mayflower* Pilgrims, a distinguished former professor of history at Harvard University offered a tribute to the men and women who risked so much to lay the foundations of the republic. The year was 1936—316 years after the signing of the Mayflower Compact—when Professor Samuel Eliot Morison spoke these words. Why should anyone still care about the Pilgrims today?

> Here is a story of simple people impelled by an ardent faith in God to a dauntless courage in danger, a boundless resourcefulness in face of difficulty, an impregnable fortitude in adversity. It strengthens and inspires us still, after more than three centuries, in this age of change and uncertainty. . . . The story of their patience and fortitude, and the workings of that unseen force which bears up heroic souls in the doing of mighty errands, as often as it is read or told, quickens the spiritual forces in American life, strengthens faith in God, and confidence in human nature. Thus the Pilgrims in a sense have become the spiritual ancestors of all Americans, whatever their stock, race, or creed.[26]

If only we could somehow persuade all Americans to grasp the truth and importance of those words. But for one of the leading icons of the secular Left, Professor Noam Chomsky of MIT, the story of the American founding is a dark saga—an example of over-the-top religious extremism. In an interview for *The Humanist*, he said, "There's that something about the history of the United States, going back to the Pilgrims, that I would call religious extremism. It's a major theme in this society and culture."[27] The villain for this humanist isn't the persecution that brought the Puritans to this country but their religious fundamentalism, along with a penchant for exploiting the natives.

I would propose that it is Chomsky's views that are extreme, but he is not alone. There are other Americans, including some very much in the public eye, who are only too glad to assure the world that America is not a Christian nation. During a press conference in Turkey on April 6, 2009, President Barack Obama said, "One of the great strengths of the United States is . . . we do not consider ourselves a Christian nation. . . . We consider ourselves a nation of citizens who are bound by ideals and a set of values."[28] The only problem with the statement is, it's not true. Upward of 80 percent of Americans today say they are Christians—the highest percentage of any industrialized nation—and it has been that way for the last three hundred years.

A 2006 ABC News poll found that 83 percent of Americans self-identify as Christians while 2.2 percent say they are Jewish, and just under 1 percent are Muslim. In fact, the total number of Americans of "other faiths" is less than 4 percent.[29] A 2006 Gallup survey reported that 42 percent of Americans say they attend church or synagogue every week or almost every week. The numbers vary from state to state, from 60 percent in the South to less than 25 percent in Vermont.[30]

The president's words may cheer secularists, but the words of the Founders—along with the history we have seen in these pages—make it clear that the Christian faith was the single most dynamic force in the discovery, population, and unification of America. Over and over again throughout our history, this fact has been reinforced in public declarations.

James Madison, the father of the Constitution, said, "We have staked the whole future of American civilization, not upon the power of government, far from it . . . but upon the capacity of mankind for self government; upon the capacity of each and all of us to govern ourselves, to control ourselves, to sustain ourselves according to The Ten Commandments of God."[31] The revolutionary-era patriot Patrick Henry agreed, saying, "It cannot be emphasized too strongly or too often that this great nation was founded, not by religionists, but by Christians; not on religions, but on the Gospel of Jesus Christ."[32]

A century later in 1846, the Supreme Court of South Carolina rendered the judgment that "Christianity is a part of the common law of the land, with liberty of conscience to all. It has always been so recognized . . . it is the foundation of those morals and manners upon which our society is formed; it is their basis. Remove this and they would fall."[33] Forty-six years later, after an exhausting ten-year review of all the founding documents of the republic, the United States Supreme Court said in its 1892 Trinity decision, "There is a universal language pervading them all, having one meaning: they affirm and reaffirm that this is a religious nation. These are not individual sayings, declarations of private persons: they are organic utterances; they speak the voice of the entire people . . . that this is a Christian nation."[34] And later still, in *Zorach v. Clauson* (1952), liberal justice William O. Douglas announced the majority opinion of the United States Supreme Court, declaring, "We are a religious people whose institutions presuppose a Supreme Being. When the state encourages religious instruction or cooperates with religious authorities by adjusting the schedule of public events to sectarian needs, it follows the best of our traditions. For it then respects the religious nature of our people and accommodates public service to their spiritual needs."[35]

No one would argue that America in the twenty-first century is a paragon of virtue or that we still exhibit the same strength of character, resilience, and moral fiber of the founding generations. But no one can deny that the nation rose to greatness in large part because of the beliefs and behaviors of the men and women who gave birth to this nation; and those beliefs were, above all, a gift of their profound Christian faith.

Our challenge today is to live up to those high standards, and I believe that can still happen; but when it does, it will not be some jumped-up man-made affair. But I am getting ahead of myself. Before returning to this subject, let us turn the page and step back briefly to consider the achievements of the first generation of English colonists who paid a tremendous price to establish the Colony of Virginia. Theirs is a very different story, but it is an essential link in the history of American independence.

Three

WHAT THE FOUNDERS BELIEVED

By the mid-sixteenth century, it was becoming commonplace. English seafarers made landfall in North America at least a half-dozen times, accompanied by groups of wealthy adventurers eager for riches and personal acclaim. It is astonishing how many of these gentlemen were quick to publish their journals and sketchbooks. A few even managed to bring back Native Americans they had captured in the wilds of Virginia for exhibit in London. But none of the early expeditions had been resourceful enough to establish even one successful colony in the New World, and we can't help but wonder why. Why were the earliest expeditions so different from the landing at Plymouth just a few years later?

Unlike the English colonies in New England that had begun with strong Puritan roots and noble aspirations, the first colonies in Virginia were commissioned with more conventional objectives. The earliest groups of explorers from Britain were sent abroad with instructions to search for gold and silver, and if possible to locate a westward passage to the Pacific Ocean. They succeeded in none of those objectives, but rather than spending time clearing land, building permanent dwellings, or planting the crops necessary for their own survival, the would-be settlers quarreled among themselves constantly.

The most notorious attempt to exploit the uncharted wilderness of North America was the English settlement at Roanoke Island, just off the coast of North Carolina. Walter Raleigh, who was knighted by Queen Elizabeth I in 1584, was given a charter that year to organize an expedition to colonize North America. With royal patents in hand, Raleigh christened the new territory Virginia, in honor of the Virgin Queen. An Oxford-educated gentleman and a court favorite, Raleigh wisely chose not to make the journey himself, but by the spring of 1585, he managed to outfit seven ships and a party of 108 able-bodied men to undertake the adventure.

The expedition would be led by Raleigh's cousin, Sir Richard Grenville, who was a military officer and scientist, along with one experienced explorer, Ralph Lane. They set out from the port of Plymouth, England, for the coast of North America, where they intended to establish a new plantation. The Atlantic crossing was unusually rough, and the two gentlemen Raleigh had put in charge were constantly at odds with each other. When they finally reached their destination after ten weeks at sea, Ralph Lane assembled work parties and began construction of a makeshift outpost on the island. Then, just days later, Richard Grenville and most of the ship's crew said their brief farewells and set sail for England, leaving the remaining colonists to fend for themselves.

Ralph Lane acted as governor on the island. He organized scouting parties to go into the wilderness, searching the entire region in a 130-mile radius. The laborers and carpenters in the group made good use of the abundant timber in the area and built a small fort to protect themselves during the frequent surprise visits from the local Indian tribes. However, by the time the English privateer Sir Francis Drake stopped briefly at the site in June of the following year, Lane and the others were exhausted, hungry, and profoundly dispirited. Lane was only too glad to give up on the experiment and return with Drake to London.

Walter Raleigh, however, refused to admit his plan had failed, and one year later he dispatched three more ships to continue the Roanoke experiment. The newly mounted expedition set sail with 150 settlers on May 8, 1587, under the command of a new leader, Captain John White. The party arrived at Roanoke three months later, in mid-August, at which time the settlers participated in the first recorded Protestant service in the colonies.

Later that month John White's daughter, Elenor, who was married to Ananias Dare, gave birth to the first English baby born on American soil, Virginia Dare. Finding little of the previous settlement still intact, and painfully aware that the provisions they had brought with them would be insufficient for their long-term needs, John White decided to return to England to gather additional food, tools, and supplies. Unfortunately, the English navy was fully occupied when White returned, waging war against the Spanish, and it would be four long years before he was able to arrange passage back to America.

When he finally landed at the site of the Roanoke settlement in 1590, there was nothing left. His family was gone, the fort he helped build was broken and deserted, and there was no sign of what may have happened to the colonists. His daughter and grandchild were nowhere to be found. Today, more than four centuries later, the "Lost Colony of Roanoke" remains one of the most perplexing unsolved mysteries of the founding era.

Despite the misfortunes of the Roanoke colonists, the men who helped launch the age of English exploration in the New World—including the two Anglican clergymen Richard Hakluyt and Samuel Purchas who were such prolific writers and travel enthusiasts—continued to lobby king and Parliament for additional forays into North America where, they said, vast wealth and unrivaled imperial glory were ripe for the taking.

DAZED BUT UNDAUNTED

News of the Roanoke debacle aroused doubts and disappointment in London and could have ended the efforts to colonize North America except for the relentless ambition of the merchants and promoters. Although the prospect of great treasure now seemed much less likely, the colonists had discovered an important new crop in the New World, tobacco, that would eventually provide sufficient motivation and revenue to persuade the financial backers to continue pouring money into the expedition.

In 1606, King James I, who succeeded Elizabeth as monarch in 1603, granted two trading companies exclusive rights to establish colonies in America between the thirty-fourth and forty-first degrees north latitudes. On December 20, 1606, the London Company sent 143 settlers on three ships—*Godspeed*, *Discovery*, and *Susan Constant*—under the command of Captain Christopher Newport. Most of the passengers, according to at least one eighteenth-century report, were poorly suited for survival in an untamed wilderness. The ships landed first at Cape Henry near the mouth of Chesapeake Bay on April 26, 1607; then they moved farther inland. Two weeks later on May 14, they named the new settlement Jamestown, in honor of the king.

These "reprobates of good families,"[1] as the Virginia diarist William Byrd would refer to them later, apparently made the voyage expecting the sort of lush vistas, abundant crops, and fat cattle that promoters like Richard Hakluyt had promised. What they actually discovered was a mosquito-infested swamp in the middle of a jungle, with the constant threat of attack by hostile "savages." There were no conveniences of any sort. What was needed at Jamestown was back-breaking labor. For the most part, however, these men and women were utterly unsuited to work of any kind. Many simply refused to work. Instead, they sat around fanning themselves, expecting to be fed and cared for by their social inferiors.

In time the newcomers managed to construct a stockade, a

palisade of tall timbers laid out in the shape of a large triangle. It included a central storehouse, a church, and several small buildings where the settlers could take shelter. In the first seven months the settlement was nearly wiped out by disease, famine, and unceasing attacks. The total number of settlers, which was just over a hundred souls in May 1607, was less than half that number the following September. Indians had attacked before the fortifications were in place, and no sooner had the living quarters been completed than fire broke out, destroying several houses, the church, and chaplain Robert Hunt's entire library.

Unlike Walter Raleigh and the men he had previously given leadership roles, the leader of the Jamestown expedition, Captain John Smith, was not an English gentleman. He was a practical man of modest means who was not averse to hard work and was, fortunately for the settlers, a compassionate, determined, and capable leader. It was his energies during the worst of times that kept the colony going. And Smith's most able assistant during all this time, the young Anglican chaplain Robert Hunt, had left a young wife and two small children back in England, feeling that God had called him to accompany the Jamestown colonists as their minister.

The colonists, on the other hand, could be loud and offensive, "little better than Atheists," one settler quipped. But they showed dutiful respect for their young preacher. On April 29, 1607, on the morning of their third day in the New World, the colonists planted a cross made of solid oak at water's edge—they had brought the cross with them from England for that purpose. Hunt prayed first, then the whole company joined him in offering prayers of thanksgiving to God for their safe arrival.

In his official capacity Hunt served as minister, vicar, and chaplain of the settlement, but he was always quick to lend a hand in every important task. No job, regardless how menial or exhausting, was too much for him. He had dedicated the new colony in the name of God on the day of their arrival, but he was glad to take up tools and share in their daily chores. "We are all laborers in a common vineyard," he told them. He led public prayers every morning and evening, preached two sermons on Sundays, administered communion, and ministered to the souls of his flock.

Surviving in this environment proved to be much more demanding than any of the settlers had anticipated. Yet the Reverend Robert Hunt was never heard to complain, even when his precious books and personal effects went up in flames. He nursed the sick and prayed for the dying. From beginning to end, Hunt was the most even-tempered and considerate member of the group, and when he came down with a fever and died just one year after the arrival in Jamestown, many of the colonists were heartbroken.[2]

The preacher's death left a vacuum, but his Christ-like example of self-sacrifice and devotion was a blessing and served as a poignant reminder of the original charter for the Virginia Colony that cited "propagating of Christian Religion" as one of the expedition's primary purposes. An inscription on the bronze plaque honoring Robert Hunt at the Jamestown historical site today bears the words of the settlers who knew him: "We all received from him the Holy Communion together, as a pledge of reconciliation, for we all loved him for his exceeding goodness. He planted the First Protestant Church in America and laid down his life in the foundation of America."[3]

Life in the colony was a day-by-day affair, and life was never easy. Food they had stored in crates and sealed lockers rotted before it could be eaten, and precious supplies simply disappeared. They were constantly plagued by rats and vermin of all kinds; and famine, sickness, and malarial fevers were a never-ending threat. All these things took a tremendous toll on the population, and it began to feel as if they were cursed. It wasn't until the Powhatan Indians came in peace, offering to trade food and other common necessities for glass beads and implements made of iron and copper, that the settlers were able to rest at all. But this act of benevolence was no guarantee of safety.

The attacks may have slowed temporarily, but they would continue indefinitely. The settlers were ravaged by diseases, but at times they were their own worst enemies. The uncertainties of their precarious existence were taking a toll on their souls as well as their bodies, and it showed. Less than two years after they had built it, the church the men erected to replace the temporary structure John Smith had rigged up with old canvas sails and cedar poles was on the verge of falling apart.

When Sir Thomas Gates arrived as the new governor in 1609, he made a thorough inspection of the living quarters, fortifications, and other facilities within the compound. Much of it was serviceable, he said, but he was disappointed to see the pathetic condition of the church. It symbolized the state of religion in the colony, and he ordered the settlers to immediately begin restoration. As a distinguished military officer, Gates had been sent by the London Company to take whatever steps might be needed to strengthen the colony and get the men back to work. He realized that the vitality of their Christian faith was every bit as important as their commitment to building a productive economy.

One of Gates's first official acts was to call for a renewal of religious services. From that point on, there would be two Sunday sermons each week and a Weekday Sermon every Thursday. In addition, a bell was to be rung every morning at ten o'clock and every evening before supper, calling each man to a time of personal prayers. The governor believed a revitalized faith would help the settlers deal more effectively with the hardship of their daily lives.

Equally important, the governor wanted to emphasize the majesty and solemnity of the worship service. When he went to church on Sunday, he was accompanied by his councilors, captains, and officers. There was also a company of fifty armed soldiers, called halberdiers, surrounding him in their brilliant red tunics. The governor took his seat in the choir where everyone could see him, and vice versa. He sat, as Frank Lambert reports, "in a green velvet chair, with a velvet cushion before him on which he knelt, and the council, captains, and officers sat on each side of him, each in their place."[4]

THE FINGER OF GOD

Very much like the Pilgrims in New England (who would not arrive in the New World for another eleven years), the Jamestown colonists suffered through their own "starving time" in 1609–10. All but 60 of the original 214 settlers died during that fateful winter. For many of the men and women in the settlement, the losses, defeats, and constant struggles were unbearable. To make matters worse the ship they expected to arrive in the fall of 1609, bringing food and desperately needed provisions, did not survive the voyage. Without the new cargo, which included clothing, tools, and many other staples they desperately needed, the settlers knew there was no way they could survive.

But this would be one of the most amazing miracles of the entire Jamestown saga. During the passage from England to Virginia, the cargo ship *Sea Venture*, carrying all the provisions for the struggling colony, went aground off the coast of Bermuda, and the entire crew was given up for dead. The colonists waited expectantly, searching the horizon day after day for any sign of hope, but the ship never came, at which point the men voted to bury their cannons and armor, abandon the colony, and return to England at the first possible opportunity. If they had left the colony, the settlement at Jamestown would have gone the way of all the other failed attempts. But on June 10, 1610, the day before their planned departure, Providence intervened, and the ships bearing their new governor, Lord de La Ware, and all the goods and supplies for which they had been praying suddenly appeared at the mouth of the James River. When the captain and his crew came ashore, the colonists learned the *Sea Venture* crew had not been lost at sea after all. They had not only survived the shipwreck but also managed to save the entire cargo, then built new ships. As soon as they were able, they continued the journey to Virginia.[5]

There was no doubt in the minds of any of the Jamestown settlers that this was a miracle from heaven, and when the news reached England, preachers on both sides of the Atlantic declared the rescue to be an act of divine mercy. And just as important, they believed it was a sign from heaven that the English flag was meant to fly over the New World. In Virginia the Reverend Alexander Whitaker wrote, "The finger of God hast been the only true worker here." In London the Reverend William Crashaw agreed, saying, "If ever the hand of God appeared in action of man, it was here most evident: for when man had forsaken this business, God took it in hand."[6]

Many of the men and women who had been the most childish and unreasonable before the relief ship arrived were seemingly transformed by the experience. They could see that miracles do happen and that obedience to God and king was essential for their survival. They realized God is sovereign—God rules in the affairs of men—and He intervenes in ways that sometimes defy human reason. The wreck of the *Sea Venture* and the relief of the colony convinced the colonists that—just as He had spared the children of Israel from the wrath of Pharaoh—God could and would suspend the laws of nature for His faithful servants.[7]

Although they had been saved from disaster in the nick of time, the struggling colony was by no means in the clear. Their "seasoning time" would continue for years to come, but occasional shipments of goods and fresh provisions from England, along with the success of the tobacco plantations established by John Rolfe, gave the settlers renewed confidence and good reasons to go on. Rolfe's marriage in 1614 to the Indian princess, Pocahontas, who was the daughter of the Powhatan chief, Wahunsenacawh, improved the settlers' prospects for a while, but it was still no guarantee of lasting peace.

Despite their efforts to appease the local tribes, the troubles never ceased. It was painfully clear that something had to change. Then in 1618, representatives of Sir Edwin Sandys, the London Company's treasurer, suggested the colonists try and integrate the families into the settlements. At that point several Indian groups were given houses, and schools were built for their children so they would be introduced to the Christian religion and English customs.

The colonists assumed the Powhatan nation would be grateful for their benevolence and welcome the opportunity to participate in English community life, but that was not the case. Furthermore the Powhatans did not miss the fact that most of the settlers held them and their way of life in contempt. "There is scarce any man among us," one sympathetic settler wrote, "that doth so much as afford them a good thought in his heart, and most men with their mouths give them nothing but maledictions and bitter execrations."[8]

By the year 1622, the Powhatan elders realized the English intended to claim all of their nation's lands, expanding English towns and villages across Virginia. They saw this as a threat to their way of life. The colonists' offer to educate their children was seen as an even greater threat—an effort to steal their children's hearts and eradicate their native customs. At that point the Powhatan chief, Opechancanough, conceived a plan he hoped would drive the foreigners out of Virginia once and for all.

The attack of March 22, 1622, began with a clever bit of deception when a large group of Powhatans came into the English village, bearing gifts of meat and fruit. The following morning they returned to the settlement and moved from house to house, greeting the colonists warmly. Then at a given signal the natives suddenly grabbed their weapons and other implements and began butchering as many settlers as they could find. They massacred entire families in their homes and killed all their servants and field hands. By the time the mayhem was done, the Powhatans had killed 347 men, women, and children. Then, to make sure no one failed to get the message, they desecrated the bodies of the dead, burned the villages, and destroyed the remaining livestock and crops.[9]

When news of the attack and the colony's devastating losses reached London, King James was livid. He canceled the London Company's charter in 1624, and the entire colony of Virginia along with its governing body, the House of Burgesses, was placed under royal control. That was how things continued for the next half century until September 1679, when the fortress and village of Jamestown were finally burned to the ground during a violent clash between the settlers and their governor, William Berkeley, known as Bacon's Rebellion. When the capital of the Virginia Colony was moved to Williamsburg in 1699, the Jamestown settlement was abandoned and fell into ruin. A re-creation of the original village can be seen today at the site, thanks to a project funded by the Colonial National Historical Park.

CLERGY UNDER DISTRESS

The Virginia commonwealth of the mid- to late-seventeenth century did not look much like the settlements of New England, but the citizens of all the English colonies had many things in common, including their religious faith. Most of the ministers who came to Virginia during those years were Anglicans. They were Episcopalian in doctrine and demeanor but subscribed to Calvinist teachings regarding salvation by grace through faith, and they preached in the Puritan plain style. Regardless of style, they all believed the Church of England provided the best expression of the Christian religion.

While the Puritan churches in Massachusetts maintained their Congregationalist identity, the churches in Virginia were becoming more aggressively Anglican with each passing year. An act of the House of Burgesses in 1632 made uniformity of belief and practice a matter of common law, ensuring the Church of England would be the official faith of the colony and that the Episcopalian form of worship would be the norm. As some of the other colonies were doing, Virginia also enacted anti-Quaker laws to avoid schism in the church, even prescribing the death penalty for Friends who refused to stay away.

The middle colonies, however, were much more tolerant of minority denominations. Quakers, Amish, Mennonites, and various other sects were welcomed in Pennsylvania and the colonies of Delaware, New York, and New Jersey. Rhode Island was chartered by Roger Williams as a refuge for those of a more democratic spirit. Pennsylvania was established as a Quaker colony by a royal land grant to the English Quaker, William Penn, in 1638; but none of these denominations would have been welcome in either the northern or southern colonies until late in the following century.

By the end of the seventeenth century, the church in Virginia was still growing, but it lacked the intensity of the congregations farther north. James Hutson, who is the author of a Library of Congress publication tracing the history of faith in America, writes that "religion was the salt that flavored life in seventeenth-century British North America."[10] But there were many Virginians in the closing decades of the century who feared the salt was losing its savor.

A half century after the demise of the Jamestown settlement, the Anglican church held a virtual monopoly on religion in the colony; however, as Hutson points out, the churches were so widely scattered that regular church attendance was often difficult, and next to impossible in bad weather. Some Anglican ministers were assigned multiple widely separated parishes, which made Sunday and weekday services incredibly stressful, and officiating at the growing number of weddings, baptisms, funerals, and other special occasions was next to impossible. In some instances, specially trained laymen were allowed to conduct services, but the end result was a general decrease in the orthodoxy and level of Christian commitment in many parts of the colony.

There were never enough ministers, and there never would be as long as the life of the typical pastor remained stressful as he was underappreciated and underpaid. The Virginia legislature attempted to introduce measures to make life a little easier for the clergy by offering to increase salaries, which were often paid in tobacco and corn. But many parishes failed to provide even a modest living for their ministers. Each community was required to set aside a certain amount of property, called glebe land, where crops were cultivated for the benefit of the clergy. But one English visitor to the Virginia Colony wrote that ministers there were condemned to "see their families disordered, their children untaught, the public worship and service of the great God they own neglected."[11]

Some parishes, on the other hand, could complain that their preachers were receiving better support than they deserved. A certain percentage of the ministers who came to the colonies had done so to escape bad debts, bad marriages, and other problems. This situation eventually became so common that the House of Burgesses issued a decree: "Ministers shall not give themselves to excess in drinking, or riot, spending their time idly by day or night playing at dice, cards, or any other unlawful game; but they shall . . . occupy themselves with some honest study or exercise, always doing the things which shall appertain to honesty, and endeavor to profit the Church of God." Apparently, however, the government's caution had little effect. Another English visitor remarked a decade later that Virginia seems to attract mainly the kind of ministers who "babble in a pulpit" and "roar in a tavern."[12]

THE OLD DOMINION

The contrast between the colonies of Virginia and New England in the late seventeenth century was striking. The population in both areas was still mainly English, but while the citizens of the northern colonies were staunchly Puritan with separatist sympathies, Virginia was resolutely Anglican with loyalist sympathies. And while the Puritans were evangelical and passionate about soul-winning, the Virginians avoided displays of enthusiasm or emotion in the churches. Furthermore in New England practically every man, woman, and child could read and write, whereas in Virginia education and learning were reserved mainly for the ruling class.

New England was also supported by numerous trades, crafts, and budding industries while Virginia was all about agriculture, mainly centered around the tobacco trade. Not least, while New England was generally democratic in spirit, Virginia retained the attitudes and habits of an Old World aristocracy. As historian Francis Parkman points out, Virginia society was stratified with slaves, indentured servants, and poor whites at the low end of the social spectrum, farmers and small planters in the middle, and the landed gentry who made up the ruling class at the high end. Parkman writes:

> Many of them were well born, with an immense pride of descent, increased by the habit of domination. Indolent and energetic by turns; rich in natural gifts and often poor in book learning, though some, in the lack of good teaching at home, had been bred in the English universities; high-spirited, generous to a fault; keeping open house in their capacious mansions, among vast tobacco fields and toiling negroes, and living in a rude pomp where the fashions of St. James were somewhat oddly grafted on the roughness of the plantation . . . [13]

But what the Virginia planters lacked in formal schooling, Parkman adds, was compensated for by power and position, along with a bold spirit of independence and a patriotic attachment to the Old Dominion. "They were few in number; they raced, gambled, drank, and swore; they did everything that in Puritan eyes was most reprehensible; and in the day of need they gave the United Colonies a body of statesmen and orators which had no equal on the continent."[14]

The Pennsylvania Colony, by contrast, was by design a wild mixture of races and creeds—English, Irish, Germans, Dutch, and Swedes, who were Quakers, Lutherans, Presbyterians, Catholics, Moravians, and many other denominations. The Quaker tradition, to which William Penn and the colony's founding families all belonged, dominated in the eastern part of the colony while German Lutherans, most of whom were simple farmers, were most numerous in the middle parts of the territory, and Scots and Irish immigrants occupied the western regions.

Because of this wide diversity it was only natural that Philadelphia would play a key role in the revolutionary period. Second only to Boston, Philadelphia was the largest town in British America and the intellectual hub of the colonies. Ironically the Quaker influence suggested that Pennsylvania would be pacifist and noncombatant in the revolutionary era, but the colonies were under increasing stress from British policies, and even the most deeply rooted beliefs can change in such circumstances.

The Colony of New Netherland was settled by Dutch traders in 1614, and remained under Dutch control for the next fifty years. The English navigator Henry Hudson was the first to explore the region on behalf of Dutch merchants, but when James I learned of Hudson's involvement, he commanded him to cease all such efforts. The town of New Amsterdam, on the western end of Long Island, was home to Dutch Calvinists, French Huguenots, and German Lutherans, as well as large numbers of Independents, Scottish Presbyterians, and others of little or no religion. In 1664, James laid claim to the territory for England. Unable to defend his prior claim, the Dutch governor, Peter Stuyvesant, had no choice but to accept a bloodless defeat. New Amsterdam was then renamed New York, in honor of the king's brother, the Duke of York.

The Colony of New Jersey was mainly farm territory while Maryland, very much like its larger and more prosperous neighbor to the south, was a tobacco-growing region. Unlike Virginia, however, Maryland had been established as a home for Roman Catholics who were out of favor everywhere else. The Colony of Delaware, established by Virginia's former governor, Lord de La Ware, was essentially an extension of Pennsylvania, and the southern colonies—North Carolina, South Carolina, and Georgia—were predominantly agrarian societies with a mixture of English plantation owners, poor white farmers, and large numbers of slaves, indentured servants, and castoffs from the British Isles.

The attitudes of all these colonies toward each other are hard to imagine today. Their only source of unity was the fact that they were European immigrants with an allegiance to the English king. As Francis Parkman points out, communication between the colonies was slow and tedious. Messengers traveled over rough roads poorly cut through dense forests. In addition, there were long-held animosities between some of them because of land disputes and commercial rivalry. Each man considered his own colony to be his native land; the concept of a united North America simply did not exist.

THE LAND OF OPPORTUNITY

As social and political institutions in the colonies increased in maturity and status, and as the populations of all the colonies became more numerous, it was obvious on both sides of the Atlantic that these Americans were building an economic powerhouse. There were still poverty and hardship in many places, particularly in the western territories where communities of any size were few and far between, but business was booming in the cities and towns. After a century of toil and constant uncertainty, there was now a gratifying and unprecedented level of prosperity.

The wealth of the colonies began with agriculture. Land was plentiful, and the climate was ideal for growing a wide variety of cereals, fibers, fruits, and vegetables that were highly prized in Europe. Rice, wheat, corn, hemp, and tobacco were grown commercially on both small and large farms. There were highly productive fisheries in Massachusetts Bay and all along the Atlantic coast, and every colony could boast of a thriving trade in horses, cattle, sheep, pigs, and poultry. South Carolina became the wealthiest of the thirteen colonies in the mid-eighteenth century, thanks primarily to the large number of rice plantations cultivated there by slave labor.

America's forests were seemingly endless, and the timber merchants harvested tremendous quantities of oak, poplar, elm, cedar, and pine for construction projects in the colonies as well as for shipbuilders in the maritime colonies and the overseas trade. In addition, there were now mines in the mountains of Carolina, Virginia, and Pennsylvania, producing iron ore, copper, and lead. These and many other commodities—including animal hides, whiskey, rum, sugar, and tobacco—contributed to the colonies' growing economic strength.

Cotton and other fiber-producing plants were grown and harvested in the southern colonies for the looms in England. Weaving was still a cottage industry in the early years, but by the end of the eighteenth century, there would be large textile mills in Carolina, Delaware, and the middle colonies. Wool products, however, were not produced commercially until the end of the century, due to trade restrictions imposed by Parliament. Sheep, goats, and wool products had been a mainstay of England's economy for centuries, and the last thing the lawmakers in London wanted was competition from America.

Thanks to abundant natural resources, business was thriving in the early years of the eighteenth century. Wages for American workers were as high as or higher than those in England at the time, but fewer than half of the working men owned their own homes or land. Tax records from the period indicate that the bottom 30 percent owned nothing, but from the beginning there was a strong work ethic in the colonies. Thanks to low tax rates and a less rigid class system than that of the Old World, it was possible for a common man with a quick wit and a strong back to acquire wealth and rise in society.[15]

Benjamin Franklin, as perhaps the most conspicuous example, was born into a middle-class family. His father, Josiah, was a soap and candle maker. The elder Franklin hoped his youngest son would become an Anglican minister, but Benjamin had other ideas. He was obstinate, independently minded, and curious about many things; but he was not a good student. He was much too impatient and undisciplined and, consequently, spent just two years in grammar school before taking an apprenticeship with his older brother, James, who was a printer.

Once he had learned the trade, Ben left his father's home in Boston and headed to Philadelphia, where he worked in several print shops before he decided to go into business on his own. It wasn't long before

Ben and a financial partner, Hugh Meredith, purchased one of the colony's first periodicals, the *Philadelphia Gazette*, and turned it into the most successful newspaper in the country. Franklin is also credited with creating the first political cartoon, "Join, or Die." The cartoon appeared in the *Gazette* on May 9, 1754, calling for the American colonies to unite against further encroachments by Parliament and King George II.

Almost every American home at the time had a copy of the King James Bible, but Franklin believed there was a need for other kinds of literature as well. Relying upon his quick wit, a quirky sense of humor, and an ear for a colorful anecdote, he composed *Poor Richard's Almanac*, which would become, second only to the Bible, the most popular book in the country. At a time when the entire population of Philadelphia was less than twenty-five thousand, the almanac reportedly sold more than ten thousand copies a year.[16]

In time Franklin would become a successful inventor, postmaster, humorist, scientist, political commentator, statesman, diplomat, and ambassador to France. He taught himself to read French, Spanish,

Italian, and Latin, and he was considered by delegates to the Continental Congress to be among the most illustrious members of that body. He never denied his working-class background, but by age forty-two he had achieved enough wealth and status to turn over the day-to-day management of his business to others. By any standard Franklin was exceptional. Not many men could equal his achievements, then or now. But the point is that in England such a career would have been inconceivable while in America every man had the opportunity to rise to whatever level his skill and determination would allow.

A CHANGING LANDSCAPE

What was happening in America in the early years of the eighteenth century was unique in human history, a fact that did not go entirely unnoticed in England. The explosion of prosperity and the rise of an independent spirit in the colonies, which ought to have been cause for celebration, actually contributed to a growing rift between England and America. Sir Robert Walpole, known as "England's first Prime Minister," was the voice of the British government between 1721 and 1742, and he was a vocal supporter of a policy of "salutary neglect" regarding the colonies. This had been the unofficial policy of Parliament ever since Jamestown, enabling colonial governments to achieve autonomy and efficiency without undue interference from London. Walpole said, "If no restrictions were placed on the colonies, they would flourish."[17] And the more the American colonies flourished, he believed, the better for Britain.

The American alliance was opening up new territory for Britain in the West; it brought them new and exotic commodities, and it added much-needed revenue to the Exchequer through taxes, fees, and duties on certain American goods. A laissez-faire policy made perfect sense, he believed, but not everyone in London agreed with Walpole's assessment. England was deeply in debt as a result of back-to-back wars in Europe, Canada, and the British Isles. Strapped for cash and with English troops strung out halfway around the world, it was inevitable that both king and Parliament would look to America for relief, in the form of new and higher taxes—along with intervention in many other areas.

The Navigation Acts, which dated to the mid-seventeenth century, prohibited the colonies from trading with nations other than England, Scotland, and Ireland. These policies raised little or no alarm in the beginning since foreign trade was not yet a major concern, but as America's factories, farms, and mills became more and more productive, English laws restricting commercial growth and taxing profits were suddenly a sore spot for the colonies. Domestic taxes were lower in America than in Britain, but each new increase provoked an angry response, and the increases were suddenly coming more and more often.

The Molasses Act of 1733 placed a duty on sugar and sugar-based products but caused little stir in America because the rum manufacturers in New England ignored it. They found that smuggling was a much better alternative. The colonies continued to trade lumber, furs, and agricultural products for sugar from the West Indies without paying duties, but thirty years later when Parliament passed the Sugar Act with stricter enforcement, resentment spread throughout the colonies. The Sugar Act—along with the Stamp Act, passed in 1765—became one of the first irritants leading to the eventual showdown between America and Britain.

But prosperity had other consequences as well. As life in colonial America continued to improve materially and economically, there was a growing sense that something was being lost in the moral and spiritual vitality of the nation. The pace of expansion along with improvements in mobility and economic opportunity led, not to euphoria, but to anxiety, and the fallout could be felt in all sectors of society—especially in the churches, which were losing members and influence. As historian William McLoughlin reports,

The ministers no longer elicited deeply felt responses but rather a vague and undefinable discomfort. Men and women in every colony recognized that their efforts to succeed in this world were compelling departures from older behavior patterns and values. Businessmen had to cut corners to compete with their rivals. Farmers had to charge high prices to pay off mortgages on new land. Political leaders distorted the truth to win votes or gain influence. Town fathers enriched themselves and slighted the needs of the community. Lawyers and judges seemed unable to reach verdicts recognizably just to both parties. Legislators seemed to yield to special interests instead of serving the general welfare. On the frontier, where institutional restraints were weakest, men increasingly took the law into their own hands—against Indians, horse thieves, or an interloper overreaching himself.[18]

The result was social and political disorder. But the most important reaction was a new level of soul-searching, particularly in the churches of New England that had been wrestling with the issue of doctrinal purity for some time. Throughout the founding era, there had been strict adherence to Scripture and the principles of the Reformed faith. Calvinism taught that man is by nature sinful and in need of redemption, which comes through belief in the atoning death of Jesus Christ and is only attainable by a sincere confession of sin, repentance, and conversion.

Church membership and the sacraments of baptism and holy communion were limited to those who could give evidence of a salvation experience. But a new kind of rationalism was being preached in many Congregationalist churches in New England, best exemplified by the Halfway Covenant of 1662, which in its original formulation allowed the children of church members to receive baptism without making a profession of faith. Fifty years later the covenant was being applied to those wishing to join the church, whether or not they were confessing believers.

In the beginning the idea was to make sure that unbaptized children of members would remain in the church family as adults, but the new liberalized policies made full fellowship available to all adults who wished to be affiliated, regardless of their reasons. Many public offices at the time required evidence of church membership, and this brought some people into the churches purely for expedience, not because of religious conviction.

Pastors initially approved of the idea because it increased church attendance, but the actual effect was a watering down of theological integrity. Halfway churches offered membership to all comers—any so-called "moral person" was welcomed. Offering the sacraments to nonbelievers was, liberal clergy argued, a "means of grace" by which the Holy Spirit might work upon the souls of the unconverted and draw them into fellowship. "Better to have them in the church than out of it," they said. But in time this weakening of long-established tradition would have serious repercussions. "By 1720," as McLoughlin writes, "the vast majority of ministers were telling their parishioners that regular prayer, church attendance, right behavior, and responsible citizenship were all means of preparation for the salvation God would send when the time was ripe."[19]

The new doctrine offered congregants the assurance that man is not inherently evil, as the traditionalist preachers had insisted, but is basically good and capable of great things. God does not condemn His children to hell but wants the best for them. In this environment even the most unprincipled and profane members of the community were inclined to think of themselves as the best of men. But deep down there were lingering uncertainty and spiritual malaise.

THE ROOTS OF AWAKENING

The Reverend Solomon Stoddard was among the best-known Congregationalist preachers in New England at the time, and one of the most controversial. His enthusiastic embrace of the Halfway

Covenant put him at odds with a number of his peers in Boston, yet by opening church membership to any man of moral character, Stoddard doubled his congregation in Northampton while more orthodox congregations were shrinking. Ironically Stoddard's staunchest critic turned out to be his own grandson, Jonathan Edwards, who would offer the most formidable challenge to the rationalist approach. In 1741, Edwards preached the sermon that, more than any other, has been credited with launching the Great Awakening.

Jonathan Edwards (1703–1758) was the son of a Congregationalist minister in East Windsor, Connecticut. He was a brilliant student, entering Yale College at the age of thirteen where he studied Hebrew, Greek, Latin, geometry, rhetoric, and logic. Near the end of his second year, the young man experienced a dramatic conversion that transformed his life and his understanding of Scripture. After completing his baccalaureate in 1720, he spent the next two years at Yale studying theology; then at the age of eighteen, he was named pastor of a small church in New York.

Edwards held that position for only a few months before the church ran out of money. He then returned to Connecticut and accepted a position as a teacher and administrator at Yale. After several years in that post, he was called to his grandfather's church in Northampton, Massachusetts, where he served as assistant pastor for two years. When Solomon Stoddard died in 1729, Edwards was elevated to the position of senior minister. The problem he wrestled with in this new position was that he had never agreed with the Halfway Covenant his grandfather supported. He served as pastor of the church for twenty years before he made his feelings known, and, at that point, he was summarily dismissed by the congregation.

For the next seven years Edwards served as a missionary to the Indian communities at Stockbridge, Massachusetts, and devoted himself to study. During this time, he wrote four of the most respected theological works of the Puritan era, including "Freedom of the Will" and "The Great Christian Doctrine of Original Sin Defended." But the contributions for which Edwards is remembered today are two works composed during his time at Northampton: "A Faithful Narrative of the Surprizing Work of God in the Conversion of Many Hundred Souls in Northampton," published in London in 1737, and the sermon "Sinners in the Hands of an Angry God," which he preached at Enfield, Massachusetts, on July 8, 1741.

The revival that broke out in the Northampton Church in 1733 took Edwards and many others by surprise. He was unquestionably a gifted preacher, but Edwards insisted that what happened there over the next seven years was not an act of man but a move of God. The revival began among the youth of the church, then spread from Northampton to surrounding communities with such passion that it could not be restrained. Edwards later wrote:

> The congregation was alive in God's service, everyone earnestly intent on the public worship, every hearer eager to drink in the words of the minister as they came from his mouth; the assembly in general were, from time to time, in tears while the Word was preached; some weeping with sorrow and distress, others with joy and love, others with pity and concern for the souls of their neighbors.[20]

More than three hundred men and women joined the church in 1734 alone. The power of the Holy Spirit was so strong, changing the daily routines of so many citizens in Northampton, that local shop owners complained they were being driven out of business by the revivalists.

By 1735, the revival reached across the Connecticut River valley, as far away as New York and New Jersey. When news of what was happening in America reached England in 1735, the revivalists John and Charles Wesley immediately took notice, as did their colleague and fellow member of the "Holy Club" at Oxford University, George Whitefield. John Wesley, who had been ordained in 1728, was widely known as the leader of the Methodist movement, so named for the group's diligent study of Scripture and devotion to works of charity. He was anxious to see America for himself and to find out what the Awakening was all about.

The Wesley brothers sailed to America on October 14, 1735, hoping to preach to the Indians. However, the governor of the Georgia Colony, James Oglethorpe, insisted John speak in the churches. After two years John and Charles returned to London, deeply disappointed and consumed by doubts about their own salvation. The Anglican churches in the South had been insulted by Wesley's insistence that faith in Christ demands a personal salvation experience, and the Indian groups who received him were not the least impressed by his style of preaching. All of this precipitated a spiritual crisis in Wesley's own life that led, in 1738, to a miraculous conversion experience and the blossoming of his ministry in England.

Up until that time John Wesley had taken a dim view of his friend Whitefield's enthusiastic style of preaching. Nothing quite like it had been seen in the Church of England, and many accused the young man of insanity or worse. He had been ordained as a priest, but he was never given a church appointment because of his evangelistic fervor. Nevertheless Whitefield, like Wesley, was determined to go to America to see for himself what was happening there.

When he arrived in Massachusetts in 1738, George Whitefield was a novelty. Traditional Anglican congregations, very much like those in England, were offended by Whitefield's style of preaching. When he began preaching at open-air services in the countryside, however, dozens, then hundreds, and ultimately tens of thousands came out to hear him preach. Older and more traditional ministers, such as the Reverend Charles Chauncy of Boston, claimed that Whitefield's "enthusiasm" was a form of mental derangement. But rather than being deterred by such comments, Whitefield was inspired by them and preached more powerfully. Wherever the sound of his voice was heard, the presence of the Holy Spirit was undeniable, and before long it was apparent that the Awakening that started at Northampton in 1734 was just the beginning.

As an indication of what was about to happen in the American churches during the Great Awakening, we have stirring accounts from individuals whose lives and attitudes were transformed. Nathan Cole was a member of a Congregationalist church in rural Connecticut. In his journal Cole writes that he was an "Old Light," meaning a died-in-the-wool pew-sitter of the old order, until he ventured to a camp meeting in 1741 to hear Whitefield preach. He was changed, he says, and became a "New Light." It took a while to summon the strength of will, but he eventually resigned from his church because of the Halfway Covenant and the easy acceptance of nonbelievers. He became a separatist first, then a Baptist and a lay pastor.[21]

Herman Husband was the son of a tobacco planter in Maryland and a member of the Anglican Church. At age fifteen he went to hear Whitefield preach and, like Nathan Cole, was radically transformed. Over the next several years he went from the Anglican to the Presbyterian church and then to Quakerism, where he became involved in ministries to the poor, the widow, the orphan, and others in need of God's love.[22]

As James Hutson relates in his history of religion and the American founding, Christianity in rural areas of the colonies was essentially a "do-it-yourself" project throughout most of the eighteenth century. Ordained ministers with school training were few and far between, except in the larger cities, and those larger congregations attracted mainly sedate and scholarly ministers who still preached in the old style. Outside the cities, congregations often depended on devout laymen or schoolmasters to read from books of collected sermons that were very popular at the time. Hutson writes:

> These groups, often close in spirit to primitive Christianity, existed in every colony, although they were far more numerous south of New England. Some German Reformed and Lutheran

congregations in frontier Maryland, for example, operated for decades, until ordained ministers, who were greeted with "tears of joy," caught up with them.[23]

Scotch-Irish Presbyterians, steeped in the Reformation doctrines of their Calvinist forebears, were quick to adapt to this situation, forming churches with dedicated lay pastors until trained ministers were available. These men and women had come from Northern Ireland in large numbers, and they contributed greatly to the "frontier spirit" and the "spirit of independence" that would be so important during the revolutionary period. As James Hutson writes, "Recent scholarship has put an even higher estimate on the strength of their religious convictions. Scotch-Irish Presbyterians now appear to have introduced as much religious energy into the eighteenth-century middle and southern colonies as the Puritans did in seventeenth-century New England."[24]

BIRTH OF THE AMERICAN SPIRIT

Between 1730 and 1750, there was an explosion of faith from one end of America to the other. It is touching, Hutson writes, to read accounts of the "thirst for the gospel" among the men and women who were building the settlements and family farms during the eighteenth century. Itinerant preachers and "circuit riders" were begged to stay. The members of some frontier congregations were "willing to sell their coats and the rest of their clothing to help support a preacher." Communities in many places formed cooperatives and built new churches on speculation, in the hope that God would send them a minister who might be willing to accept a call.[25]

Letters, journals, and other accounts of community life in the mid-seventeenth century tell of churches packed to the rafters with men and women who were hungry for the Word of God. In some cases itinerant pastors preached to congregants who were "forced to stand without doors and others hanging out the window." In other cases entire families would pack into tiny oxcarts or walk "10 to 12 Miles with their Children in the burning Sun, so earnest, so desirous [were they] of becoming good Christians." There are also reports of individuals who joined other denominations, different from the ones they had known, "being willing to embrace anything that looks like a religion, rather than have none at all."[26]

Such strong reactions were remarkable because, then as now, denominational distinctions were not a small matter. As discussed in the previous chapter, New England Congregationalists and the Anglicans in the middle and southern colonies held firmly to very different views on matters of church polity. Church officials in the middle and southern colonies, where the Anglican communion was strongest, soon began to feel threatened by denominational differences. Concerned about the prospect of losing members, they immediately began taking steps to fortify the local churches.

The establishment of religion was not an issue in the eighteenth century. All the colonies had established churches, funded by the government until after the American Revolution. The Anglican Church had been established in New York since 1693, while the Church in Maryland was established in 1702, South Carolina in 1706, and North Carolina in 1715. In addition to the state support they received, the churches began cooperating in the founding of colleges and other educational institutions to train their ministers, and associations were created to regulate denominational standards and encourage uniformity.

Along with the wave of conversions that came from the Awakening, these organizations reaped the benefits of a sustained boom in new church formation. The number of Anglican congregations increased from 111 in 1700, to more than 400 by 1780. Meanwhile Baptist congregations grew from 33 to 457, Congregational churches went from 146 to 749, German and Dutch Reformed parishes increased from 26 to 327, Lutherans from 7 to 240, and the Presbyterian churches from 28 to

475.[27] It has been estimated that during the first half of the eighteenth century—encompassing the years of the Great Awakening—between 75 and 80 percent of the entire population of North America attended church on a regular basis.[28]

One writer suggests that the type of Christianity we recognize today as evangelicalism actually began in the 1730s through the preaching of men such as Jonathan Edwards, George Whitefield, Gilbert Tennent, James Davenport, and others who had no idea they were starting a movement. Instead, they saw themselves as throwbacks to the old-fashioned Calvinist preaching. Edwards claimed he was preaching nothing but "the common plain Protestant doctrine of the Reformation." Likewise, the Methodists believed they were "restoring the 'old divinity' of the Reformation." But the men and women who experienced the Awakening firsthand were under no illusions: they knew that they had been touched by the hand of God.[29]

Before the Great Awakening the colonies had very little in common. They didn't even like each other very much. But as the Awakening began to spread from town to village throughout the country, there was a new sense of connection and cooperation between the colonies. Whenever the people of one colony heard that one of these famous preachers was going to be anywhere in the area, they would pack up their families and travel miles, even hundreds of miles, to the campsites where they could hear the messages.

This was a tremendous social phenomenon. And the more it happened, the more the colonies came together, not only politically but spiritually. This was really the first widespread sense of brotherhood that allowed Americans of the eighteenth century to see themselves not merely as unrelated communities of farmers and merchants, but as men and women with a common bond—as citizens of the united colonies of America.

This new sense of unity eventually developed into what we would recognize today as the American Spirit. It would take a great deal of unity for these same men and women to rebel against King George.

Even after the first shots were fired at Lexington and Concord in 1775, most Americans resisted the Revolution—they thought of themselves as Englishmen and subjects of the Crown, and it would be very hard for them to break that bond of kinship. But in due time the provocations and punishments inflicted on them by the English would overcome their resistance. At that point, the understanding of spiritual and political liberty infused in them through the Great Awakening gave them the courage and resolve to break their bonds.

Four

THE BIRTH
OF THE AMERICAN SPIRIT

18TH-CENTURY POPULATION IN THOUSANDS[1]		
	1700	1780
NEW ENGLAND COLONIES		
MAINE	.1	49.1
NEW HAMPSHIRE	5.0	87.8
VERMONT	.1	47.6
PLYMOUTH/ MASS. BAY	55.9	268.6
RHODE ISLAND	5.9	52.9
CONNECTICUT	26.0	206.7
SUBTOTAL:	93.0	712.7
MIDDLE COLONIES		
NEW YORK	19.1	210.5
NEW JERSEY	14.0	139.6
PENNSYLVANIA	18.0	327.3
DELAWARE	2.5	45.4
SUBTOTAL:	53.6	722.8

SOUTHERN COLONIES		
MARYLAND	29.6	245.5
VIRGINIA	58.6	538.0
NORTH CAROLINA	10.7	270.1
SOUTH CAROLINA	5.7	180.0
GEORGIA	.1	56.1
KENTUCKY	.1	45.0
TENNESSEE	.1	10.0
SUBTOTAL:	104.9	1,344.7
ESTIMATED TOTALS:	251.5	2,780.2

Colonial America had come a long way since the first settlements at Roanoke and Jamestown. By the year 1700, there were nearly 100,000 inhabitants in New England, just over half that number in the middle colonies, and another 105,000 in the southern colonies with Virginia the largest and most prosperous. Thanks to a high birthrate and the steady flow of immigrants from all parts of Europe, the population of British North America was suddenly booming.

Throughout the colonial period immigration continued to accelerate, surpassing the natural rate of increase. Between 1607 and 1700, as many as 200,000 Europeans made the journey to America, including large numbers of English, Irish, Scottish, and Welsh, along with growing numbers of Germans, Italians, and Scandinavians. Notably missing in these totals were the French settlers who journeyed farther north to Quebec. Later, when the French began occupying new lands in the west, as part of the Louisiana Territory, communities of French-speaking Europeans settled at St. Louis and other sites along the Mississippi River, as far south as New Orleans, which had been colonized by the French Mississippi Company in 1718.

Between 1700 and 1763, immigrants from the British Isles arrived seeking the freedom and autonomy they had been denied in their native lands. Settlement in North America was now possible for men and women of all classes and backgrounds, not merely the young and adventurous or the persecuted and discontent. An expanding network of shipping companies, land promoters, bankers, plantation owners, and merchants offered passage to British America on credit. Some colonists came bearing royal charters that enabled them to establish large plantations or entire colonies, as was the case with William Penn in Pennsylvania and James Oglethorpe in Georgia. However, for those of lower estate who could not afford the cost of passage, the most common alternative was to sign a letter of indenture. It has been estimated that fully two-thirds of all English-speaking settlers in the seventeenth century came to this country as indentured servants. And as many as 80 percent of those who came in the eighteenth century were either indentured servants or "redemptioners."[2]

Many who came from central Europe were convinced to make the journey to America by couriers carrying letters between Pennsylvania and Germany. Known as "newlanders," these couriers were former emigrants themselves, either returning home for a visit, collecting debts, or claiming an inheritance. They were paid by their neighbors to carry letters and conduct business in their former homelands. By recruiting others to emigrate, the newlanders could earn free passage back to Philadelphia, along with a modest commission in the process.[3]

Thanks to advancements in shipping at all levels, from the improved seaworthiness of English vessels to the greatly reduced threat of piracy, transatlantic crossings were becoming more frequent and reasonably safe. There was a steady stream of information, merchandise, and people traveling back and forth between Europe and America. The number of transatlantic crossings tripled from about 500 during the 1670s to more than 1,500 each year by the late 1730s. The increased traffic also meant lower costs for shippers and merchants, which led in turn to a greater abundance of goods of all kinds.

Scottish emigration to the colonies soared to more than 145,000 between 1707 and 1775. Generally poorer than the English, the Scots also had greater incentive to emigrate because of the oppression they had endured in their own country. The Act of Union, which united England and Scotland under the banner of Great Britain in 1707, accelerated the process by encouraging thousands to abandon their ancient homeland in search of greater freedom in the New World. Good reports from early emigrants who prospered, particularly in the middle colonies, attracted large numbers of emigrants through "chain migration," reuniting them with family members who had come earlier, or in some cases actually relocating entire communities from Scotland and other parts of Europe to the New World.

Nearly half of the Scottish emigrants came from Ulster, Northern Ireland, which had been colonized by lowland Scots in the 1690s. Like the Highlanders, who were driven from their ancestral lands by the English during the eighteenth century, the Ulster Scots sought to escape punitive laws (particularly regarding religious freedom) at home. Scottish settlers tended to emigrate in groups organized by their Presbyterian ministers, who negotiated with shippers to arrange passage. When they arrived in the colonies, they generally settled in the Carolinas or on the western frontier, where land was cheap and regulations were few. In America all these Scottish immigrants were known as Scotch-Irish even though the name only applies to the Ulster Scots.

Estimates based on colonial records, personal letters, newspaper reports, and other fragments of data from the period suggest that in 1763 about 50 percent of the population was English, 18 percent Scottish or Scotch-Irish, 18 percent African slaves, 6 percent German, and 3 percent Dutch; the rest were a mixture of all the other European nationalities who immigrated to North America. By the mid-eighteenth century, intermarriage was already making America a melting pot.[4]

A NEW SPIRIT OF UNITY

In this environment the Founding Fathers faced a monumental task: How would they ever form a unified nation of men and women from such an ethnically, linguistically, and economically divided population? When Thomas Paine published his powerful diatribe, *Common Sense*, on the threshold of the American Revolution, he began it by saying, "The cause of America is in a great measure the cause of all mankind." It was one thing to say that all men desire freedom from oppression and the opportunity to succeed, but Paine didn't miss the fact that eighteenth-century America was now a land inhabited by people of many nations:

> This New World has been the asylum for the persecuted lovers of civil and religious liberty from *every part* of Europe. Hither have they fled, not from the tender embraces of the mother, but from the cruelty of the monster; and it is so far true of England that the same tyranny which drove the first emigrants from home pursues their descendants still.[5]

Large parts of America had been settled by Englishmen, but there were other parts where the citizens spoke languages other than English and celebrated customs that were quite different from those of their British neighbors. But Paine realized that there were two things all these people had in common—love of country and love of God—and in *Common Sense* he appeals to both of these emotions. Regarding the common bond of national unity, Paine says:

> The sun never shined on a cause of greater worth. 'Tis not the affair of a city, a county, a province, or a kingdom, but of a continent—of at least one-eighth part of the habitable globe. 'Tis not the concern of a day, a year, or an age; posterity are virtually involved in the contest, and will be more or less affected even to the end of time by the

proceedings now. Now is the seedtime of continental union, faith, and honor.[6]

The writer makes it clear that regardless of where they emigrated from, the men and women of this country were engaged in a universal struggle for freedom and the right of self-determination. Everyone who made the pilgrimage to America, or whose fathers and mothers had risked everything to make a new life for their children, had a stake in America's success. They had all come here to escape oppressive circumstances, and they were united in their love of liberty and their common bond of citizenship in this "New World." Even though most had rarely (or perhaps never) thought about the possibility of rebellion or the formation of an independent republic—the consequences of which were literally unthinkable—they nevertheless understood the appeal to union, faith, and honor.

Paine knew very well that his readers would have plenty of objections, so then, addressing himself to the shift of loyalties from the British monarchy to the Monarch who rules over all men, he writes:

> But where, says some, is the king of America? I'll tell you, friend, he reigns above, and does not make havoc of mankind like the royal brute of Britain. Yet that we may not appear to be defective even in earthly honors, let a day be solemnly set apart for proclaiming the charter; let it be brought forth placed on the divine law, the word of God; let a crown be placed thereon, by which the world may know that, so far as we approve of monarchy, that in America *the law is king*.[7]

The impact of Paine's words, contained in a slim volume of barely fifty pages, was tremendous. Word of mouth spread quickly, and the pamphlet sold upwards of 120,000 copies in the first three months, and more than a half million copies in the first year. These were unprecedented numbers. The pamphlet went through twenty-five printings in the first year of the Revolution, but to demonstrate the sincerity of his words, Paine donated all royalties from the sale of the work to the Continental Army, under the command of General George Washington.

Much has been made of the fact that Paine was not a Christian in any orthodox sense. He has been described as a Deist, leading some critics to suggest he was simply exploiting the religious sentiments of the colonists to provoke the reaction he desired. Based on later writings, such as *The Rights of Man* (1791) and *The Age of Reason* (1794), which echo the liberal sentiments of the French Revolution more clearly than our own, that would seem to be a reasonable evaluation of Paine. As an Englishman, Paine witnessed religious controversy firsthand before coming to this country, and he adopted the rationalist worldview.

He may have been an Enlightenment thinker, but Thomas Paine understood very well that the Puritans and many others had come to America, first and foremost, for religious liberty. Most of all, he understood that the Christian religion was the one common denominator uniting all Americans, regardless of their origins or condition of life. It was the one thing they all believed. His appeal to faith, honor, and union had the desired impact, but it did so because the groundwork had been laid by Jonathan Edwards, George Whitefield, Gilbert Tennent, and all the great preachers of the Great Awakening a generation earlier.

PREPARING THE HARVEST

When Jonathan Edwards preached his famous sermon, "Sinners in the Hands of an Angry God," in 1741, he worried that the churches of New England had grown cold and halfhearted in their worship. Unlike their Puritan fathers and mothers who had survived deadly winters, diseases, Indian attacks, and the challenges of building new lives in an alien environment, many eighteenth-century Americans were now prosperous, comfortable, and complacent. The New England meeting-house, in Edward's estimation, was in danger of becoming a clubhouse, where well-fed and overly self-righteous ladies and gentlemen came on a Sunday, not to prostrate themselves before a holy God but to be seen and admired by their neighbors.

In 1727, less than ten years before the first tremors of the Great Awakening, the area around Boston had been struck by a devastating earthquake. Contemporary reports tell of a period of several months in which there was severe drought followed by weeks of high winds and flooding throughout the region, culminating in the Boston Earthquake of October 29. Many people felt as if the colonies were being chastened, driven to their knees by God Himself.

As a result, Ellis Sandoz writes, there was "a quickening of religious impulses," which prepared the population for the spiritual awakening that was to come, not only at Northampton but in many other places over the next five or six years.[8] In Jonathan Edwards's powerful sermon he deliberately reminded the congregation at Enfield of that earlier time, and he assured them that God is omnipotent, omnipresent, and omniscient. That is, He is all-powerful, present in all times and places, and all-knowing and all-wise. For those who might be inclined to neglect their religious duty and fall into sin with no fear of eternal judgment, Edwards warned, "The world would spew you out, were it not for the sovereign hand of him who hath subjected it in hope." Then in his characteristically solemn and measured tones, Edwards added that, "There are the black clouds of God's wrath now hanging directly over your heads, full of the dreadful storm, and big with thunder; and were it not for the restraining hand of God, it would immediately burst forth upon you."[9]

There is no question that Jonathan Edwards anticipated the impact of his words. What he had in mind was a general and widespread revival in the churches of New England. For much too long, he believed, a generation of staid and sedentary pastors had made it all too easy for congregants to ignore the warnings of Scripture and the very real dangers of eternal damnation. So in that sermon he says, "How dreadful is the state of those that are daily and hourly in the danger of this great wrath and infinite misery! But this is the dismal case of every soul in this congregation that has not been born again, however moral and strict, sober and religious, they may otherwise be."[10]

Some of Edwards's critics in his own day and many more in ours have accused him of shameless alarmism, trying to frighten people into making a religious conversion. But Edwards did not leave that option open. The alarm, he said, was a genuine forewarning of imminent disaster. In the sermon he says that any minister who would set out to terrify the people with lies, to create pandemonium by making the case out to be worse than it actually is, ought to be condemned. But he also says that if the message is not of men but of God and if the people are justifiably frightened by it because of their sinful ways, then the minister who brings the warning is more than justified and ought to be commended.

In his book *Some Thoughts Concerning the Present Revival of Religion*, published in 1742, one year after the sermon at Enfield, Edwards writes:

> When consciences are greatly awakened by the Spirit of God, it is but light imparted, enabling men to see their case, in some measure, as it is; and, if more light be let in, it will terrify them still more. But ministers are not therefore to be blamed that they endeavor to hold forth more light to the conscience. . . . To say any thing to those who have never believed in the Lord Jesus Christ, to represent their case any otherwise than exceeding terrible, is not to preach the word of God to them; for the word of God reveals nothing but truth; but this is to delude them.[11]

The objective of all his preaching was to call the men, women, and children within the sound of his voice to repentance. At the conclusion of his famous sermon, Edwards reached out to the congregation in steady and unemotional tones, saying, "Let every one that is yet out of Christ, and hanging over the pit of hell, whether they be old men and women, or middle aged, or young people, or little children, now hearken to the loud calls of God's word and providence. . . . Therefore, let every one that is out of Christ, now awake and fly from the wrath to come."[12] Despite the mixed reactions the sermon has received ever since, many thousands have heard that warning and responded.

THE GREATEST AWAKENER

By the time that sermon was given in New England, the evangelist George Whitefield was already traveling from one end of North America to the other, awakening the hearts of the colonists to a message of repentance. Like Edwards, he warned of the bondage of sin and offered his listeners the hope of emancipation from their shackles through the liberation that only comes through the gospel of Jesus Christ.

During seven separate visits to America, he traveled between his base in Savannah, Georgia, and the towns and villages of New England. In each of these tours he encountered a backlash from the pastors of the established churches who disliked his theology and resented his ever-growing popularity. But nothing could dissuade the evangelist from preaching to the massive crowds—often as many as twenty thousand men, women, and children of all types and all races—who came from miles around to hear him.[13]

Whitefield was widely known for his powerful speaking voice. But the most impressive demonstration of his gifts took place during an outdoor sermon in Boston in which he compared the violence of an approaching thunderstorm to the storm of God's judgment of sin. At the very instant he raised his arm and pointed a finger toward heaven, a brilliant flash of lightning illuminated the sky, and a blast of thunder shook the earth, to which Whitefield roared, "See there! It's a glance from the angry eye of Jehovah! Hark!" Then, after a dramatic pause, he once again declared, "It's the voice of the Almighty as He passed by in His anger."[14] It is not hard to imagine how the people would have reacted to such an amazing display.

His passionate delivery drew thousands upon thousands from cities and towns in every part of the country, leading to thousands of dramatic conversions, often accompanied by physical manifestation, such as uncontrollable trembling, ecstatic prostration, glossolalia, and many other signs and wonders. These manifestations were described by detractors as shameful displays of enthusiasm and emotion, but Whitefield's impact on the men and women of North America for more than a decade cannot be overestimated. More than any other evangelist of the day, he helped to usher in the Great Awakening, without which the unification of the American people and the success of the American Revolution may not have happened.

It is stunning to realize how much he accomplished. Whitefield preached an average of five hundred sermons a year throughout his active life, each sermon lasting from one to two hours. He often preached forty hours in a week, and sometimes more. This was in addition to everything else, including travel and correspondence, building and promoting an orphanage in Savannah, Georgia, and raising funds for missions work. In addition he made a preaching tour of England almost every year, traveled to Scotland fourteen times and Ireland three times, and also made several trips to Wales. He crossed the Atlantic thirteen times, traveling back and forth to the colonies, and he reached an estimated ten million souls during three decades of ministry.

Whitefield's eloquence was legendary. One famous story relates the reaction of the renowned British actor David Garrick, exclaiming, "I would give a hundred guineas if I could only say 'Oh!' like Mr. Whitefield." Benjamin Franklin was not necessarily a candidate for baptism; he had been raised as an Anglican but showed little interest in spiritual matters for most of his life. Nevertheless, being worldly-wise and curious about most things, he went to hear Whitefield in his professional capacity—a newspaper publisher looking for a story. In his autobiography he describes the experience:

In 1739 arrived among us from Ireland the Reverend Mr. Whitefield, who had made himself remarkable there as an itinerant preacher. He was at first permitted to preach in some of our churches; but the clergy, taking a dislike to him, soon refus'd him their pulpits, and he was oblig'd to preach in the fields. The multitudes of all sects and denominations that attended his sermons were enormous, and it was matter of speculation to me, who was one of the number, to observe the extraordinary influence of his oratory on his hearers, and how much they admir'd and respected him, notwithstanding his common abuse of them, by assuring them that they were naturally *half beasts and half devils.*[15]

Franklin's comments were only partly in jest because he understood very well that men who are convinced of their iniquity and inclined to petition heaven for forgiveness and undertake a course of moral reform were likely to be better citizens. Then he says,

It was wonderful to see the change soon made in the manners of our inhabitants. From being thoughtless or indifferent about religion, it seem'd as if all the world were growing religious, so that one could not walk thro' the town in an evening without hearing psalms sung in different families of every street.[16]

In one of the most amusing anecdotes from his autobiography, Franklin reveals just how persuasive Whitefield could be:

I happened soon after to attend one of his sermons, in the course of which I perceived he intended to finish with a collection, and I silently resolved he should get nothing from me. I had in my pocket a handful of copper money, three or four silver dollars, and five pistoles in gold. As he proceeded I began to soften, and concluded to give the coppers. Another stroke of his oratory made me asham'd of that, and determin'd me to give the silver; and he finish'd so admirably, that I empty'd my pocket wholly into the collector's dish, gold and all.[17]

The changed lives of Whitefield's hearers were even more impressive than the preacher's oratory. One New England farmer who heard Whitefield preach described the experience in his journal, where he wrote: "He looked almost angelical, a young slim tender youth. He looked as if he was clothed with authority from the great God. A sweet solemnity sat upon his brow. My hearing him preach gave me a heart wound. . . . I saw that my righteousness would not save me."[18] The preacher's words hit home in similar fashion and transformed untold thousands of hearts, and in time the message of repentance and redemption would change the spiritual landscape.

PREPARING FOR REVOLUTION

True religion for George Whitefield, the scholars tell us, meant "a thorough, real, inward change of nature, wrought in us by the powerful operations of the Holy Ghost, conveyed to and nourished in our hearts, by a constant use of all the means of grace, evidenced by a good life, and bringing forth the fruits of the spirit."[19] Like their Calvinist forebears, prerevolutionary Americans believed Christ's commandment to "render to Caesar the things that are Caesar's" (Mark 12:17) meant not only that each man ought to be obedient to the ruling authority but that each man had the right and duty to hold the ruler accountable when reasonable boundaries were crossed.

For this reason the transformation of the spirit taking place in the hearts of tens of thousands of Americans would have dramatic political implications as well. "The political culture of this country," historian and legal scholar Ellis Sandoz writes, "was deeply rooted in the core religious consciousness articulated above all by the preachers; theirs were the pulpits of a new nation with a privileged, providential role in world history."[20] Because the churches were such an essential part of community life, this was where the beliefs and actions of the men and women who would become the patriots of 1776 were shaped. As Daniel Boorstin explains:

> The New England meeting-house, like the synagogue on which it was consciously modeled, was primarily a place of instruction. Here the community learned its duties. Here men found their separate paths to conversion, so they could better build their Zion in the wilderness, a *City upon a Hill* to which other men might in their turn look for instruction. As the meeting-house was the geographical and social center of the New England town, so the sermon was the central event in the meeting-house.[21]

All these things taken together led not just to a deeper spiritual commitment but to a transformation of "the American mind." The awakening of the spirit would have a direct impact not only on American Protestantism but on the political consciousness of an entire generation.[22]

The call coming from eighteenth-century pulpits for a renewal of faith translated into a call to resist all forms of tyranny, which elicited an impulse to resist the kinds of intimidation endured under British rule. These were the provocations making their lives miserable. Each new insult—whether it was the Tea Tax, the Stamp Tax, the Currency Act, the blockade around the Port of Boston, the Boston Massacre, the quartering of British troops in American homes, or the Quebec Act (a direct assault on the Protestant churches)—was further reason for rebellion. The men and women of colonial America had been educated in the school of liberty by their ministers, and in the process they were being prepared to stand their ground when the time came.

It was in this spirit that Samuel Adams, often referred to as the father of the American Revolution, wrote, "He therefore is the truest friend to the liberty of his country who tries most to promote its virtue, and who, so far as his power and influence extend, will not suffer a man to be chosen into any office of power and trust who is not a wise and virtuous man. . . . The sum of all is, if we would most truly enjoy this gift of Heaven, let us become a virtuous people."[23]

Between 1765, when the Stamp Act was passed, and 1775, when the first shots of the Revolution were fired at Lexington and Concord, a visible transformation had taken place in the American Spirit. Inspired by the call to duty, honor, and love of country, a new generation was prepared to consider the prospect of a separation from its English masters. The colonists were prepared to take up arms against the most powerful military force on earth. This would prove to be the greatest moment in American history. It was the moment when the flame of faith that had been lit during the Great Awakening burst forth, helping to shape the character and destiny of a nation.

Two and a half centuries after that great explosion of righteous anger, we are still humbled by what they accomplished. The more I have studied that fifty-year period preceding the American Revolution, the more amazed I am by the transformation that had taken place in the hearts and minds of the people. As we have seen in previous chapters, there was a lot of religious activity in early America but not a lot of evidence of the kind of life-changing faith that would be needed in the Revolution. There wasn't much passion, and there were no religious movements until the late 1730s. The colonists observed religious ceremonies and traditions, and a majority attended church services regularly. But there was no evidence of a deeper spiritual commitment.

If there was going to be a great spiritual revival, it would have to be a move of God, and that's precisely what it was. So what was the impact of the Great Awakening? How did the preaching of a handful of pastors and evangelists change the disposition of the people and prepare them for a war of independence? The following list, I believe, offers a reasonable summary of some of the ways the Great Awakening shaped the thinking of the patriots in the years prior to the Revolution.

THE LEGACY OF THE GREAT AWAKENING

1. A UNITY AND COMMUNITY AMONG THE COLONIES

Prior to the Great Awakening the colonies viewed themselves as separate and independent bodies. They shared few things in common. But with the coming of the revivals, they began traveling from colony to colony, and in the process they found common ground with others who had the same religious experiences. This proved to be a powerful force in laying the foundation for a unified people and ultimately a unified nation.

This new spirit of unity was a necessary element in bringing together enough of the colonists to declare independence, to fight a war for freedom, and to form a new republic. The first steps of national unity that began in the church houses, town squares, and open fields as people gathered to hear the preaching of men such as Whitefield, Davenport, and Tennent would lead ultimately to the First Continental Congress that met in Philadelphia's Carpenters' Hall on September 5, 1774.

2. A SPIRIT OF RELIGIOUS TOLERANCE

Previously, followers of one religious denomination or another would stay within the four walls of their own churches in worship, but Whitefield and other evangelists held open-air meetings that brought the people out of doors and into fellowship with those of many other traditions and doctrinal views. Some denominations saw this as a threat, and the denominational hierarchies were strongly against fanning the "fires of revival."

The eighteenth-century revivals may not have turned out in just the way Jonathan Edwards had hoped, since they led to division and rancor in some places. At times the evangelists seemed to be just one more group competing for the people's religious allegiances. However, as McLoughlin points out, "while the Awakening split the very churches its leaders set out to renew, it also secured for them a niche from which to prosecute their agenda." In spite of the quarrels that occurred among the clergy, for the most part the ordinary people paid little attention to all the fuss and found fellowship and friendships across denominational lines to be refreshing.[24]

3. A MORAL AND SPIRITUAL WORLDVIEW

Strong preaching about living out the Christian life through "good works" ignited a fire of social action, which included the beginnings of the antislavery movement in America, women's rights, and other types of civic action. This was demonstrated by the most powerful preacher of the Great Awakening, George Whitefield. Whitefield thundered that Christians were called to be "servants of all." Not only did he preach it, but he put it into practice by the formation of orphanages for underprivileged children in Georgia, and his own personal aid to clergy who suffered from financial pressures. John Wesley testified at Whitefield's funeral in 1770 regarding not only his powerful preaching but also his tenderheartedness and charitable nature. Thomas S. Kidd writes:

The convictions, however, that Jesus died to save women and men of all ethnicities and classes, and the Holy Spirit empowers each believer equally, produced mixed social consequences in the first generation of American Evangelical Christianity. Evangelical beliefs worked at times to erode traditional barriers of race, class and gender. Radical evangelicals of the eighteenth century opened up unprecedented, if ultimately limited, opportunities for African Americans, Native Americans, women, the uneducated, and the poor to assert individual religions and even social authority. Early American evangelicalism also helped pioneer the American abolitionist movement that emerged more fully in the nineteenth-century North.[25]

In fact, men such as Elisha Williams, Samuel Davies, George Whitefield, and others preached to large numbers of blacks attending their revival gatherings. At the same time, black Christians with assistance from their white brothers began building their own churches and evangelizing their own people. Two former slaves, Richard Allen and Absalom Jones, became the best-known black evangelists of the period, and they went on to found the African Methodist Episcopal denomination in Philadelphia in 1816. This "black preaching" resulted in the conversion of tens of thousands of slaves who believed the gospel message. At the first General Conference of Methodism, the owning or selling of slaves was recognized as sinful and worthy of dismissal from the church.

Among the British aristocracy, however, few acts of compassion and understanding of the rights of others took place. People of a different color, language, or national origin were normally treated either as slaves or, at best, people of a lower class. There was a clear and growing disconnect between the worldview of the leadership in the motherland and the opinions of the men and women of the colonies, concerning individual rights and the dignity of human life. This divide grew larger over time, adding to the friction between the colonists and the British. For these and other reasons, many Americans began to believe that conflict was inevitable.

4. A RISE IN THE NUMBER OF TOWERING LEADERS

Colonial preachers—such as Edwards and Tennent—along with Whitefield and Wesley were elevated to positions of leadership and esteem because of their great moral influence. Backed by favorable press reports, revivalists such as Whitefield enjoyed unprecedented public acclaim. In his book *Inventing the Great Awakening*, Frank Lambert describes the masses that attended Whitefield's meeting across New England:

> The biggest crowds assembled in colonial America's two largest cities, Boston and Philadelphia, each located in a revival region. On

each of his three preaching tours, Whitefield made Philadelphia a center for his itinerating. From his first outdoor sermon there, he attracted progressively huger crowds, from the 6,000 who first gathered at the courthouse to hear him, to 8,000, and eventually 10,000 at the farewell sermon ending his first tour. At three subsequent Philadelphia services, Whitefield reported crowds of at least 10,000, and then during spring 1740 they swelled to 15,000 and reached the amazing number of 20,000, a figure that Franklin reported without dispute. Whitefield attracted similar crowds in Boston during the one trip he made there in fall 1740. For his farewell sermon delivered on Boston Common, he reported a gathering of 20,000, but two Boston newspapers estimated that 23,000 attended.[26]

This new attitude of respect and admiration for these and other distinguished men of God paved the way for other public figures, including political leaders. Many of these men were not just politicians, but men of God who would lead the fight for independence. Thomas Jefferson, John Adams, Patrick Henry, Richard Henry Lee, and George Washington were recognized as men of courage and virtue, and they commanded the respect of all Americans.

5. A SPIRIT OF INDEPENDENCE

A personal spirit of independence developed as people embraced the idea that each man was personally accountable to God. Corporate worship was an important custom, but every man was responsible for his own "spiritual awakening" apart from the church. This new feeling of accountability and independence grew into an equal, if not greater, desire for independence from British rule. This was especially true in 1769, when King George III threatened to send an Anglican bishop to oversee the American church and "set the colonies right."

When this news reached America, the colonists were furious, fearing the loss of religious freedom altogether. The great Massachusetts lawyer and statesman John Adams viewed this as one of the most provocative acts of the Crown, sparking the spirit of rebellion. He said, "Apprehension of Episcopacy contributed . . . as much as any other cause, to arouse the attention, not only of the inquiring mind, but of the common people, and urge them to close thinking on the constitutional authority of parliament over the colonies."[27] The threat of returning to a state religion enforced by royal edict that denied religious liberty was more than the colonists could bear.

By the same token when news of the Stamp Act reached the colonies in 1765, the people felt a "heavy cloud hanging over us, big with slavery and all its dreadful attendants."[28] They looked upon the imposition of punitive taxes as one of the gravest threats to their own prosperity. They had already made the connection between civil and religious liberties; they knew that when religious liberties were threatened, the assault on civil liberties could not be far behind. And this passion for religious independence clearly carried over to governmental independence as well.

6. A New Belief in Manifest Destiny

The idea of manifest destiny was based on the beliefs of many Americans that God had a divine plan for the New World, and that each person, regardless of social or economic status, was a part of God's work in bringing about a new and better world in America. Never before had the common man been empowered in such a way; never had an entire society been given the opportunity to reach for their own goals, achieve independence, and recognize their potential. The Great Awakening ignited the flames of an inclusive democracy in the hearts of millions of Americans, and it spawned the vision of the New Jerusalem—a land where God had led the immigrants and prepared them for greatness.

They could see now that British rule could only inhibit the dreams in the hearts of the people; ultimately, revolution was the only answer. As William McLoughlin notes, "Part of the American culture has been the myth that we are a 'covenanted people.' As such, God has a special interest in helping, and a special reason for punishing us. The covenant applies both to individuals and to the nation as a whole. . . . But if each does his or her part to adhere to the new rules, then God promises, according to his prophets, a glorious new day of peace, fraternity, and perfection—a time in which all human needs will be met, both physical and spiritual. Thus the experience of hearing, yielding to, and experiencing this call is one of ecstatic release from the burden of guilt and fear."[29]

7. A New Appreciation for America's Natural Resources

"The earth is the LORD's, and the fulness thereof" (Psalm 24:1). This and similar texts were common in the sermons of the Great Awakening, resulting in a new appreciation for the land God had given the colonists. Like the children of Israel who had been led from bondage in Egypt to the promised land called Canaan, they had been brought through tribulation to a land of milk and honey. The settlers on the American frontier were accustomed to hard work, and they took full advantage of the land and its resources. Clearing the land, building their homes, planting and harvesting crops, and living on the abundance gave them profound respect for the environment.

But there was more, and it was something none of them had ever experienced before: the sheer awe and majesty of the North American landscape, the mountains and valleys, and the riches they contained. Even the songs of the patriots spoke of their love of nature. American artists produced images of an unspoiled landscape that enticed tens of thousands to strike out into the utopia, opening the door to the era of westward expansion. Throughout the late-eighteenth and nineteenth centuries, caravans of lumbering ox-drawn wagons crossed the prairies, from sea to shining sea, with one consuming vision: to occupy and take dominion of the new world God had given them.

The Great Awakening taught these bold travelers that God had brought them to this place: "Then God blessed them, and God said to them, 'Be fruitful and multiply; fill the earth and subdue it; have dominion over the fish of the sea, over the birds of the air, and over every living thing that moves on the earth'" (Genesis 1:28 NKJV). The art and literature of the day describe vast, unspoiled landscapes and mighty rivers; it was not until after the Industrial Revolution that the ingenuity of man would rival the power of God, and the landscape would suffer from neglect and abuse.

8. A Desire for Personal Advancement

Breaking down the barriers of a collective worldview where individual rights were few, the new era of independence that came in the wake of the Great Awakening brought with it a desire for improvements in education, material comforts, and personal wealth. Perhaps no act of resistance exemplified this new spirit better than the Boston Tea Party of 1773. When Parliament passed the Tea Act earlier that year, they intended to give the British East India Company an unfair price advantage, which threatened the profits of American merchants.

The Americans saw clearly what was happening and objected, demanding that three ships carrying English tea be sent back to London still filled with their cargo. When the British refused to leave, colonists dressed in Native American costume and war paint boarded the vessels by night and tossed the entire shipment into Boston Harbor. Predictably the English governors took severe reprisals against the colonists, but it would not be enough. A spirit of resistance had been awakened, and things would not change for eight years until the British had been soundly defeated at Yorktown and sent home to lick their wounds.

Courage, independence, self-reliance, and a willingness to stand one's ground and defend one's honor were important by-products of the Great Awakening: these were the traits that brought the colonists victory in battle and awakened in the men and women of America the belief that they could overcome any obstacles and make a better life for themselves and their children.

9. A Belief in the Value of Action over Debate

As the revivals swept through the colonies, the volume of debate among colonial-era preachers and theologians was intense, but those who had participated in the Great Awakening had experienced for themselves the "new birth." They were not interested in all the verbal gymnastics. They had placed their faith in a living, powerful, and transcendent God, and their own emotional encounters were all the justification they needed. Emotional intensity is necessary for any revolution to succeed. Emotion produces action that triumphs over debate, and that was the spirit that prevailed through the Revolution.

Some historians have suggested that the new spirit of evangelicalism gave the Revolution one of its most potent ideological resources, as the new evangelical temperament shaped the political practices of the people. "Evangelicalism," writes Thomas Kidd,

> taught the common people who embraced it that sometimes they must take matters into their own hands, a subversive tendency that exploded during the imperial crisis. The church separations and disruptions of the revivals have been identified as a "practice model" which enabled the provincials to "rehearse"— though unwittingly— . . . the arguments . . . that would reappear. . . . The evangelical revivals caused the greatest social upheaval of any movement in the colonies prior to the Revolution. This massive defiance of traditional authority must certainly have exercised some shaping influence on the Revolution.[30]

10. The Shaping of National Identity

As religious, social, and economic barriers were broken down between the colonies, a new sense of identity was being shaped. It was the beginning of what we now recognize as the American Spirit, based on belief in personal liberty and individual rights. As this new attitude became more and more common, the desire for independence and personal freedom became the defining characteristic of the nation. The men and women of America no longer thought of themselves as subjects of an English king but as Americans. The Declaration of Independence spoke boldly of "unalienable rights," among them the rights of "life, liberty, and the pursuit of happiness." The American people did not need to be told, but the Declaration affirmed that these rights are not man-made but God-given. As theologian Richard Niebuhr has said, "America cannot eradicate, if it would, the marks left upon its social memory, upon its institutions and habits, by an awakening to God that was simultaneous with its awakening to national self-consciousness."[31]

11. A CHRISTIAN COVENANT ETHIC

The development of a Christian worldview, aroused initially during the Great Awakening, meant every believer in Jesus Christ has a duty to the community. All Christians have a holy responsibility to honor God and live according to the tenets of the Christian faith, but we are also expected to contribute to the common good. The doctrine of grace teaches that we are not the authors of our own salvation, but God has shed His grace upon us and through the sacrifice of His Son made salvation available. The doctrine of works explains that while works cannot save anyone, they are the evidence of salvation. Jesus said, "Let your light so shine before men, that they may see your good works and glorify your Father in heaven" (Matthew 5:16 NKJV), and the apostle Paul gave similar counsel, saying, "For we are His workmanship, created in Christ Jesus for good works, which God prepared beforehand that we should walk in them" (Ephesians 2:10 NKJV). These were among the fundamental principles of both Wesley's and Whitefield's Methodism and are still very much alive in the Protestant ethic today. By the end of the period of the Great Awakening, more than 80 percent of all Americans shared a common set of beliefs regarding the Christian faith and its central role in the social order.

12. A NEW EMPHASIS ON EDUCATION

Before the Great Awakening it was rare for the common man or woman to have a formal education. Most colonists who possessed a higher education came from the elite families of New England. Following the Awakening there was an explosion in the founding of colleges and schools for the education of the general populace. Fully 106 of the first 108 colleges in America were founded as Christian institutions. By the mid-nineteenth century there were 246 colleges in this country, virtually all of them founded either by Christian denominations or by individuals motivated by their Christian convictions. Among these were Harvard College in 1636, the College of William and Mary in 1693, Yale College in 1701, and Princeton (formerly the College of New Jersey) in 1746. Jonathan Dickinson, Jonathan Edwards, Samuel Davies, and John Witherspoon (a signer of the Declaration of Independence) were among the first presidents of Princeton, and the preeminent figure of the Awakening, George Whitefield, was instrumental in the founding of the University of Pennsylvania in 1751.

13. BELIEF THAT FAITH IS A PERSONAL MATTER

After the Great Awakening there was universal belief that the Christian faith is not a collectivist doctrine but a personal matter. There is no such thing in Scripture as "collective salvation." Furthermore, ministers and denominations were no longer in a position to dictate what any person could or could not believe in his or her individual understanding of the Scriptures. Such a democratic spirit would have been frowned on by the established churches prior to the Great Awakening, but the explosion of faith that took place in pastures and meadows and village greens all over the country was all the proof the Americans of that generation needed that true faith is a relationship between the individual and God.

14. AN AGE OF PUBLIC GATHERINGS AND OPEN DISSENT

The open-air sermons of the Great Awakening brought together enormous crowds of people of every sort, eager to hear what the revivalists had to say. Often these outdoor rallies would be accompanied by outbursts of emotion and enthusiasm from those who attended. Instead of being condemned, however, the people were free to express their feelings. In the years following the Awakening, similar gatherings were held in public places, but this time the people were gathering to protest the unfair policies of their British governors. When these crowds assembled to express their grievances, there were no riots—these were not vandals and looters but men and women who had learned to make their voices heard. In time, the widespread feeling that something had to be done to bring an end to British oppression prepared the way for the American Revolution.

THE CONSENT OF THE GOVERNED

When I think about the preaching of the great evangelists like George Whitefield, I often wonder what it was that made their ministries so powerful. Whitefield was anointed to preach the Word, that's true. He had experienced a genuine religious conversion in the courtyard of Christ Church at Oxford, England, in 1735. But what was it that transformed him so thoroughly and prepared him for the amazing ministry he would have just three years later in the New World? Something like that could only come from God.

Even the most secular men of the era were changed. We see the hand of God as He moved upon men such as Benjamin Franklin, a newspaper printer and publisher with a secular bent. Franklin was not a religious man, yet he began spreading the word by publishing the sermons of many of the leading preachers of the day. We might even say that the printers and publishers of the colonial era made it possible for the Great Awakening to happen.

Sermons were the most popular literature in the colonies, and as a result of the publicity he received, George Whitefield became one of the best-known public figures in the country. Without that kind of exposure, it is doubtful the Great Awakening could have happened. Benjamin Franklin, with all his civic, scientific, and political clout, was the one man who had the ability to publicize the man who came to America to publicize the Savior.

As far as he was personally concerned, Benjamin Franklin was a skeptic. He was offended that so many people would go to hear Whitefield and then give him all their money, but after hearing the evangelist for himself, Franklin emptied his pockets. It is remarkable how God used men like Franklin.

But one of the greatest stories from the colonial period is the story of Franklin's rebuke of the First Continental Congress when he called upon the delegates to pause for a time of prayer. His words are preserved in the records of the Library of Congress, and they are just as poignant today as they were when first spoken. The delegates were having a hard time coming to terms on how their new government should respond to the Coercive Acts that, among other things, had imposed martial law on the colonies. The Massachusetts delegates couldn't agree with the Virginia delegates, and both Delaware and New Jersey were on the verge of leaving in a huff. When the bickering and name-calling escalated, and the hope of a resolution appeared to be vanishing, eighty-one-year-old Benjamin Franklin rose to his feet and asked for an opportunity to speak, which was immediately granted. Stepping forward to a place where he could be seen by all the delegates, he said,

> I've lived, Sir, a long time, and the longer I live, the more convincing Proofs I see of this Truth—That God governs in the Affairs of Men. And if a sparrow cannot fall to the ground without his Notice, is it probable that an Empire can rise without his Aid? We have been assured, Sir, in the Sacred Writings, that except the Lord build the House they labor in vain who build it. I firmly believe this,—and I

also believe that without his concurring Aid, we shall succeed in this political Building no better than the Builders of Babel: We shall be divided by our little partial local interests; our Projects will be confounded, and we ourselves shall become a Reproach and Bye word down to future Ages.[32]

Needless to say, all eyes were fixed on the illustrious old man. But he wasn't finished. Seeing that the truth of his remarks had hit the mark, Franklin continued, "I therefore beg leave to move that henceforth prayers imploring the assistance of Heaven, and its blessing on our deliberations, be held in this Assembly every morning before we proceed to business, and that one or more of the clergy of this city be requested to officiate in that service."[33]

After a very brief discussion there was quick and humble concurrence with Franklin's proposal. Several names were submitted of local clergymen who might be prevailed upon to open the deliberations with prayer. The members decided on the Reverend Jacob Duché, who was widely known as an eloquent orator and pastor of the best-known Anglican parish, Christ Church in Philadelphia.

But as further evidence of the spirit of compromise that had suddenly arisen among the delegates, it is interesting to note that it was Sam Adams, a staunch Congregationalist, who first recommended Duché, despite the feeling expressed by several delegates that the Anglicans, who were strongly identified with the Church of England, were too closely connected to the British Crown. The Revolution was still fresh in the minds of all Americans, but Duché was unanimously chosen, and he made the trip from his church each morning to open every session of the First Continental Congress with prayer.

Benjamin Franklin had a reputation—and deservedly so—as a rogue. Nevertheless, God used him in a remarkable way. Isn't it amazing that God can use every sort of person to accomplish His will? But, here again, such a spirit of compromise and cooperation could only have happened as a consequence of the changes brought about by the

Great Awakening. Before going to hear Whitefield preach, it is doubtful that Franklin would ever have spoken in such a way. But the writer of Proverbs assures us, "The king's heart is in the hand of the LORD, like the rivers of water; He turns it wherever He wishes" (Proverbs 21:1 NKJV). When Franklin's heart was turned, he became a vocal advocate for Christian virtue.

The Bible says, "where the Spirit of the Lord is, there is liberty" (2 Corinthians 3:17), and the people of the revolutionary era had learned that lesson very well. Along with the importance of personal holiness, the evangelists had been preaching a gospel of transformation and liberation. But considering the price our forefathers paid for the rights and privileges we enjoy today, shouldn't we be asking ourselves, "Who are the American people today? Are we living up to the high standards of the patriots who risked their lives, their fortunes, and their sacred honor for the cause of liberty? And are we prepared to stand our ground when we're confronted by men and women promoting some very dangerous ideas and beliefs?"

There is no question that we owe our freedom to the patriots of 1776, but I have to wonder if we still have that kind of courage. The men who composed the nation's founding documents belonged to one of the best-informed, best-educated, and most conscientious generations in history. Historian Barbara Tuchman refers to the Founding Fathers as "the most remarkable generation of public men in the history of the United States or perhaps of any other nation."[34] Who could doubt it? These men had read Plato, Cicero, Locke, Montesquieu, and all the great classical scholars. They understood that every democracy eventually descends into mob rule. That's what happened in France in 1789, just thirteen years after the American Revolution. The cry of the French Jacobins for *"liberté, égalité, fraternité"* led not to liberty and justice for all but to anarchy and mob violence, which soon became the blood bath known as the "Reign of Terror."

The American Founders believed that individual liberty was a sacred right, which is why they enshrined in the Declaration of

Independence the affirmation that we are "endowed by our Creator with certain unalienable rights, that among these are life, liberty, and the pursuit of happiness." But they also understood that the best form of government is a republic in which the citizens empower their elected representatives with authority to manage the affairs of state. As citizens of a democratic republic, we have the duty to elect honorable men and women to serve in public office, but it is We the People, not the government, who are the ultimate power and authority.

In America that authority is spelled out in clear and unambiguous terms in the Constitution of the United States, which specifies that elected representatives are subject to "the consent of the governed." No doubt this is why so many people in Washington today spend so much time trying to avoid living by those statutes. The progressives in Washington want us to believe the patriots gave us a "living, breathing Constitution"—a document that provides some general guidelines for government but is, in fact, simply a set of suggestions: not binding law. But the Founders did not leave them that option.

James Madison, the principal author of the Constitution, makes it clear in Federalist 51, which was written to clarify the intentions of the Founders, that the Constitution is the nation's best guarantee of an "ordered liberty." The efficiency of the document is stunning—a mere 4,500 words without amendments—yet the Constitution provides time-tested guidance for administering the political affairs of a nation of 300 million people. The reason it has survived so long with so few amendments is because it is so logical and straightforward, based on the Framers' hard-won understanding of law, liberty, and justice.

The Constitution *is* the law. It is the foundation of our government. "But what is government itself," Madison asks, "but the greatest reflection of human nature?" He continues,

> If men were angels, no government would be necessary. If angels were to govern men, neither external nor internal controls on government would be necessary. In framing a government which is to

be administered by men over men, the great difficulty lies in this: you must first enable the government to control the governed; and in the next place oblige it to control itself.[35]

The government of a free people, the Framers insisted, can never be arbitrary. To be a credible instrument of such a government, the Constitution cannot be altered, ignored, or amended haphazardly but must be respected by all men at all times. This is what the Founders believed. This is what they gave us.

In his Farewell Address, delivered in 1796, just twenty years after the signing of the Declaration of Independence, President George Washington expressed the hope that future generations of Americans would never forget the price his generation had paid for the liberties we enjoy. It was his hope that the spirit of unity that emerged during the Revolution might endure. It was his fervent prayer, he says, "that the free Constitution . . . may be sacredly maintained; that its administration in every department may be stamped with wisdom and virtue." And he affirmed that the Constitution, as written and adopted by the several states, demands full confidence and support from every American:

> Respect for its authority, compliance with its laws, acquiescence in its measures, are duties enjoined by the fundamental maxims of true liberty. The basis of our political systems is the right of the people to make and to alter their constitutions of government. But the Constitution which at any time exists, till changed by an explicit and authentic act of the whole people, is sacredly obligatory upon all.[36]

To understand how the Founders' understanding of ordered liberty has shaped the nation, we need only consider America's record of success over the past 235 years. Through wars, natural disasters, depressions, recessions, and emergencies of every kind, the American Spirit has prevailed. Faith in God has remained constant in the hearts of millions despite the efforts of humanists and progressives to wipe it out. The faith of our fathers may not be as widespread or as vigorous as it was during the founding era, but it survives in millions of homes and churches, and more and more today in civic and political life.

A FATEFUL TRANSFORMATION

We are still "one nation under God." As author and Heritage Foundation researcher Matthew Spalding points out, "We still hold these truths to be self-evident, that all men are created equal, endowed by their Creator with certain unalienable rights. In a world of moral confusion, and of arbitrary and unlimited government, the American founding is our best access to permanent truths and our best ground from which to launch a radical questioning of the whole foundation of the progressive project." Contrary to the claims of progressives that conservatives in this country want to drag America back to the Dark Ages, ignoring the progress of the last two hundred years, Spalding writes:

> Renewing America's principles doesn't mean going back to the eighteenth century, or some other time for that matter. Think of principles as the unchanging standards that inform changing experiences. The question is not, "What Would the Founders Do?" but what will we do as we go forward toward an unknowable future with these fixed principles as our trustworthy guides? It is not about looking back to the past, but rather looking down at our roots in order to look up to our highest ideals.[37]

When you consider all of these things, you soon realize many if not all of these elements are present and active in American society today. Furthermore, I am convinced we are on the verge of a second American revolution—not a revolution of guns and bullets but a revolution in the voting booth and in the major forums of public opinion. It is a revolution of principle, demanding accountability from our public servants and everyone else engaged in government at any level.

I am deeply committed to getting people out to vote. The fact that I am a pastor of a large suburban church doesn't disqualify me from speaking resolutely about the need for character and moral discipline in our elected officials. It is not a matter of voting for Republicans or Democrats. At least 65 million evangelical Christians in this country are eligible to vote, but in a typical presidential election, barely half of them are registered. And, sadly, not all who are registered actually show up at the polls. Apathy is not what the Founders had in mind.

In the eighteenth century the sparks of revolution were fanned into flame by what became known as the Black Robe Regiment. These were the pastors and revivalists who taught the people the importance of personal liberty and challenged them to obey the call of conscience. Today we are seeing a new wave of pastors who are boldly speaking out about the abuses of power by our public officials and the importance of restoring honor in all areas of life. We are going to see a new demand for accountability in our public servants, above and beyond what this nation witnessed in the eighteenth century. I believe this is one of the things we learned from the 2010 midterm elections.

The Declaration of Independence and the Constitution were given to us by the Founding Fathers to set the standards by which we administer the government. But they are also documents of accountability. As our public officials (and particularly the courts) have chipped away at them, doing their best to weaken the Constitution—reinterpreting it in ways the Founders never envisioned, and saying that it is a "living, breathing document" that changes with the times—they are, in reality, destroying their own credibility with the American people.

One of the most important things we can do is to follow through as the Founders did, not only by changing our representatives in the legislatures but by holding all leaders accountable and insisting that they serve as our representatives and not as self-styled dictators. It is not just that we are in the midst of a popular revolution today; these things have all happened before. Thanks to the lessons of history, we have copious examples of how such things have transpired in the past, which tell us where the nation may be headed. But this we know: the action we take today will affect the lives of our children and grandchildren for decades to come.

What this book proposes is a revolution that is far superior to a violent rebellion. It is a revolution of faith and ideas, a new commitment to a higher cause. It is a revolution that will fulfill the charge our forefathers gave us during the founding era. It means knowing who we are and what we are all about. A tremendous hunger for restoration of accountability exists in this country, and the popular reaction to the progressive agenda in Washington may be a blessing. Excessive control and burdensome taxation are driving the people of this country back to basics and, hopefully, leading to a renewal and resurgence of the American Spirit.

I occasionally come across good people who are quick to tell me they are not political. I have friends who simply neglected to vote or take any interest in politics until they woke up one day and realized that the country is headed in the wrong direction. They suddenly understood what the promise of "hope and change" really meant. Now those same people cannot get enough information. They are surfing the Internet, listening to talk radio, or watching cable TV most of the time, and they are becoming engaged in the battle for the soul of America.

People need a creed and a cause, and millions of patriotic Americans are finding their voices. Thomas Jefferson, who was the principal author of the Declaration of Independence, wrote that governments are established to secure the rights of the people. But when government fails to protect our rights and liberties, the people have the right to demand change. They can abolish the government entirely, or they can become personally involved and change it for the better. Today we have some big decisions to make about the future of the republic and about the authentic Source of our rights and liberties. But the good news is, we are listening, we are tuned in, and we are not going home until we get what we came for.

Five

FAITH IN THE TWENTY-FIRST CENTURY

W hen did America become a secular nation? When did we decide "the faith of our fathers" is no longer a vital concern? There's no question that this country is more secular today than it was during the founding era, and no one would deny that anti-Christian words and deeds are more common in the twenty-first century than ever before. But have we really given up on this nation's remarkable heritage of faith? Are we becoming the kind of country that celebrity atheists like Richard Dawkins, Christopher Hitchens, Bill Maher, and Michael Newdow would like us to be?

It can be amusing to read some of the inflammatory rhetoric of secular liberals, claiming this country isn't just secular but was never a Christian nation in the first place. Anyone with even a superficial knowledge of history knows that's false. Nevertheless, in the days following President Obama's April 6, press conference in Ankara, Turkey, during which he stated, "We do not consider ourselves a Christian nation," the policy director of a left-wing think tank in Washington,

DC, called out the cheering section in an article for the liberal website Salon.com titled "America Is Not a Christian Nation." The writer, Michael Lind, was seemingly ecstatic that an American president had finally said what Lind always believed.

While admitting that George Washington and other Founders used religious language from time to time, he questioned their motives. He recited the famous lines from Washington's Farewell Address, "Of all the dispositions and habits, which lead to political prosperity, Religion and Morality are indispensable supports," and even included the less-often-cited portion of that quote: "The mere Politician, equally with the pious man, ought to respect and to cherish them." But then he claimed such statements were simply a cheap way of enforcing good behavior. In other words, the Father of His Country and the man whom Parson Weems tells us "could not tell a lie" was simply exploiting religious language for a secular purpose. Lind writes, "In Washington's day, it may have been reasonable for the elite to worry that only fear of hellfire kept the masses from running amok, but in the twenty-first century it is clear that democracy as a form of government does not require citizens who believe in supernatural religion. . . . Most of the world's stable democracies are in Europe, where the population is largely post-Christian and secular, and in East Asian countries like Japan where the 'Judeo-Christian tradition' has never been part of the majority culture."[1]

It is hard to fathom why anyone would hold up Western Europe as a model of anything, especially a stable democracy. There isn't much stability in Europe these days, and many of those secular cultures are on the verge of social and economic collapse. In a 2006 book called *Menace in Europe*, Claire Berlinski offers a chilling portrait of a continent in the midst of profound spiritual and political crisis. Wracked by an unending series of labor strikes, bomb threats, and terrorist attacks, along with declining birthrates, out-of-control taxes, and crippling levels of immigration from Third World countries, Western Europe is on the ropes. Add to this fifty years of destructive socialist programs and the rising threats of Islamization and neo-Nazism, and you soon discover that Europe is hardly a model for America. And these are just the problems that make headlines; there are many others.

Weekly church attendance in Europe is less than 5 percent today, compared to more than 40 percent in America. So what does that tell you? Berlinski reports, "A poll conducted in 2002 found that while 61 percent of Americans had hope for the future, only 42 percent of the residents of the United Kingdom shared it. Only 29 percent of the French reported feeling hope, and only 15 percent of the Germans." These statistics, she says, suggest that "without some transcendental common belief, hopelessness is a universal condition." Berlinski concludes, "I do not believe it is an accident that Americans are both more religious and more hopeful than Europeans, and more apt, as well, to believe that their country stands for something greater and more noble than themselves."[2]

I couldn't agree more, and that's why the evangelistic ministry I lead today is called There's Hope. Since our first television broadcast in 1984, There's Hope Ministries has extended the hand of fellowship to millions around the world, supplying food, clean water, and other much-needed supplies to suffering people in Africa, and offering the unconditional hope of God's love to millions more in this country and abroad who might otherwise never hear the gospel message.

Hopelessness is always tragic, and the people of Western Europe have turned away from the Author of hope to pursue the empty promises of secularism. But the glories of secularism are greatly overrated. Columnist and author Don Feder, who reported on Berlinski's book, concurs with her assessment: "No one ever founded a republic, or freed slaves, or created a great work of art, or wrote a symphony, or established a charity or a university based on a secular worldview."[3] All those things happened here in America, a Christian nation, because faith in God stimulates hope, compassion, and mercy. "Faith, hope, love," the Bible says in 1 Corinthians 13:13 NKJV. They belong together.

But ever since the French Enlightenment, secular liberals have been proclaiming the death of God. The German nihilist Friedrich Nietzsche famously declared, "God is dead, and we have killed him!" Religion is dead, the skeptics roared. The shackles of religion have been forever broken, and science has won the day! But there's just one problem: Nietszche is dead, the Soviet Union is dead, but God is very much alive. Our Judeo-Christian heritage is untarnished and those secular liberal countries are all in serious trouble—morally, culturally, and economically—while the Christian faith grows stronger every day, not just in America but around the world.

AN UNFAILING PROMISE

No matter what country it is—whether it is America or the former Soviet Union—cultural foundations come from what we believe, and more to the point, values and morals are determined by our religious beliefs. The historian Russell Kirk put it this way: "Civilization grows out of religion: the morals, the politics, the economics, the literature, and the arts of any people all have a religious origin. Every people, no matter how savage or how civilized, have some form of religion: that is, some form of belief in a great supernatural power that influences human destinies."[4]

Even large and powerful nations such as the former Soviet Union, which tried to deny the existence of God and eradicate any memory of the Christian faith, soon discovered they could not eliminate the need for an informing belief in God. They could not erase the supernatural from the minds of the people. Communism attempted to replace Christian theology with the doctrine of "dialectical materialism," which was at best a caricature of religion. But that man-made creed failed to restrain the darker impulses of the citizens and gave them no higher calling, no moral purpose, and no altruistic values to which to aspire.

As a result, the Soviet Empire collapsed, overcome by greed, duplicity, suspicion, and sloth, which were the direct by-products of that wicked philosophy. When the iron curtain came down and the

Berlin Wall was crushed to rubble by the men and women who had been prisoners of that system, the people immediately cried out for Bibles. They begged for preachers and teachers to come and help them rebuild their churches. To the age-old question, "Can man live without God?" the answer of the men and women of Eastern Europe was a resounding *no!*

In September 1994, shortly after the fall of the iron curtain, I went to Moscow to meet the Russian people and preach with Dr. Jerry Falwell in Moscow's Olympic Stadium. It was an amazing opportunity to share the Word of God with people who had been under communist oppression for more than seventy years.

The Moscow Ballet Theatre was performing a new presentation on the life of Christ, and our hosts thought it would be a nice touch to have a couple of Christian ministers come in and tell the audience the story of Jesus as part of the program. The ballet was in two acts, the early life of Jesus and then the ministry years, leading up to the crucifixion. So after the dancers had performed the first half of the story, I explored the question "Who Is Jesus?" Then after the dance company performed the second half, which ended with the resurrection, Dr. Falwell explained "How You Can Know Jesus as Your Savior."

Several of Russia's top officials were there. The KGB was there, of course, but everyone was curious about the Christian faith. We had already spoken to the leaders of the Russian Orthodox Church, and they gave us their blessing. They also told us we were free to say whatever we liked—they wanted the Russian people to know Jesus. They didn't know very much about Jerry Falwell or me before we got there, but apparently someone had recommended us. They just knew we were American pastors, and they had been told our ministries were dedicated to telling people around the world about Christ.

The most surprising part was when Dr. Falwell finished his sermon and asked for all those who would like to know Jesus to stand up—no one moved. I didn't know what to make of that at first because there was no way to witness that performance and hear the testimony of Scripture and not be moved to tears. Dr. Falwell just stood there with his arms extended, but nobody moved. Seated all across the front row were the leaders of the Orthodox Church—the patriarch along with several bishops, priests, and prelates, all in their elegant black robes and head coverings.

We stood there for several minutes, and then, way back in the auditorium, slowly one elderly woman stood up—we could barely see her over the heads of the crowd. The people all looked around to see if anyone was standing—they were watching each other to see who would go first—and when they saw the older lady stand, others stood up, first a few, then a few more, and then thousands all across that massive building. It looked like the morning tide rolling in, and maybe that's what it was. It was a moving sight.

When the commotion stopped and thousands were standing, we asked them to pray with us, and we led them in the prayer of salvation. Then, as men and women all across the building were standing, one of the officials of the Orthodox church walked up to the microphone and told the audience of more than ten thousand men and women that the things we had been telling them were all true, and he hoped all the people would believe what we said and accept Jesus Christ as their Savior.

At that point many who had been hesitant to get up suddenly leaped to their feet and indicated they wanted to know Jesus too. Before all was said and done, more than five thousand men and women had prayed for salvation. Fortunately, we had brought thousands of Bibles in the Russian language with us, and the organizers had ordered thousands of copies of my book, *The Unfailing Promise*, in Russian. All of them were offered to the people as they left that evening, and the Russians literally snapped them up.

Here was an entire culture that had tried to eradicate any mention of Jesus or the Christian faith, but it didn't work. It couldn't work because, as Saint Augustine said, there is a Christ-shaped void in every human heart that can only be filled by Christ Himself, the

One who is the genuine object of our faith. You can try to fill that void with every kind of amusement, philosophy, or political or intellectual substitute you can think of, but you will never be satisfied by anything but the presence of Jesus Christ Himself. Any world system that denies the deep-down hunger for the presence of God in our lives is destined to fail.

The Russian people had been evangelized a thousand years ago, during the Byzantine Empire, and Russia remained a devout Christian country until the Bolsheviks came to power in 1917 and made Christianity a crime against the state. The people's religious beliefs had been stolen from them, but there was residual hunger for the Word of God. I think they always knew that life under the communist system was wrong. It was utterly immoral. Life was much too hard, and the state that claimed to be their god could not save them.

The new socialist order that began with a wave of excitement and promises of material abundance and well-being quickly turned into a nightmare of villainy, greed, ignorance, and starvation. But through all of that, the hope of a Christian revival never completely disappeared: there was something in the collective memory or maybe something in their DNA. They knew there had to be a better way, and I believe they were holding onto the hope of a restoration of the Christian faith.

A KEEPSAKE TO REMEMBER

Former president George H. W. Bush was vice president when Leonid Brezhnev died in 1982. Brezhnev had been general secretary of the Communist Party in the Soviet Union. For some reason President Reagan could not attend the funeral himself, so the vice president went over as the American representative. When he returned from Russia and spoke about what took place at the funeral, he said he looked on as Brezhnev's mother bent over and kissed her lifeless son. What surprised him, however, was when she reached out and made the sign of the cross on his forehead. Even though the state was officially atheistic and even though her son had been a promoter of the communist dogma for most of his life, the flame of Christianity had never died. Beneath all the trappings of power and politics, the embers of faith were still alive, and they are very much alive in Russia today.

One afternoon my wife, Judy, and I left the hotel with our guide and took a walk around Red Square, which is still the ceremonial heart of Russia. It is the place where soldiers, tanks, and rockets are paraded every year to remind the world of Russia's military strength. We could not help being impressed by the Kremlin's colorful domes and some of the buildings surrounding the square, but the overall effect was depressing—everything else we saw was very gray and lifeless.

At one point I asked our guide, "Why is everything so drab? The cars, the people, the buildings are all so plain and dull."

He said, "Sir, it's because we don't want to be noticed. Nobody stands out in this country. Nobody wants to be different from all the rest."

When he said that, I realized what had happened. It was because of the loss of freedom under the Communists. Under socialism the state always comes first, and the individual comes last. The Soviets stripped away the freedom, the pride, and the sense of individuality from the people in order to build the power of the state. If the American people had remained under the thumb of King George III during the eighteenth century, we could well have been in a similar situation today. Life without Christ is futile, and without personal liberty, freedom of conscience, and all the rights and privileges the Founders insisted upon, the American story could have had a very different ending.

Without liberty life loses its appeal, and everything fades into boring sameness. The Bible says, "Now the Lord is the Spirit; and where the Spirit of the Lord is, there is liberty" (2 Corinthians 3:17 NKJV). No philosophy, no ideology, no collection of beliefs or principles can overcome the feelings of emptiness when the love of liberty that comes from a resilient faith in Jesus Christ is missing. Life without God is going to be empty and dull when there is no greater purpose and no hope of eternity, and any society that attempts to eradicate the knowledge of God will inevitably perish.

The Russian people must have instinctively known this, and that is why Jerry and I were invited to come to Moscow. After the concert we were asked to visit the schools and speak to the students and teachers about the Christian faith. I did not have notes or prepared remarks from which to speak. Somewhere along the way I had learned there are still leper colonies in Russia, so I decided to tell the young people the Old Testament story of Naaman the leper.

When the prophet Elisha told Naaman to go and bathe in the River Jordan to be healed of his disease, the great Syrian general was outraged. Bathing in that dirty river was beneath his dignity, he said, but a servant persuaded him to go ahead and do it anyway. Sure enough, when he obeyed the prophet's instructions and took that "leap of faith," he was miraculously healed.

With the help of an interpreter, I told them that story, and when I finished, I asked for those who wanted to know Jesus as their Lord and Savior to come to the front of the room. They just streamed forward. They were thrilled to learn that they could be children of God and know Jesus as their personal Savior. But as they were coming forward, one little girl walked over to speak to me, and she held out a little icon with the image of Christ embossed on it. When she handed it to me, the interpreter told me, "She said, 'I want to give this to you. I don't need it any longer.'"

I asked her name, and she said, "My name is Tanya." I thought that was especially nice because Judy and I have a daughter named Tonya.

One of the local pastors who had been standing with us also spoke English, so I asked him to explain what this meant. I said, "I'm grateful and touched by this little girl's generosity. It's a beautiful ornament, and I'm honored to receive it. But why is Tanya giving me such a lovely keepsake?"

He said, "Dr. Lee, this is a special gift from her family. This icon has been passed down from mother to child in her family for many,

many years. What she just said to you is, 'I don't need this picture of Jesus anymore because now I have Him here in my heart.'"

The icon is a beautiful reminder of how Christ changes lives, and I have kept it on the desk in my study ever since. Every now and then when I need a little encouragement, I will pick it up and think about what little Tanya said to me that day.

CHOOSE THIS DAY . . .

When the president spoke to the Muslim nations during his speech in Turkey, he told them the United States no longer considers itself a Christian nation. I doubt if anyone really believed that statement, regardless what skeptics may say. But even so, those words were a tacit acknowledgment of the fact that we were a Christian nation at one time. As we have seen throughout these pages, it was the dedication of the Puritans in New England and men such as the Reverened Robert Hunt at Jamestown who impressed the indelible stamp of faith upon this nation. From the first settlements in Virginia through the Great Awakening and, ultimately, through the American Revolution, the hand of God was upon the Founders, guiding them every step of the way. Since the beginning, faith has been the secret of America's success.

If we expect to remain successful and prosperous as a nation, we will never do it by following the socialist model or the European model, for that matter. And we cannot do it by trading our form of republican democracy for the social engineering schemes we have been offered by the progressives in Washington, DC. If we want to continue to enjoy freedom and opportunity and a culture of creativity, compassion, and mutual respect, then we need to stick to our beliefs and the values the Founders built into the republic.

We've had it very good in this country for most of the past 250 years—we might even say 400 years if we trace it back to the Puritan era—and the reason we have had it so good is because we were—and still are in many ways—a Christian nation. There are a lot of detractors, and the long list of books by Dawkins, Hitchens, and all the others will keep coming, proclaiming a virulent form of atheism. But that won't change a thing. Men and women just like them have been attacking Christian beliefs for centuries, trying to undermine the faith of millions. But they are just "whistling past the graveyard"—hoping there is no God because if He really exists, they know they are in big trouble.

All the carping about Christianity by skeptics on TV and the Internet can't hurt us. Faith is not determined by public opinion polls or left-wing propaganda; it is based on the unfailing promises of Scripture. Furthermore, every believer has additional confirmation through the indwelling presence of the Holy Spirit. We have endured a decades-long assault on traditional moral values from the cultural elites, and while this may have contributed to the coarseness of the popular culture, it hasn't made the gospel any less relevant or important.

But there is something we ought to consider: If great empires of the past were defeated by the moral decadence, loss of vision, deterioration in educational standards, and failure to remember the lessons of history, what's to keep this country from collapsing in the same way? As we saw in the first chapter, marriage and family are in serious trouble today. Children in many homes are growing up on their own without responsible adult supervision. Church attendance is down in some places, and many of our young pastors aren't sure how to respond.

Wherever secular liberals are in charge of the schools, we see a level of disdain for traditional moral values that is unprecedented in our history. There are signs of change in many places today, but this level of social fragmentation is dangerous anywhere, and that is one of the reasons I am encouraging Christians to become politically active. The only way America can remain strong and free is to restore the foundations of the republic while there is time; we need to take aggressive action in our communities and at all levels of government while so many Americans are mobilized and ready to respond.

Vladimir Lenin, Joseph Stalin, and other leaders of the Soviet Empire tried for more than seventy years to stamp out the traditional religious values of the Russian people. They used intimidation, mass murder, indoctrination, and every threat imaginable. They even tried exploiting religious imagery, using symbols of communism as emblems of devotion, but it did not work. Today Christianity is alive and growing all across Eastern Europe. Communism may still be the reigning orthodoxy in China, but as author and former *Time* magazine correspondent David Aikman writes in his compelling book, *Jesus in Beijing*, Christianity is thriving in that country as well. Despite the persecutions being waged against the house-church movement, the Christian gospel is the hottest thing going in China today.

The irony of all this for secular liberals is that the United States, with its deep religious roots, also happens to be the most technologically sophisticated society in history. Liberals like to characterize us as the "barefoot and pregnant brigade," clinging to our guns and religion. But in all areas of innovation and technology, Christians were there first. The nation that sent men to the moon and created the transistor and the microchip, along with all the marvels of modern mass communications, also happens to be the most Christian nation on the planet. Christian and conservative books top the bestseller lists. Christian bookstores, Christian radio and television stations, and religious programming are everywhere. You can't miss them. No wonder so many atheists are fit to be tied!

On the other hand, as Don Feder reminds us, "the worst horrors of the modern era were perpetrated by godless political creeds. The death toll from sectarian conflict over the ages is dwarfed by ideological violence, from the Jacobinism of revolutionary France to the charnel houses of communism and fascism."[5] In Proverbs, God warns, "All they that hate me love death" (8:36). Utopian schemes of every stripe always end up becoming totalitarian nightmares, merciless to those who refuse to bow to the dictates of ideology.

It was this understanding of the link between the rise of absolute power and the loss of personal liberty that led the first chief justice of the United States Supreme Court, John Jay, to write:

> Almost all nations have peace or war at the will and pleasure of rulers whom they do not elect, and who are not always wise or virtuous. Providence has given to our people the choice of their rulers, and it is the duty, as well as the privilege and interest, of our Christian nation to select and prefer Christians for their rulers.[6]

This is not to say that Christian leaders are perfect or always blameless: it was, after all, the warfare between Catholics and Protestants that caused the Puritans to seek shelter in this country in the first place. But nothing in history comes close to the atrocities of the Holocaust, the Soviet gulags, or the Chinese Cultural Revolution. The dream of state socialism has been one of the most persistent social and economic experiments in history, and it is responsible for the deaths of more than 128 million men, women, and children in the twentieth century alone, as well as almost 30 million in the wars and rebellions it provoked.[7] Submission to utopian ideologies has led to the greatest disasters in human history.

FAITH IN ACTION

The Founding Fathers knew their history; they knew that no nation could survive unless it was built on a sound moral foundation, and they believed that the Christian faith was the best way to ensure the health and longevity of the republic. Some liberal scholars will admit that the Founders were religious, but they are quick to say that the Founders established a secular government based on the doctrine of "separation of church and state." But that's false. All the colonies had established churches at one time, but the Founders had witnessed the dark side of establishment in England—centuries of religion-inspired bloodshed. That wasn't what any of them wanted.

Their idea of "separation" did not mean, however, that religion should have no influence in government. It was our second president, John Adams, a Unitarian, who said, "Statesmen . . . may plan and speculate for Liberty, but it is Religion and Morality alone, which can establish the Principles upon which Freedom can securely stand."[8] Their concern was not that religion should be disestablished but that no single denomination should be favored. Consequently each colony separated church and state by ending tax-funded subsidies to the churches. In 1833, John Adams's home state of Massachusetts became the last to disestablish the state church, the Congregationalist denomination, which had been tax supported since the founding.

You can't read far into the lives of any of the signers of the Declaration of Independence without discovering that these were deeply religious men who believed that religion and morality were essential for good government. This was precisely what George Washington meant when he referred to them as "indispensable supports." The journals of our first president leave no doubt he was a man of sincere Christian convictions. In the book *Sacred Fire*, Peter Lillback gives powerful examples of the depth and richness of George Washington's personal beliefs.

America needed an awakening in 1776, and that is why the pastors, teachers, and evangelists of the Great Awakening had such a tremendous impact on the nation. One pastor who was deeply disappointed by conditions in New England in the years just prior to the Great Awakening worried about the large number of legal disputes and courthouse battles taking place in that part of the country. The Reverend John Cleaveland described it as "a want of brotherly love." There were disputes over the use of the common lands, and everyone was up in arms over the kinds of currency to be used in trading between the colonies. But rather than resolving the disputes amicably, Cleaveland complained, everything ended up in court.[9]

The remarkable thing was not that the colonies were struggling with such questions but that as soon as the first signs of revival began to appear, there was "a tempering of the fierce social, economic, and political antagonisms that had racked the colonies since the beginning of the century."[10] For many who witnessed these changes, the surprising thing about the revivals of the 1730s and '40s was the restoration of social and civic harmony. In 1741, the same year he delivered his most famous sermon, Jonathan Edwards said he was delighted to see that the people of New England had ceased their usual quarrels, and there was a greater measure of peace and unity than that he had seen in the previous thirty years.[11]

As the troubles with England intensified, that sense of unity helped foster resistance to British policy. Eventually it would be the pastors known as the Black Robe Regiment who helped mobilize their congregations for the Revolution, and many of these men went on to serve as chaplains in the army. Despite his disappointment with the changes taking place in colonial society, Cleaveland had been a revival leader during the mid-1760s. He wrote a series of articles for the *Essex Gazette* between 1768 and 1775, decrying the actions of king and Parliament that were pushing the colonists toward armed rebellion. Regarding the Townshend Acts, he said it is the "Birth Right of Englishmen to be free." The Townshend duties were unjust, he said, and he asked, "wherein . . . we differ from the Slaves" if Parliament can levy taxes without the Americans' consent?

As the prospect of war grew nearer, Cleaveland's tone became more insistent, calling for boycotts of British goods. He urged New Englanders to pray that God would "maintain our Rights and Privileges, civil and religious; and above all Things to make us a holy, a truly virtuous People." Then, putting teeth to his request, he called for a boycott of British merchants who refused to support the actions of the patriots, and he called for the names of colonial merchants who resisted the boycotts to be published.[12]

When news of the battle at Lexington and Concord reached him at his home in Ipswich, Cleaveland lost all patience with the British Parliament and penned his strongest diatribe yet, saying, "Great Britain adieu! no longer shall we honour you as our mother. . . . King George the third adieu! no more shall we cry to you for protection! no more shall we bleed in defence of your person—you breach of covenant!" Then to the British general Thomas Gage, that "profane, wicked—monster of falsehood and perfidy," he said, "The God of glory is on our side and will fight for us." Days later Cleaveland put his strong faith into action as he and his four sons enlisted as privates in the New England militia.[13]

The spirit that had arisen in men such as John Cleaveland was not ideology but righteous indignation. They tried everything in their power to reason with the English governors and the Parliament in London, but they were met with one insult after another. Perhaps no act of Parliament better illustrates the growing tensions than the Declaratory Act of 1766, which was enacted shortly after the repeal of the Stamp Tax. In it the English lawmakers declared that regardless of what the Americans might say or do, the colonists were subjects of the Crown and were obliged to obey any and all laws of Parliament. It was, in effect, a slap in the face and one of the most unforgivable provocations for the coming war.

WHERE THERE IS LIBERTY

The Black Robe Regiment played an important role in recruiting members of their congregations for the patriot cause, and one of my favorite examples is the story of the Reverend Peter Muhlenberg, who was pastor of an Anglican congregation in Woodstock, Virginia. As the youngest son of a family of German immigrants, Muhlenberg had been cautious about criticizing King George III, but when it became apparent that war could not be avoided, he was more than prepared to respond.

His sermon on Sunday, January 21, 1776, was from Ecclesiastes 3, which begins, "To everything there is a season, a time for every purpose under heaven: a time to be born, and a time to die; a time to plant, and a time to pluck what is planted" (vv. 1–2 NKJV). He read through the passage eight times, and when he came to the eighth verse, which says, "a time of war, and a time of peace," he laid aside his text, turned to the congregation, and said, "and this is the time of war." At that point Muhlenberg untied his clerical robe to reveal the uniform of a colonel in the Continental Army.[14] At the conclusion of the service, the men of the church turned to kiss their wives and children; then they all marched outside to enlist as the sound of the regimental drums echoed through the church.

Muhlenberg's nephew reported later that 162 men signed up for military service that day, and the following day the minister took command of a company of 300 men from the surrounding county. Muhlenberg, who had been recruited by George Washington, led the Eighth Virginia Infantry throughout the war and eventually retired as a major general of the Continental Army.

When King George refused every offer of reconciliation from the Continental Congress, the Americans felt they had no choice but to take up arms. The king had rejected the Olive Branch Petition offered by Congress in 1775, and he, instead, issued a proclamation declaring the colonies in open rebellion against the Crown. At that point King George ordered all American ports to be closed as he had done to Boston the previous year. This time the king's decree would be enforced by the British navy and marines, who were already laying siege to several towns along the coast.

When it became clear that peace was no longer an option, John Adams, Samuel Adams, Richard Henry Lee, and several other members of Congress began calling for a declaration of independence. As that momentous proposal was being debated and discussed by the delegates, members of the Black Robe Regiment petitioned for a day of "fasting, humiliation and prayer," and the Continental Congress formalized their request by decree. The motion was introduced by William Livingston of New Jersey, who once served as a missionary to the Mohawk Indians.[15]

The motion was approved, and the date was set for May 17, 1776. To make sure everyone was informed of this important day, the Congress placed public notices in the colonial newspapers, recommending that all Americans spend the day in fasting and prayer, humbly seeking God's favor and asking for His protection. The resolution concluded with a prayer that God "would be graciously pleased to bless all his people in these colonies with health and plenty, and grant that a spirit of incorruptible patriotism, and of pure undefiled religion, may universally prevail; and this continent be speedily restored to the blessings of peace and liberty, and enabled to transmit them inviolate to the latest posterity."[16]

No one doubted the seriousness of the request or the urgency of their situation. The prospect of war with the English would have been terrifying to anyone. How could a ragtag army of farmers, merchants, townspeople, and clergymen ever hope to prevail over such an awesome force? In fact, the conflict had been going on since the skirmishes at Lexington and Concord in April 1775. The colonies had offered a peaceful compromise, but the British were incensed by the arrogance of their subjects and fully intended to make the Americans pay.

Because of their faith in God and their allegiance to the American cause, the colonies put aside everything else and flocked to the churches to seek the will of God. Meanwhile the delegates to the Continental Congress, who represented a wide range of sympathies and emotions regarding the prospect of war, ceased all their deliberations and took the day off to attend worship services in Philadelphia.

One week earlier John Adams had put forth a motion calling for each colony to declare independence from England. This, he thought, would be a first step toward a declaration of independence for all colonies, but not all the delegates were so optimistic. The previous month, the legislature of North Carolina passed a unanimous resolution calling for independence. The Virginia House of Burgesses did the same thing on June 29, declaring Virginia's independence from Great Britain and naming a committee to draft the state's first constitution. The Virginia legislature then ordered their delegate to the Continental Congress, Richard Henry Lee, to call for a vote on independence for all the colonies.

On Friday, June 7, 1776, Lee stood before the delegates in Philadelphia to offer the resolution: "That these United Colonies are, and of right ought to be, free and independent states, that they are absolved from all allegiance to the British Crown, and that all political connection between them and the State of Great Britain is, and ought to be, totally dissolved." The vote for the resolution was unanimous. Every delegation was in favor of independence, which meant the thirteen colonies would cease to exist and the United States of America was about to be born.

On June 11, Congress appointed a committee to prepare a draft Declaration of Independence. Thomas Jefferson, John Adams, and Benjamin Franklin were the principal architects. Jefferson worked on the initial draft in his rented room on High Street in Philadelphia between June 11 and 28; when he returned to Carpenters' Hall, Adams and Franklin read the document and made changes. A revised draft was presented to Congress on July 2, following adoption of the independence section put forth by Richard Henry Lee. The members of Congress each read the document and offered changes or revisions; this process lasted most of the day on July 3 and half of the following day. On the afternoon of July 4, the Declaration of Independence was formally adopted.

The Declaration was printed July 5, bearing only the names of John Hancock, who was president of the Continental Congress, and Charles Thomson, secretary. On July 19, Congress ordered that the Declaration be engrossed on parchment[17] with the title "the unanimous declaration of the thirteen united states of America." On August 2, John Hancock signed the engrossed copy in enormous, bold strokes that even a half-blind English king could read. Then, according to protocol, each of the remaining members signed the document, beginning with the northern states and continuing down the list to the southernmost, Georgia. Fifty-six delegates signed the document. Robert Livingston of New York and two other delegates were not present to sign.[18]

RETHINKING THE AMERICAN SPIRIT

The Declaration of Independence, as drafted by Jefferson and revised by the members of that body, was a work of genius that would become a source of inspiration and a model of political wisdom to freedom-seeking peoples everywhere. After reviewing the initial draft, John Adams wrote to his wife that July 2, the day the Declaration was approved, ought to be celebrated as the nation's birthday, with "pomp and parade, with shows, games, sports, guns, bells, bonfires, and illuminations, from one end of this continent to the other. . . ." He proposed that Independence Day forever after should be a day of thanksgiving to God for His deliverance.[19]

Today's secular liberals like to say the Declaration of Independence was a humanist manifesto inspired by the writings of Locke, Hume, Voltaire, and other Enlightenment figures. Jefferson, who was well versed in French thought and a man of science, may not have been a Christian in any traditional sense. Nevertheless, he had written in the front of his Bible, "I am a real Christian, that is to say, a disciple of the doctrines of Jesus. I have little doubt that our whole country will soon be rallied to the unity of our creator." In reality, the Declaration of Independence reflects not just Jefferson's views but the Christian worldview of the men who signed the document "with a firm reliance on the Protection of Divine Providence," and mutually pledged to each other "our Lives, our Fortunes and our sacred Honor."

I first began thinking about writing this book when I was doing some research into the philosophical and spiritual mindset of the Founders. I remember writing in my notes the words, "The Rise of the American Spirit." I had been asking myself: *What is the American Spirit? And where did it come from*? Today, after many long months of study, I am convinced the American Spirit came from the Great Awakening. It is the essence of who we are as a people. Even though that spirit has been through some difficult times of testing, I believe it is still there.

What concerns me most is that so many Americans no longer

seem to recognize it or to regard the American Spirit as highly as they ought. If the American people do not know who they are, they cannot respond appropriately in times of crisis. If our politicians do not know who we are as a nation, they cannot represent us and make decisions on our behalf as well as they should. But if We the People do not know who we are, how can we expect our leaders to know?

With the unexpected emergence of the Tea Party movement in 2009–10, I realized, *That's the Spirit of America. That's the voice of millions of Americans who believe in the achievements and values of our forefathers, and they want to prevent those values from being eroded.* If the spirit that has been so important for more than three hundred years is still there, it will rise up. We have seen it rise up before, especially in times of war and during various national emergencies. We certainly saw it in the aftermath of 9/11, and I am convinced we saw it again in the 2010 midterm elections.

All those Tea Party events that took place over several months were evidence that the American Spirit is not dead. The huge number of people who came to the Restoring Honor event on the Washington Mall made it clear that there is a deep yearning in the hearts of millions of men and women—from sea to shining sea—for a renewal of that marvelous something that made this the greatest country on earth. I doubt if all of them could name it, and many were too young to have learned very much about the history of their country in the public schools, but they knew instinctively that something was missing, and they wanted it back.

If you were to ask the average person if he or she loves America, you would probably hear, "Sure, I love my country!" But what the person is really saying is, "I love the Spirit of America." That needs to be identified, and I believe that spirit will lead us into what I have described in these pages as the Coming Revolution. That revolution is simply a reawakening of the spirit that made us what we are. It was visible during the American Revolution more than 230 years ago. It was put forth foundationally in the Great Awakening. It began to crystallize and come to fruition in the years leading up to the Revolution, and it has been strong with us through all the years since. But today it is being corrupted by the radical left and the gradual incursion of socialist policies from the 1960s by unelected judges and bureaucrats in the nation's capital. That is why we need to start holding their feet to the fire and making some serious changes.

I was in a meeting not long ago with a group of pastors, and one of them was a young man in his midthirties. He is the pastor of a large church of upwardly mobile suburbanites, and when we began talking about the importance of patriotism and respect for this country, he listened in silence for a few minutes. Then he interrupted the conversation and asked, "Can I say something?" We all nodded, and he said, "I'm as much of a patriot as anyone around this table, but if I start talking about patriotism to the people in my church, they won't know what I'm talking about. They don't have any concept of what it means to be an American."

As shocking as it is to think about what he was saying, no one at that meeting was entirely surprised because we have seen it coming for years. The education establishment has been turned upside down, and no one is teaching America's young people about the tremendous privileges they have as citizens of this country. They take our freedoms for granted and assume this country is no better than any other—even though most of the world is still in the hands of dictators and tyrants. To make matters infinitely worse, they and their children are being taught that America is greedy, corrupt, and unworthy of respect.

As a result, millions of young people have no concept of the American Spirit. They don't know what it is. They have been denied the privilege of sharing in the dream that has drawn tens of millions of men, women, and children from every continent to these shores. Now we are seeing a generation coming up who are the children and grandchildren of the men and women who fought, bled, and died for our freedom, and they have been robbed of their inheritance as Americans.

It started with the rise of communism in the 1920s, mainly in

Europe but also among the intellectuals and academics in this country. It really took off during the 1960s with the hippies and flag burners and war protesters. That spirit of anti-Americanism got a boost from President George H. W. Bush when he started talking about the New World Order. Many people were surprised to hear him use that term. Was he making some sort of prophecy? Did he know something we didn't? The fact is, the New World Order was an idea that had been in circulation for decades among the intellectual elites and backroom deal makers of the foreign policy establishment.

But what all those great minds thought should lead to peace and harmony in the world has not had the effect they imagined. The long-term goals of the European Union, the move toward a unified world currency, the purposeful devaluation of the dollar, and so many other things that the progressives have been plotting and planning for generations were unfamiliar and unnatural for most of us. Those ideas did not ring any bells, but the globalists have not given up. They are moving right ahead with their one-world agenda, unabated and unabashed. And I have to admit, if they are trying to create global unity by stomping out the flames of the American Spirit, they have done a pretty good job of it so far.

THIS EXCEPTIONAL NATION

The whole idea of American exceptionalism has been under attack for decades, as if the uniquely valuable role this country performs by lifting untold millions out of poverty is something for which we should be ashamed. This is a serious problem that needs to be addressed, but I have hope that things are changing for the better in all these areas. You do not have to be a Tea Party advocate to see it, but there is a revival of the American Spirit taking place all around us, and it is transforming the social and political landscape.

It is not the kind of hope and change we were promised by the Obama administration; instead, it is a reaction from the heartland against the unrelenting pressure from the Left to deny what we truly are and to make us into something else. This is the change that is making headlines, and the Tea Party movement is evidence that the attempt to remake America into a socialist state is not going over very well with large numbers of Americans.

If you even try to mention the idea of manifest destiny in a classroom in Europe—as I did on one occasion during a lecture at Oxford—the academic elite will go ballistic. The idea that America has had a providential role in history or that this country has a very special destiny is more than it can handle. But our forefathers certainly believed it. You cannot read the history of this nation without seeing just how uniquely and providentially we have been blessed. And America has been a blessing to the nations of the world ever since.

American military might stopped the Nazis, the Japanese Empire, and Mussolini's Fascists. It shut down the concentration camps at the end of World War II. From 1947 to 1951, the Marshall Plan helped bring Europe back from the brink. Economic development in Germany and Japan after the war was spearheaded by American businessmen, allowing those countries to become two of the most competitive and successful economies on the planet. For more than a hundred years, America's wealth has fed the poor, rescued the downtrodden, and fought to help nations recover from disasters and diseases of every kind. This country's record of compassion and service to the world is unrivaled, and we have never done it for profit; we do it because that's the kind of people we are. We do it because this is a Christian nation— an exceptional Christian nation.

In a 1776 letter to family friend Mercy Otis Warren, John Adams wrote, "Public virtue cannot exist without private; and public virtue is the only foundation of republics." He continued,

> There must be a positive passion for the public good, the public interest, honour, power, and glory, established in the minds of the people, or there can be no republican government, nor any real liberty. And this public passion must be superior to all private passions. Men

must be ready, they must pride themselves, and be happy to sacrifice their private pleasures, passions, and interests, nay their private
friendships and dearest connections, when they stand in competition with the rights of society.[20]

That is a powerful statement of the American Spirit, arising from the
wellspring of faith. The men and women of the founding era understood
that the judgment of history was upon them. If they fought so valiantly
to gain independence from Britain and then gave us a government run
by selfish, mean-spirited, and corrupt bureaucrats lacking all concern
for the public good, they would have failed. How would this country be
any different from the European monarchies they had escaped? Adams
spoke for all the Founders when he said that commitment, self-sacrifice,
and personal devotion are essential if there is to be "real liberty."

I am also reminded of the words of other leaders who faced equal or
greater challenges in their lifetimes. For example, President Franklin
Roosevelt at the outset of the D-Day Invasion of Europe, June 6, 1944,
knew that millions of lives already had been lost in the Second World
War and that the fate of millions more would soon be at stake. He went
on the radio to inform the American people of the landings in France
and to offer a heartfelt prayer for our servicemen and the success of
their mission. This is what he said:

My Fellow Americans:

Last night, when I spoke with you about the fall of Rome, I knew
at that moment that troops of the United States and our Allies were
crossing the Channel in another and greater operation. It has come
to pass with success thus far. And so, in this poignant hour, I ask you
to join with me in prayer:

"Almighty God:

"Our sons, pride of our nation, this day have set upon a
mighty endeavor, a struggle to preserve our Republic, our

religion, and our civilization, and to set free a suffering humanity. Lead them straight and true; give strength to their arms, stoutness to their hearts, steadfastness in their faith.

"They will need Thy blessings. Their road will be long and hard. For the enemy is strong. He may hurl back our forces. Success may not come with rushing speed, but we shall return again and again; and we know that by Thy grace, and by the righteousness of our cause, our sons will triumph. They will be sore tried, by night and by day, without rest—until the victory is won. The darkness will be rent by noise and flame. Men's souls will be shaken with the violences of war.

"For these men are lately drawn from the ways of peace. They fight not for the lust of conquest. They fight to end conquest. They fight to liberate. They fight to let justice arise, and tolerance and goodwill among all Thy people. They yearn but for the end of battle, for their return to the haven of home. Some will never return. Embrace these, Father, and receive them, Thy heroic servants, into Thy kingdom. And for us at home—fathers, mothers, children, wives, sisters, and brothers of brave men overseas, whose thoughts and prayers are ever with them—help us, Almighty God, to rededicate ourselves in renewed faith in Thee in this hour of great sacrifice.

"Many people have urged that I call the nation into a single day of special prayer. But because the road is long and the desire is great, I ask that our people devote themselves in a continuance of prayer. As we rise to each new day, and again when each day is spent, let words of prayer be on our lips, invoking Thy help to our efforts.

"Give us strength, too—strength in our daily tasks, to redouble the contributions we make in the physical and the material support of our armed forces. And let our hearts be stout, to wait out the long travail, to bear sorrows that may come, to impart our courage unto our sons wheresoever they may be. And, O Lord, give us faith. Give us faith in Thee; faith in our sons; faith in each other; faith in our united crusade. Let not the keenness of our spirit ever be dulled. Let not the impacts of temporary events, of temporal matters of but fleeting moment—let not these deter us in our unconquerable purpose.

"With Thy blessing, we shall prevail over the unholy forces of our enemy. Help us to conquer the apostles of greed and racial arrogances. Lead us to the saving of our country, and with our sister nations into a world unity that will spell a sure peace—a peace invulnerable to the schemings of unworthy men. And a peace that will let all of men live in freedom, reaping the just rewards of their honest toil.

"Thy will be done, Almighty God.

"Amen."[21]

Those powerful words brought the reality of war home to millions in a way nothing else could have done. These were not the punched-up and calculated exhortations of the political soapbox but a passionate cry from every heart for the men who were at that very hour descending upon the most ambitious military landing in history. This was a prayer for America's sons, fathers, friends, and loved ones and a commitment to continue in prayer for as long as it would take to achieve victory.

Whatever you may think of Franklin Roosevelt, no one can deny the depth of faith he demonstrated in that hour. Because of his genuine compassion for the American people, he was able to speak for all of them with words that could not help but touch the heart of God. And we know God did answer that prayer by giving the American forces and our Allies the victory. The war in Europe would continue for eleven long months until the final German surrender on May 2, 1945, but the die was cast when the president and all of America prayed.

This is how Americans have dealt with adversity for more than three hundred years, by prayer and humble supplication and by the appeal for divine guidance combined with a fierce determination to conquer whatever obstacles may lie before us. When we appeal to heaven, God does not expect us to come to Him with some grand scheme. He wants us to be willing to seek His face, to do His will, and to follow His leading—which can be awfully hard to detect at times. When God called Abraham to leave Ur of the Chaldeans, Abraham had no idea where he was going. When God instructed him to sacrifice his son, he had no idea that God would provide another sacrifice—a ram—so that Isaac could be spared. But as Paul tells us, "Abraham believed God, and it was accounted to him for righteousness" (Romans 4:3 NKJV).

Throughout Scripture we see the same pattern: God is seeking those who will step out in faith, believing that He still causes all things to "work together for good to those who love God, to those who are the called according to His purpose" (Romans 8:28 NKJV). The fact that our forefathers and foremothers, with remarkably few exceptions, actually believed that promise and acted on it, would—if nothing else—make this a truly exceptional nation.

Six

THE COMING REVOLUTION

If you wanted to take one of the world's largest and most dynamic economies and fundamentally change it from top to bottom, what would you do? Where would you begin? This was the question the young lawyer asked himself. He was full of questions, full of ideas. He dreamed of doing something big and important, but he didn't know where to begin. He had grown up in a middle-class family; both of his parents were teachers who were socially and politically aware. His father always said there were too many poor people, all of them working too hard for too little pay, and too many rich people who never seemed to work at all. Couldn't somebody do something about that?

The young man was a mediocre student—his teachers said he was too impatient and undisciplined—but he was a man of action, and he believed he could do something. He could be somebody. Like his older brother, Alex, Vladimir Ulyanov wanted to challenge the status quo. He just needed a plan. After college he worked as a small-town lawyer for a while, but he hated the job. He knew he was destined for bigger things. So he kept thinking, kept reading, and by his mid-twenties Vladimir had found his plan. He found it in the writings of the revolutionary thinkers and philosophers of the previous generation, but the plan was big and ambitious: so big, in fact, that he would need thousands of volunteers to make it happen.

That is what he decided to do. He would write articles, papers, and books; he would get out in public and give speeches so he could raise the people's awareness, change the public consciousness, and raise an army of volunteers motivated by a vision of hope and change. Before all was said and done, his plan would lead to a total transformation of society. He would change the culture and reshape the economy, beginning with the graduated income tax, centralized control of banking and credit, and nationalization of the media, mass communications, and transportation. It also included government control of the environment and farming and the confiscation of public lands.

Unionization and regimentation of the labor force were essential—this was the foundation of his army of volunteers—along with control of public education and the universities. And the biggest and grandest plan of all, the abolition of private property and the confiscation of inherited wealth would pay for everything he hoped to accomplish. With all these things in place, Vladimir Ilyich Ulyanov—now known as V. I. Lenin—turned his attention to the one obstacle that stood in the way of his "Worker's Paradise," the one thing preventing final and absolute control of the economy and the success of all his plans: the Christian faith of the Russian people.

Unlike Karl Marx, who had originally conceived and published a plan for world domination in the *Communist Manifesto* of 1848, Lenin was never one for subtlety. If Marx was the academic and the theorist, Lenin was the agitator and the warrior. Marx provided the nail, but Lenin had the hammer. As Malachi Martin writes:

> Marx's dry discussions and the touch of poetic pretense in his forecasts contrast with the bloody realism of Lenin, whose predictions were far from idyllic. His plans all were aimed at a complete and bloody break with the past, and at the violent death and final

entombment of capitalists and capitalism. . . . The one poetic touch in Lenin's otherwise abrasive mind, in fact, concerned that almost dreamlike "Worker's Paradise" he foresaw at the end of the proletarian rainbow. To find a parallel, you would have to go back to the early Hebrew prophets and their forecast of the Messianic Age. . . . On the near side of that rainbow, however, the reality Lenin foresaw and worked so feverishly to bring about was the grinding tyranny that has been witnessed by the world for seventy years and more.[1]

Lenin referred to the war against Christianity and the universal acceptance of atheism as "the cause of our state."[2] Christianity made the people soft, he believed, and unwilling to join the revolution. Orthodox Christians were content with their lives and tended to believe that with God's help they could overcome their own limitations and the disadvantages life had thrust upon them. For Lenin, who had long since renounced morality and religion, that kind of thinking was infuriating. He needed an army of zealots to help him carry forward his revolutionary dream. Christianity would have to go.

After the Bolshevik Revolution in 1917, Lenin created the Communist International (the Comintern), and his followers launched a massive campaign against the churches. Nothing would stand in their way. During the seventy-year history of the Soviet Union, millions of churches were desecrated, burned, or converted to secular purposes (turned into shops, offices, theaters, museums, and warehouses). The few houses of worship that were not destroyed or converted to other uses became state property, and the charitable programs previously run by the churches were taken over by the government.

Orthodox monasteries were turned into prison camps, and millions of believers were persecuted, tortured, or killed. Some Christians and Jews who refused to renounce their faith were sent to labor camps or mental hospitals. Thousands more were exiled and shipped off to other countries, but believers of all faiths were ridiculed and harassed, and by 1925, official courses in atheism were being taught in all the schools and colleges.

From the start the Communists used whatever language they needed to mislead the people. In the midst of all the social and political turmoil of the post–World War I era, words like *socialism* and *democracy* sounded reassuring. Many people still feel that way: What's so bad about socialism? What's wrong with democracy? Lenin knew these terms could be useful because they allowed the government to increase control over the people (the bourgeoisie), and socialism was just the first step toward Lenin's ultimate objective, full-blown communism. This was what he meant by "democracy." But for the initiated, Lenin spelled out his meaning in the "Program of the Communist International" (1928), in which he said,

> The Soviet form of State, being the highest form of democracy, namely, proletarian democracy, is the very opposite of bourgeois democracy. . . . The Soviet State is the dictatorship of the proletariat, the rule of a single class—the proletariat. Unlike bourgeois democracy, proletarian democracy openly admits its class character and aims avowedly at the suppression of the exploiters in the interests of the overwhelming majority of the population.[3]

Lenin made sure the Comintern understood the objective was total and absolute domination by any means necessary, and he added ominously, "The Soviet State completely disarms the bourgeoisie and concentrates all arms in the hands of the proletariat; it is the armed proletarian State."[4]

In the wake of the Bolshevik Revolution, Lenin promised tolerance for dissent, but that was a lie. It was simply a talking point he never intended to honor. When Czar Nicholas II, his wife and four daughters, and his son and heir, Alexis, were brutally murdered in July 1918, the story was immediately spread that local anarchists were responsible for the crime, but that was also a lie. After an investigation that included a detailed review of archival material from Lenin's personal bodyguard, the Russian historian Edvard Radzinsky was able to confirm in 1990 that Lenin had ordered the executions. In fact, his bodyguard had delivered the order to the telegraph office and then saved the original telegraph tape as a record of the secret order.[5]

In the words of the Orthodox priest and dissident Gleb Yakunin, "Russia turned crimson with the blood of martyrs." In the first five years after Lenin's army of radicals and labor organizers seized power, 28 bishops and more than 1,200 priests were murdered in cold blood. Later under Joseph Stalin, who ruled as general secretary of the Communist Party from 1922 to 1953, the level of state-authorized terror only increased, and, according to records from the era, "by the end of Khrushchev's rule [1953–1964], liquidations of clergy reached an estimated 50,000."[6]

THE GREAT LIBERAL DREAM

Karl Marx, who died in 1888, did not live to see the tragic results of his big idea, and Lenin, who died in 1924, just seven years after the Bolsheviks seized power, never saw the great "Worker's Paradise" he had envisioned. But the tyranny they unleashed on the world would not die so easily, and it has continued to haunt the planet ever since. In January 2011, the religious watchdog group Freedom House reported that freedom is in decline around the globe. In 2010, just 87 countries qualified as "free countries," and 25 of the world's 194 countries faced significant deterioration in the levels of personal freedom.

"Authoritarian regimes like those in China, Egypt, Iran, Russia, and Venezuela," the report stated, "continued to step up repressive measures with little significant resistance from the democratic world."[7] Not surprisingly, Marxist-Leninist ideology is implicated in every case. More recently we have seen a wave of violence and instability in Mexico and South America, along with riots and insurrection all across the Middle East inspired by equal parts of Islamic extremism and Communist agitation. Our own government, instead of calling for order and an end to the violence, has apparently taken sides with the rioters calling for revolution, supporting the spread of Islamic Sharia law, encouraging groups like the Muslim Brotherhood while turning its back on leaders who have been supportive of U.S. policy in the past and forcefully condemning the only democratic nation in the region, the state of Israel.

But some will ask, why should all these things matter to me? They matter because we have good reason to fear for our country when American foreign policy no longer represents the beliefs of a majority of the citizens, and when lawmakers in Washington continue creating outrageously expensive new programs that rob people of their self-reliance and push the nation further down the road toward socialism. As Russell Kirk pointed out in *The American Cause*, tyrants of all stripes draw their strength from their ideologies, and ideology is always the enemy of faith in God. People whose lives have been turned upside down by war or famine or disasters will naturally look for comfort wherever they can find it. In the absence of genuine faith in God, many will give their allegiance to any charismatic leader who can offer a vision of peace and plenty. But this is an environment ripe for exploitation.

During the French Revolution liberal ideologues calling themselves "New Men" promised a classless society where all men would be happy and prosperous, but those promises were empty and resulted in the "Reign of Terror" and more than fifty years of social and political anarchy. During the Enlightenment's assault on both church and state, the boulevards of Paris ran red with the blood of its victims, and the promise of liberation became a death sentence for thousands.

By the same token, communism, which is an even more insidious ideology, has claimed the lives of more than 100 million men, women, and children worldwide. Despite the widely celebrated collapse of the Soviet Union in 1989–90, the Marxist ideology is very much alive, still attracting followers, and still wreaking havoc in this country and around the world.[8] What the destitute and hungry are being offered today is a false vision of utopia, the promise of a world in which war and sorrow and inequality will no longer exist. But as discussed in the first chapter of this book, that is a promise no one on this earth can keep.

When the Russian dissident Aleksandr Solzhenitsyn came to this country in 1974, he was shocked to discover that while communism was already in decline in the Soviet Union, it was thriving in America's newsrooms and on our university campuses. How could "the best and brightest" in academia and the news media have fallen for the Communist lie when so many in his own country were waking up from a decades-long nightmare and praying for the collapse of the socialist regime?

The great man never received a satisfactory answer, but in 1994, after twenty years in this country, during which he was vilified by liberal elites for his Christianity and his conservative political views, Solzhenitsyn returned to Russia, where he could serve as a witness of his resolute faith in God and his hope for an authentic democracy in that country. By the time he died in 2008, however, the former KGB director Vladimir Putin was president of Russia.

To comprehend why liberals are so inclined to support socialist policies and condemn those who hold traditional values, it is important to understand that liberal ideology rejects the doctrine of "original sin." The Bible teaches that sin separates mankind from God and only belief in the substitutionary death of Jesus Christ can restore a right relationship with the Father. Liberal ideology, on the other hand, teaches that humanity is naturally good and even perfectible when given the right opportunities. As defined by James Burnham, "Modern liberalism . . . holds that there is nothing intrinsic to the nature of man that makes it impossible for human society to achieve the goals of peace, freedom, justice, and well-being that liberalism assumes to be desirable and to define 'the good society.'"[9]

The Founding Fathers went to great lengths in the Declaration of Independence and the Constitution to protect the rights of the individual. The entire Bill of Rights is a defense of personal liberty and a limit on the power of the state. Unfortunately, this is not what liberals in America are after. In his book *Liberty and Tyranny*, author and attorney Mark Levin writes that liberals are intellectually committed to the supremacy of the state rather than the rights of the individual. "For the Modern Liberal," he says, "the individual's imperfection and personal pursuits impede the objective of a utopian state. In this, Modern Liberalism promotes what French historian Alexis de Tocqueville described as a *soft tyranny*."[10] Consequently Levin argues that today's liberals ought to be characterized as statists because their main concern is empowering government while curtailing the rights and privileges of individual citizens.

One of the best definitions of liberalism comes from a twentieth-century liberal, the former vice president under Lyndon Johnson, Hubert Humphrey, who said *change for the sake of change* is the hallmark of political liberalism. In an article in the *New York Times Magazine*, Humphrey said, "It is this emphasis on changes of chosen ends and means which most sharply distinguishes the liberal from a conservative in a democratic community . . . liberals recognize change as the inescapable law of society, and action in response to change as the first duty of politics."[11]

What each of these definitions tells us is that in liberal ideology the belief that public officials can make radical changes to our government while basically ignoring the will of the people is perfectly legitimate. This was never what the Founders had in mind. However, I believe this is why presidential candidate Barack Obama chose the slogan Hope and Change for his 2008 campaign. This was the language of the ultraliberal communities in which he had spent his entire life. From boyhood on Mr. Obama was exposed to no other point of view, and he concluded that this was what a majority of the voters wanted to hear. Apparently he guessed right since they elected him president. But I doubt if even a fraction of the voters had any idea what that promise would ultimately entail.

THE JUDEO-CHRISTIAN ETHIC

Standing in dramatic opposition to the liberal view of human nature and the socialist vision of the perfectibility of mankind is the Judeo-Christian ethic, which was embraced without exception by the Founding Fathers and the generations afterward who laid the foundations of American democracy. I described this in the opening pages of *The American Patriot's Bible*, published in 2009, but I think it is important at this point to outline briefly the seven principles that "people of the book," meaning Christians and observant Jews, have traditionally embraced.

1. THE DIGNITY OF HUMAN LIFE

Without respect for human life at all stages, from conception to natural death, any claim of decency and morality is meaningless. Jesus said, "I have come that they may have life, and that they may have it more abundantly" (John 10:10 NKJV). Because Americans hold all life in high regard, millions of men and women have come to this country from around the world. This is also why we send missionaries, aid workers, and military forces to foreign lands: we believe human life is precious. But we are far from blameless, and history will take a dim view of some of our policies regarding human life. With a blood-stained history of more than thirty-five years and 50 million deaths, the abortion industry has left an indelible stain on this nation's honor. The good news, however, is millions of Americans are beginning to see the light and are changing their views on abortion. If the American people cannot show compassion for the most innocent human life, the unborn child in his mother's womb, we have no right to speak about human dignity. This is God's standard, and it ought to be our hope and prayer that the evil practice of abortion will be ended very soon.

2. THE TRADITIONAL MONOGAMOUS FAMILY

There is nothing more natural or more essential to the health and well-being of the community than the traditional two-parent family.

This was God's plan from the beginning, and the very first institution He created. Before the community, before the church, and before government, God created man and woman as partners, each with unique strengths and attributes that would be needed to raise happy and healthy children and build stable communities. While there are times when the loss of a spouse or loved one may alter this arrangement, any deliberate attempt to circumvent God's design—to change this natural balance that is common throughout nature—will have serious and long-term consequences.

3. A National Work Ethic

Dating back to the landing at Plymouth Rock, what has sometimes been called the "Protestant work ethic" has been one of the most important characteristics of the American way of life. The Bible says, "If anyone will not work, neither shall he eat" (2 Thessalonians 3:10 NKJV). The Pilgrim Fathers knew they would not survive if each man and woman did not do his or her part, and the success of those first settlements was a testament to the determination and energy they exhibited.

In times of stress—the Great Depression of the 1930s, for example, or the economic difficulties in America today—it's not always easy to find work, but God expects each of us to be willing and ready to contribute when we can. The fact that millions of Americans have done their part to support their families and earn an honest living is one of the main reasons this country has been such a beacon of hope to the rest of the world. Any government policy that subverts the right to work or holds individuals and families in bondage in the name of welfare threatens this most basic human right.

4. The Right to a God-Centered Education

Any society that fails to teach its children the proper relationship between mankind and the Creator will experience hardship and sorrow. If children do not understand the vertical relationship between themselves and God, they will have difficulty understanding the role of parents, teachers, and other authority figures, and consequently they will have problems with the horizontal relationship with their peers. The Founders had no misgivings about the importance of a God-centered education: they believed the purpose of education at all levels was to inculcate the virtues and moral values essential for good citizenship.

This is why all the universities of the founding era were established as seminaries. Every academic discipline, whether it is science, mathematics, history, literature, or the arts, has deep Christian roots; it is impossible to read about the origins of any of them without encountering the godly men and women who paved the way. When our schools, in the name of diversity and tolerance, deny children the privilege of a proper understanding of our Judeo-Christian heritage, they handicap their understanding of the world and, worse, dishonor the very Source of wisdom and prosperity.

5. THE ABRAHAMIC COVENANT

One of my favorite verses in the Bible is Psalm 33:12, which says, "Blessed is the nation whose God is the LORD, the people He has chosen as His own inheritance" (NKJV). There is no question that America has been blessed by God. Columbus believed God brought him to these shores for the purpose of establishing a godly nation. The Pilgrims, who began their journey in the New World with a covenant called the Mayflower Compact, survived overwhelming odds, upheld by their strong faith and fervent prayers, and God allowed them to prosper.

Every American president has honored God, at least in his public statements, and we have built a "city on a hill." When God made a covenant with Father Abraham, He promised to bless and prosper the patriarch and his descendants forever if they would remain faithful and never forget where their blessings came from. I believe God has allowed this country to undergo severe hardships in recent years largely because America is at risk of forgetting those things.[12] If we really want to see our situation take a turn for the better, we need to get back on our knees, ask for forgiveness, and honor this nation's covenant with the Creator.

6. COMMON DECENCY

Is there anything more gratifying than being treated with decency and respect? And is there anything more exemplary of the American Spirit than showing common courtesy to other people, regardless of their race, religion, or social status? The radicals of the French Enlightenment promised equality and opportunity for all, but the *nouvelle regime* they created in the eighteenth century was a disaster because they deliberately left God out of the picture and showed respect for no one. If we understand, as the Bible says, that we are created in the image of God, then we honor the Creator when we treat others as we wish to be treated. "Therefore," Jesus said, "whatever you want men to do to you, do also to them, for this is the Law and the Prophets" (Matthew 7:12 NKJV). Demonstrating respect and common decency toward others is recognition of the Christian belief that "I serve myself best when I serve you."

7. OUR PERSONAL ACCOUNTABILITY TO GOD

Modern sociologists are apt to say that criminals and other kinds of offenders are victims of society. Rather than placing the blame for wrong choices where it actually belongs, they prefer to blame some vague institution called *society*. But God is under no such illusion. The belief that each person is accountable to God and will have to answer for his or her choices in life is one of the most basic principles of the Judeo-Christian ethic.

Generations of Christians have believed the words of Saint Peter: "The eyes of the LORD are on the righteous, and His ears are open to their prayers; but the face of the LORD is against those who do evil" (1 Peter 3:12 NKJV). Knowing that God hears and sees every word and deed ought to be a source of great comfort because, as the Bible assures us, "He cares for you" (1 Peter 5:7 NKJV). But a sense of personal accountability is equally important because it reminds us that when this life is over, there will be a day of judgment.

LIVING UP TO OUR IDEALS

Why does America send soldiers, aid workers, and cultural emissaries around the world to extend a helping hand to the people of other nations? Because Americans are decent people who care about the welfare of others. We believe national defense and military readiness are essential, and we understand that we must be willing to stand our ground against the forces of evil in the world. For the most part, Americans have never shirked their civic duty in these areas.

On the other hand, concern for the well-being of others was a major failing of the Soviet Union. Because of the corrupt system in which they were trapped, the people became corrupt, self-centered, and skeptical of everything and everyone. The government poured billions into armaments and made a huge display of Russia's military strength, but deprived of faith in God, the people lost their common decency; and as the Soviet economy was slowly grinding to a halt in the 1980s and '90s, no one would risk his or her own safety for the well-being of others.

Just think of what happened with abortion in that country. I have been told the average woman in Russia today has had four abortions.[13] Obviously for these women abortion is not about the health of the mother. It is simply a contraceptive. If the pregnancy is deemed inconvenient, she can just get rid of it. How sad to realize that much the same thing is now happening in this country, especially on the college campuses where sexual promiscuity is actively encouraged. Nevertheless, there is also good news that many people are beginning to see abortion as a sin against human nature. I am seeing more and more reports each year indicating that a growing number of Americans believe that abortion is wrong and ought to be legally ended.

There's Hope Ministries sponsors a pregnancy clinic in the Atlanta suburbs. We helped save the lives of 72 babies in 2010 alone; these are all beautiful children who would otherwise have been victims of the so-called *pro-choice movement* if we had not intervened. Unfortunately we can't save them all. We could save ten times that number if we had the funds and manpower to expand our outreach. But even with all we know about the horrors of abortion and with the loss of more than 50 million lives to the abortion holocaust since the Supreme Court's 1973 *Roe v. Wade* decision, it is difficult to raise money for crisis pregnancy centers in many communities. Too many people have decided the abortion crisis is somebody else's problem. The Left has done a good job of politicizing the debate, and it is uncomfortable to protest for the rights of the unborn, so many people just look the other way and stay home.

Unfortunately the government has no problem using our tax dollars to promote abortion, advocating for abortion services through the Department of Health and Human Services and pouring millions into organizations such as Planned Parenthood, which is the largest abortion provider in America. Despite the efforts of conservative lawmakers and constant protests from pro-life groups and concerned citizens, the Obama administration increased funding for Planned Parenthood from $350 million in 2009 to $363 million in the 2009–2010 fiscal year. For political liberals in Washington and in state legislatures around the country, this is the defining issue of their public life, and they are not about to back down—which says a lot about what motivates people on that side of the aisle.

Every time we turn around, government is digging deeper into our pockets, creating new and more expensive social programs that invariably fail to deliver the benefits they promised but always lead to higher taxes. Liberal social programs have been a disaster for America, leading to higher levels of crime, joblessness, generational dependency, poverty, and profound resentment, not only among the recipients of these services but from the taxpayers who are required to fund them. The American family has been devastated by well-meaning but misguided sociology. Entire industries have been driven to the point of bankruptcy and beyond, so now our economy stands on the threshold of collapse.

A big part of the resentment expressed by members of the Tea Party movement is due to government's inability to deliver on its promises. But even more troubling, too many Washington policy makers and bureaucrats refuse to admit that we are already over our heads in debt and the American economy is sinking fast. Even with a national debt of $14 trillion, a $1.6 trillion budget deficit in fiscal year 2011, and the threat of foreclosure by China and the other countries funding our debt, liberal lawmakers do not seem to know when to stop.

The Democratic majority that took control of Congress after the 2008 general election has expanded the size of government in almost every area. Policies the voters overwhelmingly rejected have been forced down our throats, pushing the nation deeper into debt and further into the grip of state socialism. At this pace, by the end of President Obama's term, the government will have borrowed as much money in four years as it had in the previous 223 years since the Constitution was adopted in 1789. According to the administration's own numbers, the accumulated debt will top $19 trillion by the year 2021, consuming 80 percent of the nation's gross domestic product (GDP).[14]

Many young people have been persuaded in their schools and colleges that socialism is a good thing, a compassionate way of caring for the less fortunate. At the same time they are being taught that capitalism is a bad thing because it exploits workers and empowers the rich. The vast majority of Americans know better than that: we have no interest in going the way of the Soviet Union or Eastern Europe or Western Europe for that matter. But unless we can convince the next generation of the profound danger of that way of thinking, it will be immeasurably harder to turn things around.

For a closer look at some of the reasons we need to resist the direction the federal government has been taking us the past few years, I would like to offer a quick review of some of the policy issues that have become major sources of irritation.

THE HEALTH-CARE DILEMMA

Despite the claims trumpeted by the mainstream media and members of the president's party in Congress that health care in this country suffers in comparison to the nationalized health services in places such as Great Britain and Canada, a new study by British researchers found that American doctors do a much better job of treating and curing serious diseases such as cancer. As reported in the August 2008 issue of the medical journal *Lancet Oncology*, American patients have a better survival rate for thirteen of the sixteen most common cancers than their British counterparts. American men are 40 percent more likely than European men to live for five years after their first diagnosis, the study says, and American women are 12 percent more likely to live at least five years longer than European women.[15]

For years we have been told the American health-care system is broken and only government can fix it. Anyone who has ever stood in line at the DMV or tried to communicate with an IRS agent about a tax problem ought to know better. Any time government bureaucrats get involved in any issue, the problem gets worse. In a recent study of key issues in the health-care debate, author and researcher Sally Pipes offers a somber observation, stating, "Health care and K–12 education are the two sectors in America that have more government involvement than any other, and they both suffer from serious quality problems."[16]

During debates leading up to passage of the 2010 health-care bill, effectively mandating nationalized health care for all Americans despite overwhelming resistance from the public, Congress began the process of simultaneously nationalizing a large segment of the insurance industry. Rather than making the system more affordable, easier to use, or less restrictive, these new laws are having the opposite effect. Before insurance companies can offer coverage to the public, each policy must be reviewed by all fifty state insurance administrations. Consumers are barred from purchasing insurance across state lines, and then they are forced to purchase one-size-fits-all packages that include many services they will never need. In 2007, there were 1,901 different federal mandates that health insurance providers must observe; this is what always happens whenever the federal government starts making the rules.[17]

Government regulations regarding Medicare and Medicaid have multiplied the amount of red tape involved in processing medical claims and complicated the process of delivering appropriate care. Bureaucratic interference hampers the work of physicians beyond any reasonable limits. Both of these programs impose strict price controls on health care by determining what doctors and hospitals can charge for their services, which has led to serious inequities and caused thousands of doctors to opt out of the government-managed programs.

According to a 2008 survey of medical services for elderly Americans, approximately a third of all senior citizens reported having difficulty finding a doctor who would accept them as patients. As Sally Pipes points out, "The government may efficiently control the costs at which doctors are reimbursed. This does not, however, account for the pain and suffering people endure waiting for care or the value of their time spent searching for a doctor."[18]

In their efforts to persuade Americans of the need to radically remake the U.S. health-care industry, congressional Democrats told us repeatedly that 47 million Americans were living in fear that they could not receive adequate care because they did not have medical insurance. The truth is, at least 10 million of the reported 47 million were not American citizens. Those individuals would have been treated without cost at virtually any American hospital. Another 18 million were between eighteen and thirty-four years of age and unlikely to purchase health insurance at all. Another 17 million, with incomes over fifty thousand dollars, could afford to purchase health insurance but decided for their own reasons not to do so. And, finally, many of the supposed 47 million were temporarily unemployed and would be eligible for benefits as soon as they returned to work.[19]

By far the greatest problem regarding the implementation of national health care in this country is the enormous financial burden it would place on the federal government. As with Social Security, Medicare, and Medicaid, all that cost eventually comes back to the taxpayers without any guarantee the government can actually deliver the goods. The government's insistence on plunging ahead with mandatory health-care initiatives despite the obvious risks and complications led syndicated columnist Michael Medved to conclude:

> The likelihood of further explosions in the national debt represent a genuine threat to national security, with real chances for out-of-control inflation, a badly battered and devalued dollar, and the disastrous downgrading of federal debt by worried creditors. The utter disregard to any sense of fiscal discipline represents a menace to our way of life at least as serious as the murderous minions of Islamo-Nazi terror.[20]

Ever since the Social Security Administration was created by the Roosevelt administration in 1935, the government has pretended there is a big trust fund somewhere in Washington where the contributions of individual wage earners are safely kept, gaining interest until the individual retires. The truth is, there never was such a trust fund, no lock box, no bank account of any kind. Instead, tax monies paid to the IRS for all these services go straight to the general budget, where they are promptly spent by Congress for other things.

Every new program, every government expense, and every promise of relief winds up being simply another way of extorting money from taxpayers for inefficient programs. In each of these programs, as former Reagan administration lawyer Mark Levin points out, "the individual is tethered to the state, literally and utterly reliant on it for his health and survival. . . . Rather than the individual making cost-benefit and cost-quality decisions about his own condition, the Statist will do it for him. And the Statist will do it very poorly, as he does most other things."[21]

There is no question there needs to be improvement in the cost and accessibility of health care in this country, but the answer is not more government inefficiency and interference in the doctor-patient relationship. Instead of allowing bureaucrats in Washington, DC, to decide what treatments are acceptable and how much they should cost, the free market system that has worked so well for most of our history—at least until the beginning of Lyndon Johnson's Great Society schemes in the 1960s—has a natural self-regulatory apparatus: if it works, people will use it, and they will pay a fair price. That's the American way. If the quality of care is poor, the results are disappointing, or the physician fails to render professional treatment at a fair price, the consumer will vote with his feet and find a doctor who can do a better job. That's how it ought to work in a free society.

MARRIAGE AND FAMILY ISSUES

Recently the Family Research Council issued a report based on 2008 Census data entitled "Index of Belonging and Rejection," which indicates that the percentage of American children growing up in intact homes with a birth mother and biological father who remain legally married to each other until the child becomes a teenager has fallen dramatically over the past thirty years. The figures in this report are deeply troubling. Just 45 percent of young people in this country manage to grow up with both parents. For whites the average is 54 percent, and for blacks it is just 17 percent. The average for Asian Americans is somewhat better at 62 percent but still disappointing.

The out-of-wedlock birthrate for blacks was 26 percent in 1965, when Daniel Patrick Moynihan first identified the problem, and the white illegitimacy rate was just 3 percent. Today it's 28 percent for whites, 72 percent for blacks, and 40.6 percent overall. As Tom Bethell writes in the *American Spectator*:

> We are living in the midst of a revolution that few want to talk about even though, if not reversed, it will spell the end of Western Civilization. Accompanying this revolution has been the collapse of fertility rates, especially in Europe. This demographic revolution, aided by contraception and abortion, ensures that income transfer programs will not be sustainable for much longer—perhaps no more than another ten years in Europe. Only the immigration to the U.S. of more fertile Latinos has postponed (but has not averted) the same outcome here.[22]

The traditional two-parent family has been the bedrock of society throughout history. Even though some cultures, such as the ancient Greeks and the French Jacobins, flirted disastrously with other sorts of arrangements, no nation has successfully challenged the value of this God-given and time-honored institution. Supreme Court Justice Joseph Story affirmed the importance of the traditional bond of husband and wife, saying, "Marriage is treated by all civilized societies as a peculiar and favored contract. It is in its origin a contract of natural law."[23] When the home is built around a faithful monogamous marriage, social welfare programs are seldom necessary. Or as the social critic Michael Novak put it, the family is the original Department of Health and Human Services.

Multiple studies show that married adults have better health, live longer, have fewer accidents, and are generally happier than single or unmarried cohabiting adults. Married women experience less domestic violence and are less likely to become victims of violent crime than single or divorced women. Equally important, children raised in traditional two-parent families perform better in school, are more likely to graduate from high school, and are less likely to be involved in juvenile crime. Girls raised in such families are much less likely to have a teen pregnancy. Married women are also less likely to experience poverty, whereas the number one predictor of childhood poverty is growing up in a household headed by a single mother. According to the U.S. Census Bureau, children living in households headed by single mothers are more than five times as likely as children living in households headed by married parents to be living in poverty—42.9 percent compared with 8.5 percent.[24]

In spite of all the evidence linking disruptions in traditional family formation to serious social pathologies, the federal government continues to issue bureaucratic mandates that reward dysfunction and penalize the two-parent family. In the 1960s, it was "no-fault divorce," which made it relatively easy for couples experiencing normal marital difficulties to separate and file for divorce before fully considering the consequences for themselves and their dependent children. Then in the 1970s, leaders of the feminist movement, such as Betty Friedan and Gloria Steinem, managed to persuade millions of women that marriage and child-rearing was a prison devised by men to keep them in bondage. Friedan later recanted and apologized for the mayhem she caused, but the damage had already been done.

When we measure the harm inflicted by all these reckless attempts to redefine the family, we have to wonder where such ideas come from. The sources of the chaos are the same ones we have run into time and time again. As reported by Jennifer Roback Morse, the socialist view of family formation, which is derived from classical Marxist dogma, has been one of the most insidious and persistent enemies of the two-parent family in our time. Marxist theory, she says, holds that relationships between men and women are characterized by conflict because of the problem of male dominance.

According to Marx and Friedrich Engels, the authors of the *Communist Manifesto*, the transition from group marriage to monogamy in primitive societies led to the subordination of women. Originally, they said, the typical household was a commune in which groups of men were the hunter-gatherers and groups of women were in charge of the household. When Betty Friedan published her bestseller,

The Feminine Mystique, in 1963, she picked up the Marxist line; but she was merely expressing the perspectives of the leftist intellectuals she had lived among during her student days at Smith College. The book became a dangerous weapon in the hands of the sixties radicals.[25]

Not surprisingly, as Dr. Morse reports, liberal divorce laws were among the first priorities of the Bolsheviks following the Russian Revolution of 1917. Although Lenin remained married to the same woman for twenty-six years, he realized that the attack on marriage and family could be a powerful way of destabilizing bourgeois society and furthering his revolutionary goals. Ever since that time, the trend in liberal family law, Morse writes, has been to "knock marriage off its perch."[26]

The state, according to this trend, has no particular interest in channeling parenthood into marriage or assigning social and legal parental rights to the biological parents. Currently the family courts have enormous discretion in allocating custody and financial support among known parents. If the family-law radicals have their way, the state will not simply be recording parentage but actually determining parentage. This will vastly increase the discretion and, hence, the power of the family courts. In fact, this happened in December 2009, when a Vermont court ordered a Christian child to be taken away from her biological mother and given to a former lesbian partner.[27]

We have to wonder how the American people allow such things to happen, but those who want to change the laws so that unspecified numbers and genders of people can claim the benefits of legal marriage have been very clever, using the language of "choice" and "rights" to gain public approval. As Dr. Morse suggests, this language has powerful appeal to many people today, but the rhetoric is deceptive and dangerous because it removes the stigma from aberrant behaviors that endanger children and their parents and ensures that the state will be involved at every level.

The government cannot seem to keep its hands off the family, constantly advocating for liberal causes that violate the sanctity of the family and the moral authority of Judeo-Christian beliefs. As an example, in February 2011, the attorney general of the United States informed Congress that the federal government would no longer enforce the Defense of Marriage Act (DOMA), which became law under President Clinton in 1996. This law, affirming marriage as the legal union of one man and one woman, effectively prohibits federal recognition of so-called *gay marriage,* which is clearly why liberals in Washington are anxious to see DOMA repealed.

At the same time the government's way of solving any problem always ends up robbing the federal treasury in order to fix the problems that government policy created in the first place. In 2008, total government spending on welfare programs such as Aid to Families with Dependent Children (AFDC) came to $714 billion. That amounts to more than $16,800 for every so-called poor person in America. As reported by the Heritage Foundation in January 2011, all of the welfare agencies and programs administered by the federal government have gotten substantial raises under the Obama administration. The 2011 federal budget increased funding for food stamps from $39 billion to $75 billion: a whopping 92.3 percent increase.

During the first year of the Obama presidency, the number of Americans on food stamps increased by 5 million—the largest single-year increase since the Carter administration of the mid-70s. The Republican majority in the House of Representatives has taken the first step in trying to get a grip on many of these unproductive schemes, including the effort to repeal the administration's nationalized health-care bill, but if we really care about what kind of nation our children and grandchildren will inherit, we will have to increase our efforts to get the nation and the economy back on track.

PROBLEMS IN AMERICA'S CLASSROOMS

Inscribed on the walls of the Widener Library at Harvard University are the words, "You shall know the truth, and the truth shall make you free." Without referring to the person who spoke those words, many people on that Boston campus would naturally assume they were spoken by a great civil rights leader or some former president. The problem is not that many people don't know that Jesus Christ is the source of the quote but that hardly anyone on the campus today believes that truth can be known.

Little by little over the past forty years, social and cultural revisionists have taken over the schools, the media, and the government institutions in this country. The speech codes enforced in some of those places would be more appropriate in Nazi Germany than "the home of the free and the brave." Despite the blowback from conservative groups, speech codes and campus civility standards are increasingly common. University administrators and faculty members condone every sort of perversion these days, but the one thing they will not tolerate is the idea that somebody might claim to have "truth." So much for Western civilization.

According to a survey of university students conducted by former education secretary William J. Bennett, more than 70 percent of the 634 college students surveyed disagreed that the values of the United States are superior to those of other countries, with 34 percent strongly disagreeing. More than a third disagreed with the statement, "The United States is the best country in the world." Eighty percent rejected the claim that Western civilization, with all our unparalleled achievements, is superior to Arab civilization. And as Bennett pointed out, perhaps the most striking finding was that a third of the respondents said they would actively evade a military draft in the War on Terrorism, while another third would refuse to serve abroad, and just one-third would be willing to fight for their country overseas.[28]

Despite the ongoing War on Terror and the tragic events of September 11, 2001, college students refused to condemn the actions of the 9/11 terrorists. The multiculturalism being taught in American schools and colleges has been taken to such an extreme that college students today embrace virtually any culture but their own. The tendency for academics and their students to "blame America first" for the world's problems—which has now apparently made its way into the highest levels of government—can't help but have a negative impact on the nation's prospects for the future.

A few years ago a review of textbook requirements in New Jersey found that the state's guidelines for history omitted any mention of the Founding Fathers, the Pilgrims, or the *Mayflower*. A history textbook being used in Florida public schools, called *A World in Conflict*, devotes the first five pages on the subject of World War II entirely to information about women in the armed forces, black soldiers on the home front, and Japanese internment camps. Surprising, perhaps, but this is typical of the situation in many school districts today.[29]

The textbooks favored by multiculturalists generally ignore the contributions of Western civilization, particularly with regard to religious tolerance, individual liberty, democratic institutions, and the rule of law. The foreword to a textbook used in one New Mexico school district, called *500 Years of Chicano History in Pictures*, states that the book was "written in response to the Bicentennial celebration of the 1776 American Revolution and its lies." The author writes that her purpose is to "celebrate our resistance to being colonized and absorbed by racist empire builders."[30]

Unfortunately the typical university classroom is not much better. Colleges are supposed to be places that encourage a free and open exchange of ideas, but that is not the case on most campuses these days. Many college courses focus on narrow areas that are highly specialized, narrowly interpreted, politically charged, and unabashedly promoting the holy grail of "race, class, and gender." For centuries men and women from every continent, race, and socioeconomic background have come to this country to escape classification, but on today's campus, the emphasis is on group identity, racial differences, and liberal social policies.

By and large, America's universities have lost sight of what a college education is supposed to be. In this environment it is no surprise that students have little respect for their cultural heritage and little knowledge of the sacrifices our forefathers made for the freedoms they enjoy. When the National Association of Scholars surveyed course offerings at the nation's top fifty universities, they found only a third of those schools required a course in freshman English. Just 12 percent required any type of math, only 34 percent required students to study science, and only 4 percent had a philosophy requirement. None of them required students to study literature. But the most disturbing discovery was that just one of the top fifty colleges in America required students to take a course in American history.[31]

Is it any wonder that so many young people do not seem to know who they are? Students arrive on campus unsure of themselves, ignorant about most things, except what is happening on Facebook or who is texting them on their iPhones. Critical thinking skills, which have been discouraged from their earliest years in public school, are often severely limited. Everything is about fitting in, not making waves, and getting a college diploma for the least possible amount of work. Students today are as bright as ever, but they have been raised in relative comfort in a country where life is pretty easy, and the vast majority have never learned to question what they have been taught.

The tragedy is that students and their parents are paying the price for what is happening on campus in more ways than one. Mom and Dad are paying tuition for an education that subjects their sons and daughters to speech codes, sexual intimidation, anti-American indoctrination, and anti-intellectual mind control. Students from inner-city schools and other low-demand environments often arrive on campus without the academic or social skills to resist this kind of indoctrination. They become easy prey for liberal ideologues and tend to accept the rhetoric of their professors without question.

Curricula in our schools and colleges rarely, if ever, focus on America's greatness or the nation's contributions to democracy, language, culture, science, and industry. Instead, students are exposed to a steady drumbeat of criticism, blaming America for slavery, cultural chauvinism, imperialism, and religious intolerance. There was a time when Americans had so much confidence in the superiority of our way of life, columnist Mona Charen points out, that we taught our values to immigrants and insisted they master the basics of American history, language, and government before becoming eligible for citizenship. Today we are not even teaching those things to our own children.[32]

A poll commissioned by the American Council of Trustees and Alumni (ACTA) examined knowledge of American history among seniors at the top fifty-five liberal arts colleges in the country. The questions covered subjects professors in the sixties would have considered high-school level, but 81 percent of those college seniors earned a grade of D or F on the exam. When they were asked to identify the source of the statement "To each according to his needs, from each according to his ability," 35 percent guessed the phrase was from the U.S. Constitution. In fact, it is a principle of Marxist communism.

More than half of the students thought Germany, Italy, or Japan were United States allies in the Second World War rather than our enemies, the Axis powers. Fewer than a third knew that the Reconstruction era had to do with the Civil War, and 40 percent could not place the Civil War in the correct half century. Only 25 percent could identify James Madison as the "father of the Constitution" while just 22 percent knew that the words "government of the people, by the people, and for the people" come from Abraham Lincoln's Gettysburg Address.[33]

If you wonder why there is such a shocking lack of knowledge in the nation's schools, consider that of the fifty-five highly rated institutions in the survey, not one of them requires a single survey course in American history. The implications of such studies should be obvious. Our schools are turning out a generation of functional illiterates who have little or no regard for the great gifts of liberty we enjoy, so how can we expect them to defend, protect, and preserve this great country when they know so little about it? Washington's solution is to simply define the problems away, but that is an unacceptable alternative.

THE CANARY IN THE MINE

A lot of things have gone right for America since the *Mayflower* landed at Plymouth Rock over four centuries ago. The first Americans barely survived that first winter, but they persevered and proved themselves worthy of their calling. They were men and women of a resolute Christian faith, and God provided for their needs. He sent help when they needed it, just as He prepared the way for their descendants for generations to come.

Many battles of the American Revolution were close calls; the patriots lost most of them for the first six years. The English army was the most formidable fighting force in the world at that time, and no one believed the colonists could defeat them. The final victory at Yorktown was nothing short of a miracle, but the Americans won because there was something even bigger at stake: God had plans for America.

God had prepared this land before the colonists ever arrived—it was to become a "city on a hill," a beacon of personal freedom and religious liberty to the world, a land where freedom could thrive. For most of our history we enjoyed unprecedented freedom and opportunity, but considering the struggles we face today from an out-of-control economy, the ongoing assault on traditional values, and the escalating threats to religious liberty, I have to wonder how much longer God will extend His hand of blessing to this nation.

As a Christian minister, I am deeply troubled by threats from the ACLU and other secular activists to change the tax status of our churches, preventing pastors from speaking freely about critical social issues from the pulpits. Without a renewed commitment to religious liberty and the freedom to speak openly in any venue, what is to prevent us from falling victim to intimidation, blackmail, and totalitarian ideologies of one sort or another? The welfare state cannot save us. Green energy will not save. us. More police, more jails, and more threats won't save us. Only God can save us, and unless the American people rise up and demand that the government get back on track, stop these predatory behaviors, and return to our founding principles, we are in for a long and bumpy ride over the next several years.

We are already borrowing money from our grandchildren to pay for the government's reckless spending. How much longer can that continue? If someone had told the people of Russia back in the mid-1980s that their economy would collapse by the end of the decade, they would have laughed. But people who ought to know are warning us now, "Stop spending! Get back to basics! We are headed in the wrong direction!"

I believe members of the Republican majority in Congress have heard the message. They are doing their best to respond, but they are also facing entrenched resistance from the liberals in the Senate and the executive branch. We have to wonder, however, what will it take for Washington to change course and take the steps necessary to avoid an impending collapse? Are the president, the Congress, and the American people willing to make the hard decisions that will be needed? Or will we have to wait until the economy collapses as it did for the Soviets? If so, there is no guarantee we can recover: there won't be anybody standing by to give us a bailout. But there are plenty of folks in the Middle East and the Far East who would love nothing better than to see America crash and burn. There are people in this nation, for that matter, who would love to take advantage of a struggling economy while we are still weak and defenseless. God help us.

In an article about religious liberty around the world, Cato Institute Senior Fellow Doug Bandow remarked that religious liberty is like the proverbial canary in the mine—advance warning that things may be going wrong. "If a state won't respect this most basic freedom of conscience," he said, "it isn't likely to respect people's lives and dignity in any context."[34] I believe that is a perceptive observation that applies not just to repressive Third World societies but to ours as well.

What we really need in this country is a restoration of Christian values and beliefs. I believe God may be withholding His judgment for the time being, giving us a chance to return to our founding principles.

That does not mean Christians expect everyone to believe as we do or to agree with us on every issue. God cannot bless an immoral nation, but freedom of conscience is an essential right. The Constitution guarantees every citizen the right to believe according to the dictates of his or her own conscience. We wholeheartedly support the principle of "religious liberty" for others, and that is all we ask for ourselves and our families. But we will never sacrifice our God-given right to defend our beliefs and to share the hope within us with the world.

Seven

WHAT YOU CAN DO

When the colonists of New England reached the point of utter exasperation with the predatory laws and policies of King George III and the British Parliament, Samuel Adams and the Sons of Liberty organized what the patriots referred to as "Committees of Correspondence." These groups were created to make sure people in all parts of the colonies were informed about what was going on in the never-ending disputes with the Crown. Adams and the others wrote circular letters and pamphlets, delivered rousing speeches in the streets, town halls, and taverns, and distributed broadsides warning the people about the provocative actions of the English authorities, constantly fanning the flames of resistance.

When Paul Revere made his famous midnight ride to Lexington, he did so as a member of the Boston committee, carrying the news that a large company of British regulars was moving in their direction. In the months leading up to the Revolution, there were reportedly as many as seven thousand members of these committees, led by Adams and such distinguished figures as John Dickinson, Patrick Henry, Richard Henry Lee, and Thomas Jefferson.

When Adams, along with Joseph Warren and James Otis, presented a "Report of the Committee of Correspondence" at Boston's Faneuil Hall on November 20, 1772, they recited a long list of grievances against the British and spelled out the core beliefs of the Founders that would be enshrined just a few years later in the Declaration of Independence and the Constitution. "Among the natural rights of the Colonists," they said, "are these: First, a right to life; Secondly, to liberty; Thirdly, to property; together with the right to support and defend them in the best manner they can. These are evident branches of . . . the first law of nature." They went on:

> All men have a right to remain in a state of nature as long as they please; and in case of intolerable oppression, civil or religious, to leave the society they belong to, and enter into another. When men enter into society, it is by voluntary consent; and they have a right to demand and insist upon the performance of such conditions and previous limitations as form an equitable original compact. Every natural right not expressly given up, or, from the nature of a social compact, necessarily ceded, remains. All positive and civil laws should conform, as far as possible, to the law of natural reason and equity.[1]

These words, so similar to the language of the Declaration, affirm the belief that all people possess a moral sense as a component of conscience and an innate sense of moral accountability. Furthermore these men believed the principles of right and wrong could be found in copious detail in the Bible, which was commonly available and generally accepted by the men and women of the founding generation as the Word of God. As the apostle Paul had written: "For the wrath of God is revealed from heaven against all ungodliness and unrighteousness of men, who suppress the truth in unrighteousness, because what may be known of God is manifest in them, for God has shown it to them" (Romans 1:18–19 NKJV).

Later, when the authors of the Declaration of Independence declared, "all men are created equal, that they are endowed by their Creator with certain unalienable Rights," this is what they were saying. They believed no man-made law should arbitrarily abrogate or interfere with these natural rights, which are imbued by the laws of nature and the laws of God. Thomas Jefferson made this clear several years later in a letter to Richard Henry Lee regarding the process of drafting the Declaration:

> This was the object of the Declaration of Independence. Not to find out new principles, or new arguments, never before thought of, not merely to say things which had never been said before; but to place before mankind the common sense of the subject, in terms so plain and firm as to command their assent, and to justify ourselves in the independent stand we are compelled to take. Neither aiming at originality of principle or sentiment, nor yet copied from any particular and previous writing, it was intended to be an expression of the American mind, and to give to that expression the proper tone and spirit called for by the occasion.[2]

Jefferson's point of view had been expressed by Samuel Adams and the Boston Committee when they wrote in their report, "In the state of nature every man is, under God, judge and sole judge of his own rights and of the injuries done him. By entering into society he agrees to an arbiter or indifferent judge between him and his neighbors; but he no more renounces his original right than by taking a cause out of the ordinary course of law, and leaving the decision to referees or indifferent arbitrators."[3]

None of the Founders denied the authority of statutory law. Crimes ought to be punished, they said, and judges and juries were established for that purpose. But there was a law greater than the laws of men. When they spoke of "the laws of nature and of nature's God," they were referring to commonly held standards of right and wrong. They believed all human beings have an inborn sense of right and wrong. While this knowledge can become corrupted, in a healthy society, they believed, the vast majority of people would naturally agree on these basic principles.

By 1768, when four thousand British troops arrived in Boston to enforce the Townshend Acts, the patriots realized there could be no turning back. They realized the English were intentionally provoking the colonists, and the Townshend Acts were just one more attempt to undermine the autonomy of the colonies by compelling American merchants to comply with British trade regulations. Very much like the Declaratory Act of 1766, which was a poke in the eye demanding unquestioned obedience to the Crown, these new articles dared the Americans to rebel by declaring the British Parliament had the right to rule the colonies and to tax them as they wished. To make the point, they immediately placed new duties on paper, lead, paint, and imported tea.

Samuel Adams and the Committees of Correspondence wasted no time publicizing these new threats. After the Boston Massacre of March 5, 1770, in which a British patrol fired on a crowd of angry colonists and killed five unarmed men, colonial outrage became even more intense. The British governor withdrew his troops to Castle Island to avoid further bloodshed, but the colonists were not appeased. Instead, they saw this as a sign of weakness. When the public funeral for the five victims of the massacre was held a few days later, more than ten thousand Americans joined the procession as a demonstration of unity. Yet when the Revolution began five years later, it was not the result of any one act but, as the Declaration of Independence expressed it, the result of "a long train of abuses and usurpations, pursuing invariably the same Object."

A NEW DECLARATION OF GRIEVANCES

The Committees of Correspondence's most important contribution in the colonial era was in providing a consistent, reliable, and readily accessible flow of information that would help mold the American people into a unified and cohesive force. Today, when the nation is confronted by a new and even more strident "train of abuses," that function is being carried out by a new generation of patriots who are making a wide range of assets available to the public over the Internet and through talk radio, cable TV, cellular telephones, and many other kinds of twenty-first-century media. And, very much like that original band of rebels, these Americans are preparing for some major changes of their own.

In a televised campaign address to his supporters on October 31, 2008, given on the campus of the University of Missouri, Barack Obama made a statement that drew little attention at the time. He said, "We are five days away from fundamentally transforming the United States of America." To many viewers it sounded like a typically arrogant boast, not uncommon in politics. But within weeks of the January 2009 inauguration and the installation of a new cast of characters in the White House, the voters began to see what Candidate Obama actually meant by those words. Since that time there has been a stunning change in the tone and emphasis of national policy, but there has also been an equally stunning change of attitude toward the direction this administration has been taking the nation.

The Tea Party movement that emerged in early 2009, seemingly out of nowhere, would soon become the most visible response of middle America to this sudden shift in policy. The movement stands for smaller government, fiscal responsibility, individual freedom, and a conservative view of the nation's founding documents. Millions of Americans, motivated by their commitment to faith, family, and freedom, are joining forces across party lines to express their concerns.

One of the first appearances of the movement came on January 19, 2009, the day before the presidential inauguration, when a group of New York stock traders, concerned that the new administration would do serious harm to American business, began sending e-mails to their colleagues suggesting that everyone send tea bags to their representatives and senators. It was a modest beginning.

In the following weeks Tea Party protests began to appear all across the country, with increasing sophistication and appeal. On February 1, 2009, the tea bag suggestion was picked up by individuals in several cities; then on February 27, an organized event was staged to protest the American Recovery and Reinvestment Act of 2009 that had been signed by the president just ten days earlier. By Tax Day, April 15, 2009, the protests were a nationwide phenomenon with more than eight hundred Tea Party events all across the country and as many as a million participants.

By July 4, 2009, the number of Independence Day events was too great to count, but Tea Party events of all sizes took place in thousands of communities from coast to coast, focused on love of country and the uniquely American Spirit of patriotism, expressing displeasure with the leftward lurch of government under the Obama administration. Millions of Americans were profoundly concerned about the direction of economic policies that, even at that stage, threatened to bankrupt the nation. By that point dozens of Tea Party organizations were being founded with sophisticated websites and a highly visible presence. These new groups began recruiting members and creating a network of like-minded citizens, most of whom had never before been politically active but who were anxious to take a stand against the bizarre vision of America they saw reflected in the White House and both houses of Congress.

Popular conservative broadcasters, such as Rush Limbaugh, Sean Hannity, and Glenn Beck, are more popular today than ever. Beck, a radio and TV celebrity, asked his audience during a December 3, 2009, broadcast,

If I would have told you last year at this time that the government would own General Motors, Chrysler, and many of the banks and financial institutions, and AIG, that they would fire the CEOs, that they would threaten the banks, that they would shut them down unless they would take that [bailout] money . . . would you have believed it?[4]

The answer was a resounding *no!* No one could have anticipated such changes, but this was the attitude of "shock and awe" that many people were feeling. And these were just some of the issues that would awaken the nation and sound the alarm for an all-out popular rebellion.

In a powerful book challenging the Obama administration's efforts to "fundamentally transform" the United States into a socialist nation on the European model, economist and syndicated columnist Thomas Sowell accused the administration of attempting to dismantle the constitutional framework of the republic by ignoring legal limitations on executive power and inventing laws to suit its own purposes, without the "consent of the governed." A century ago, he said, politicians of the Progressive Era were the first to try to rewrite the Constitution according to their own left-wing ideology.

But what we are seeing today is an even more sinister attempt to transform the nation in ways that can only lead to disaster. Sowell writes, "The Constitution was not only a challenge to the despotic governments of the time, but has been a continuing challenge—to this day—to all those who think the ordinary people should be ruled by their betters. . . ."[5] From day one the administration's idea of "betters" could be seen in the unprecedented appointment of a large number of public-policy czars with cabinet-level authority. Many of these individuals were financial experts from Wall Street firms such as Goldman Sachs and social activists with long-standing leftist connections. Within weeks the administration was carrying out a systematic raid of the public treasury. And this was accomplished with the aid of a compliant Congress intent on passing a string of massive spending bills so fast the public could not possibly keep up— laws, not coincidentally, that members of the House and Senate had not even bothered to read.

Little by little the administration was able to carry off a wholesale restructuring of government, like nothing the country had seen in more than two hundred years. It was the New Deal, the Great Society, and the Great Leap Forward rolled into one. The long-established principles of "checks and balances" and "separation of powers" were ignored, but all this has led to a loud and predictable backlash from the American people, and the 2010 midterm elections were just the first step toward a return to normalcy. Suddenly the Tea Party movement was better organized, better connected, and better prepared for the confrontation with Washington—prepared for what some deemed a second American revolution.

According to a Gallup poll taken in the second week of January 2011, just 19 percent of Americans were satisfied with the way things are going in America, and the level of satisfaction among conservatives (at 12 percent) was less than half that of liberals (at 27 percent). Topping the list of voter concerns were the troubled economy, high unemployment, and the intrusiveness of Washington policy makers in practically every area of their lives. Whether the restrictions are on drilling for oil or on McDonald's Happy Meals, most Americans believe Washington liberals are sticking their noses into places where they have no business, and growing levels of public concern are stoking a grassroots rebellion like nothing this country has ever seen.[6]

It may surprise some folks in Washington to know that, as reported by a December 2010 Rasmussen poll, more than half of Democrats (52 percent) and more than three out of four Independents (76 percent) now say the country is on the wrong track—and 86 percent of Republicans strongly agree.[7] Researchers found that 87 percent of all voters rate the ongoing problems with the economy as "very important"—the highest level since August 2008. At the same time, 67 percent rate the concerns with government ethics and corruption as "very important." And perhaps most surprising, Rasmussen researchers found that the number of adults identifying themselves as Republicans has jumped to 37 percent while the number of Democrats has dropped to 33.7 percent—the lowest level since November 2002.[8]

A February 2011 TIPP poll by *Investors Business Daily* found that the majority believe the federal government should be smaller and provide fewer services. Overall, nearly six in ten of those surveyed said the government has too much power. Not surprisingly, 83 percent of Republicans and 72 percent of self-identified conservatives believe government is too powerful, but 64 percent of Independents and 62 percent of self-identified moderates feel the same way. In their assessment of these figures, the researchers concluded, "This political alignment of Republicans with independents and the ideological alignment of conservatives and moderates make small-government supporters a force to be reckoned with."[9]

IF WE FORGET WHAT WE DID

In his farewell address, delivered on January 11, 1989, President Ronald Reagan offered a powerful statement of the importance of this nation's founding principles. He expressed his deep love for America, but he wondered if the American people really understand the dangerous challenges we face. He said,

> An informed patriotism is what we want. And are we doing a good enough job teaching our children what America is and what she represents in the long history of the world? Those of us who are over thirty-five or so years of age grew up in a different America. We were taught, very directly, what it means to be an American. And we absorbed, almost in the air, a love of country and an appreciation of its institutions. If you didn't get these things from your family, you got them from the neighborhood, from the father down the street who fought in Korea or the family who lost someone at Anzio. Or you could get a sense of patriotism from school. And if all else failed, you could get a sense of patriotism from the popular culture. The

movies celebrated democratic values and implicitly reinforced the idea that America was special. TV was like that, too, through the mid-sixties.[10]

Anyone who grew up in this country during the first half of the twentieth century was schooled in the values and beliefs of the Founders. American history was an essential part of that. We were justly proud of the patriots' struggle for independence, and we understood that our free, republican, capitalist system was an engine of prosperity, not just for Americans but for the world. We believed the love of liberty engendered here could bless untold millions if we continued to abide by those principles.

But as the levels of affluence and material comfort expanded during the second half of the century, many people began to drift away from those core values. Intellectuals, academics, and media elites who had been influenced by leftist ideologies began to question the morality of their own country so that today, as President Reagan noted in his speech, "some things have changed." He further stated,

> Younger parents aren't sure that an unambivalent appreciation of America is the right thing to teach modern children. And as for those who create the popular culture, well-grounded patriotism is no longer the style. Our spirit is back, but we haven't reinstitutionalized it. We've got to do a better job of getting across that America is freedom—freedom of speech, freedom of religion, freedom of enterprise. And freedom is special and great. It's fragile; it needs protection. So, we've got to teach history based not on what's in fashion but what's important: Why the Pilgrims came here, who Jimmy Doolittle was, and what those thirty seconds over Tokyo meant.

And then he added, more forcefully, "If we forget what we did, we won't know who we are."[11] That is the challenge we are facing at this moment in our history—to remember not only what we did but also the enormous price our forefathers paid for the liberties we enjoy.

If we expect to maintain the strength and vitality of this country for another two hundred years, we will need to insist that our children and grandchildren are taught the great and noble history of this nation, remembering the sacrifices of all the valiant warriors who paid the ultimate price for liberty. But they also need to know there are men and women, basking in the bounty of this great nation, who want nothing more than to undermine our freedoms and through persistent indoctrination bind the American people in ideological chains. The acid test of our willpower and resilience will be whether or not we still have the courage and strength to resist such people, to take a stand for righteousness, and to do whatever it takes to restore the foundations of the republic before it is too late.

The Reverend Jonathan Mayhew, who is often cited as the first member of the famed Black Robe Regiment of New England, was the pastor of the Old West Church in Boston and among the first to light the flame of rebellion in the hearts of the patriots. Refusing to be silenced by moderates and loyalists in his congregation, Mayhew dared to speak the truth regardless of the consequences. When he delivered his most famous sermon, "A Discourse Concerning Unlimited Submission and Non-Resistance to the Higher Power," there were many who felt the young minister had gone too far.

Those who expected men like Mayhew to bow to British demands cited the apostle Paul's admonition in Romans 13:1, "Let every soul be subject to the governing authorities. For there is no authority except from God, and the authorities that exist are appointed by God" (NKJV). But Mayhew was having none of it and declared, "Common tyrants and public oppressors are not entitled to obedience from their subjects, by virtue of anything here laid down by the inspired apostle." Furthermore, he said, "when [the king] turns tyrant, and makes his subjects his prey to devour and to destroy, instead of his charge to defend and cherish, we are bound to throw off our allegiance to him, and to resist."[12]

When his sermon was published a few days later, Mayhew was obliged to pen a short preface in which he warned, "Civil tyranny is usually small in its beginning, like 'the drop of a bucket,' till at length, like a mighty torrent, or the raging waves of the sea, it bears down on all before it, and deluges whole countries and empires." Then, in the text of the sermon he delivered on January 30, 1750, he said,

> We may very safely assert these two things in general, without undermining government: One is, that no civil rulers are to be obeyed when they enjoin things that are inconsistent with the commands of God: all such disobedience is lawful and glorious. . . . Another thing that may be asserted with equal truth and safety, is, that no government is to be submitted to, at the expense of that which is the sole end of all government—the common good and safety of society. . . . But it is equally evident, upon the other hand, that those in authority may abuse their trust and power to such a degree that neither the law of reason, nor of religion, requires that any obedience or submission should be paid to them: but, on the contrary, that they should be totally discarded; and the authority which they were before vested with, transferred to others, who may exercise it more to those good purposes for which it is given.

Mayhew was not a firebrand at that point—he would become one a short time later and has been credited as being the first to utter the words, "No taxation without representation!" But at the conclusion of the sermon, he admonished the congregation to be cautious: "Let us prize our freedom," he said, "but not use our liberty for a cloak of maliciousness."[13] Mayhew died at age forty-six, a full decade before the first shots were fired at Lexington and Concord, but he was memorialized years later as the first to sound the alarm, to awaken the colonists to their rights as free men and members of the family of God, and to proclaim from the pulpit that the defense of liberty in the face of tyranny is a just and righteous cause.

THE LOYAL RESISTANCE

When a new generation of patriots stands up today to resist the incursions of government, they are not doing so in a malicious spirit. There have been many attempts to link the tea parties to thugs and zealots of one kind or another, but the charges won't stick. Amid all the confusion following the shooting of Congresswoman Gabrielle Giffords in January 2011, as one example, reporters and national news anchors were too quick to suggest that this detestable act was the work of a rogue "teabagger." Within hours, however, it became apparent that the shooter was a known psychopath who was not connected to the tea parties or conservatives of any stripe but was, in fact, attracted to satanism and other crazy ideas.

Even a cursory look at the websites and literature of some of the better-known Tea Party organizations makes it clear their members are normal, everyday Americans who care deeply about the well-being and safety of their country. Confronted by trillion-dollar deficits, outrageous bailouts to Wall Street billionaires, and a laundry list of payoffs to political cronies, the Tea Party faithful are simply doing what the patriots of 1776 felt obliged to do: they are standing up and saying no to the perversion of our constitutional form of government by the unjust governing authorities.

Groups such as Tea Party Patriots, FreedomWorks, Let Freedom Ring, the Tea Party Express, and several others that are growing in size and influence were founded by average Americans who have become profoundly concerned with the leftward lurch of the federal government. All these groups have become mobilized to express the concerns of millions of men and women about the direction the progressive establishment has been taking the country. Representing a wide range of views, these folks are everyday patriots who want to make sure their voices are heard loud and clear in the nation's capital and in state legislatures around the country.

The groups include individuals who are vocal advocates of lower taxes, less government interference in our everyday lives, and a restoration of individual liberty. To accomplish all these goals, most of the Tea Party organizations recruit, train, and mobilize thousands of volunteer activists in all parts of the country, providing them with facts, information, and other important resources that will help them speak up and stand up in defense of our core values.

In general, all of them agree that congressional spending is out of control. Dating back to the first bailouts of subprime mortgage lenders by the Bush administration in 2008, the federal government has been on a spending binge that threatens not just the economy but the survival of the nation. At the same time irrational restraints on energy production and the growth of American business have dealt a crippling blow to the economy and contributed to the ongoing scourge of joblessness while new government regulations and exorbitant taxes have slowed the growth of innovation and job creation in all sectors. This is why freedom-loving groups of all kinds are speaking up, demanding economic reforms.

Another major concern of the movement is border security. With twenty million to forty million illegal aliens already in this country, it is obvious the Obama Justice Department is not interested in protecting American sovereignty. They are allowing millions of poorly educated and unskilled workers to cross into this country with little or no resistance, primarily because they believe these individuals—who have only limited knowledge of the country's history and values and even less knowledge of democratic institutions—are likely to become supporters of the president's party in the voting booth.

Job-killing measures are also a major concern of Tea Party activists. The union policy of "card check" would strip employees of the right to express by secret ballot their wishes concerning unionization. Without secret ballots, workers could run the risk of jeopardizing their personal safety and job security if they disagree with the union bosses. Conservatives are also concerned about the unrealistic demands of the Environmental Protection Agency and other government agencies that are strangling new energy development while gobbling up private property and public lands all over the country.

Finally, they support repeal of the disastrous health-care legislation passed by the 111th Congress, along with tort reform limiting the ruinous rewards currently being paid to predatory trial lawyers and their clients. Government mandates passed by presidential fiat, bypassing Congress through the use of executive orders, have been disastrous for the economy and every American. To restore balance, Congress must, at the very least, begin a disciplined study of the problems within large government programs, such as Social Security, Medicare, and Medicaid, in order to preserve what is best about each of these programs and eliminate exploitation, overregulation, and waste.

THE GREAT REPUDIATION

For many moderates, Independents, and others who may be getting their first glimpse of the Tea Party movement, there is a certain amount of curiosity and perhaps a little nervousness about what really is going on. They want to know what's behind this new attitude of dissent: What is causing so many average Americans to rebel against the government? Where do these people get their ideas, and what is motivating such a large, diverse, and apparently leaderless segment of the electorate to do what they are doing?

The spirit of rebellion we are seeing in cities and towns all across America comes from the same spirit that motivated the colonists to demand independence from the British Empire in 1776. It is the knowledge that essential principles and beliefs are being compromised by an administration with a very different idea of what this nation is all about. As author and scholar Michael Novak has recently written, this uprising is not simply a political rebellion or a rejection of Washington's out-of-control spending habits: it is "a revolution against moral decline."[14]

The spirit that came out of the Great Awakening of the early eighteenth century was a rededication by hundreds of thousands of men, women, and children to the foundational principles of the Christian faith. It was also a response to the knowledge that a righteous God will not withhold His judgment forever. This was the first full expression of the American spirit of independence, and it brought with it a willingness to stand up for what we believe to be true and right. That same spirit is alive in the Tea Party movement today.

The 2010 midterm election was a landslide victory for conservative voters. As James Ceaser has pointed out at RealClearPolitics.com, the Democratic Party suffered "the greatest defeat for a newly elected president in a midterm since the Republican Party under Warren Gamaliel Harding in 1922."[15] The Democrats lost sixty-three seats in the House of Representatives, making them the minority party. They also lost six seats in the Senate but still hold a slight numerical advantage with fifty-one Democrats, forty-seven Republicans, and two Independents in that body.

The Democrat defeat was historic not only because of the number of House seats lost but also because of the number of seats lost in any midterm election—it was the most since 1938. As James Ceaser says, it is the performance of the president's party following his first election that offers the most critical point of comparison. He writes that the 2010 midterm elections turned out to be the closest this nation has ever come to a national referendum on the "ideology" of a presidential administration.

Mr. Obama disguised his true ideology with a vague promise of hope and change during the campaign; then he immediately became the most ideological and divisive president in history after the election. Ceaser writes,

> Some of his supporters like to argue in one breath that he is a pragmatist and centrist only to insist in the next that he has inaugurated the most historic transformation of American politics since the New Deal. The two claims are incompatible. Going back to the major

political contests of 2009, beginning with the Governors' races in Virginia and New Jersey and to the Senate race in Massachusetts, the electorate has been asked the same question about Obama's agenda and has given the same response. The election of 2010 is the third or fourth reiteration of this judgment, only this time delivered more decisively. There is one label and one label only that can describe the result: *The Great Repudiation.*[16]

In the same spirit Michael Novak has written, "No president in American history has ever been so thoroughly discredited after two years as Barack Obama."[17] The loss of fifty-four House seats in 1994 was a shocker for the Clinton White House, but the debacle of 2010 was even greater because it could only be interpreted as a rejection not only of administration policies but also of its overall ideology.

In his first two years as president, Novak says, Mr. Obama convinced millions of Americans he wanted to make this country more like France or Germany or some other European welfare state, but the American people hated the idea and rebelled with undisguised intensity. The shakeup taking place in Congress and in state houses nationwide contributes to a trend that the recently elected Republican governor of South Carolina, Nikki Haley, calls a new generation of rock-star governors who don't care if they aren't reelected as long as they get results.

The most revolutionary aspect of such changes is how a popular movement with no national leader has risen up spontaneously from the grassroots and is now changing the political climate in this country and far beyond. This new generation of Tea Party patriots is not looking to opinion polls or talking points for their ideas: instead, they are looking to the Founding Fathers and to the principles of personal responsibility and limited government that have been a part of our American heritage for generations. While the Obama administration may occasionally pay lip service to these ideas, it is increasingly apparent that the administration's eyes are fixed on the European model of the welfare state. Fortunately the people are saying no to that insidious plan, and the Tea Party movement is in the process of installing speed bumps all along the way.

Drawing the attention of millions of Americans back to the authentic source of our laws and policy—the United States Constitution and the revolutionary ideas it contains regarding individual freedom and republican democracy—has been the greatest achievement of the movement. As I suggested in chapter 1, sometimes adversity can be our best ally, and the awakening we are seeing today is due in large part to the nightmare we have endured.

We are not out of the woods by a long shot. The challenges for our elected representatives have never been greater. The popular culture is still spreading its tentacles, submerging millions of America's young people in decadent, pointless, and empty lives. We have to wonder in this environment if God can continue to bless a nation so deeply immersed in sensationalism, sensuality, and sin. While many people are working hard to restore our political fortunes, the media-driven culture is, as Michael Novak writes, "becoming more and more decadent, less and less under the sway of personal moral responsibility, more relativist, less under the self-control of reason."[18]

The "superculture," he says, hangs over the nation like a miasma of moral smog. Rather than holding up an image of hope and restoration, our liberal elites have become cheerleaders for moral decline. In his classic six-volume study of ancient civilizations, *A Study of History*, the English historian Arnold Toynbee wrote that one of the signs of collapse in the great empires of the past was what he described as a "schism in the soul," which was an unresolved struggle between right and wrong that ultimately led to moral chaos. When the elites of a culture, the "creative minority," become utterly dissipated and immoral, they become an "oppressive minority," and such a nation invariably enters a "time of troubles" that inevitably leads to collapse.

The hope for America in this second decade of the twenty-first century is that we will not allow our nation to be utterly corrupted, either politically or morally, by today's cultural elites. The 2010 midterm elections were an indication that a political and moral revolution has begun; however, it is my prayer that a cultural revolution—with a new attitude of personal responsibility, compassion, and reverence for the things that truly matter—will not be far behind. We are not without resources; God forbid that Toynbee's prophecy of national decline should ever happen here.

THE PATHWAY TO VICTORY

At the close of the Constitutional Convention on September 18, 1787, a large crowd of anxious citizens had gathered outside of Philadelphia's Independence Hall, waiting to learn whether or not the delegates had successfully completed the task of drafting the new Constitution. One by one the delegates left the building, making their way home through the mass of onlookers. As he was leaving, the delegate from Maryland, James McHenry, happened to overhear a lady, later identified as Mrs. Powel of Philadelphia, calling out to Benjamin Franklin. "Well, Doctor," she said, "what have we got—a Republic or a Monarchy?" Glancing her way, Franklin replied, "A Republic, if you can keep it."[19]

Franklin knew what millions of Americans have discovered since that day. It takes a lot to keep our republic. There are always those within and without who are trying to take our liberties from us. America's Founding Fathers and early patriots gave their lives as well as their possessions to preserve and protect our freedoms. Our fathers and mothers and sisters and brothers have given the ultimate sacrifice on battlefields and beaches around the world in the effort to preserve our liberties—and those sacrifices continue even today. But what are we to do? Those of us who are here in the homeland, those of us who are the ordinary folks, those the politicians call the American People—what can we do to bring about a new revolution to preserve our nation, the greatest nation in the free world, and recapture the liberties and ideals that have been stolen from us over the past few years?

The hope and change we were promised during the 2008 campaign season has turned out to be something quite different from what most Americans had in mind. But I believe the plan for real constructive change is not all that complex or confusing: every American can become a part of the national movement for God and Country. The first step is to stop complaining and whining about the problems in Washington, DC. That won't get the job done. The second step is to take action; there are things we can do to counteract the progressive assault on America and take our country back—as Ben Franklin put it, to preserve the republic. So let me suggest a clear and honorable pathway that any generation of Americans may follow in order to protect what is right and to change what is wrong within this great nation.

FIRST: WE MUST PREPARE PERSONALLY

Preparation is a vital part of every successful endeavor. When we read about the struggles of the fifty-six signers of the Declaration of Independence in their efforts to reach an agreement on the contents of that document, we can be certain their decisions were not made without a great deal of forethought and personal preparation. The final words of the Declaration make it clear they had settled in their hearts that they were all taking a great personal risk. They knew the formation of this new nation would come at a high personal cost to each of them.

Written just above their signatures are these words: "And for the support of this Declaration with a firm reliance on the Protection of Divine Providence, we mutually pledge to each other our Lives, our Fortunes, and our sacred Honor." Once they signed their names to the document, there would be no turning back. Once their names were penned on that page, they had committed an act of treason against the Crown. After writing his name in large, bold strokes, John Hancock quipped to the assembled delegates, "Gentlemen, we must all hang together." To which Benjamin Franklin replied without hesitation, "We must, indeed, all hang together, or most assuredly we shall all hang separately."

We ought to take a lesson from the Founding Fathers: If we are willing to pay whatever price is demanded from us, to go any distance set for us, to endure any battle fought against us in order to reclaim America in our generation, then and only then, through such personal dedication we will be prepared to turn the tide of anti-Americanism that is overtaking our land. That determination is powerful and personal, but it is also essential if there is to be any chance of victory.

SECOND: WE MUST PARTNER WITH OTHERS

The strength of the Founders and those forces that achieved victory in America's first Revolution came from their sense of unity and the common goal of advancing the cause of liberty. It would be foolish to think all the colonists were in favor of the Revolution. It is doubtful, in fact, that the forces that did join together even liked each other very much. There was a great deal of distrust and friction between the colonies over a myriad of issues, but the patriots of 1776 believed the common good far outweighed the likes or dislikes of the individual. They found their desire for "a land of the free" to be a more noble passion than their petty differences.

Look across America today, and you will see millions of good and ordinary people who love this country. They go out every morning and put in an honest day's work. They honor our flag, and they get tears in their eyes at the singing of our national anthem. They don't understand why anyone would want to destroy what we have been given. These men and women are ready to go out and do something to make a difference.

Meanwhile the social elitists look down from their ivory towers with disdain for the ordinary man and woman, never realizing that if these "ordinary Americans" ever partner to recapture their land, there is no force on earth that can stop them. And the need for a dedicated, committed, unified, and unwavering band of freedom-loving patriots has never been greater than it is today. Today we are seeing signs of that unity all around us. Everywhere we look, Americans are rising up together. We see it on the Internet as literally dozens of organizations have been formed, dedicated to the idea of restoring American values. Tea Party organizations at the national, regional, and local levels are all a part of that movement, and if and when all these various groups come together for the sake of liberty, they will be a mighty force indeed.

This is not just some idea for the future; it can start now. Let's not wait to follow the groups. Individually, let's find and befriend someone else who loves America, someone else who sees it as his or her calling to stand for those foundational liberties that are so valuable and so rare.

THIRD: WE MUST LEARN THE PROCESS

Within the God-given wisdom of our founding documents, we have been granted clear and certain processes for bringing about change in those areas we perceive to be wrong for our land. From the local municipalities to the halls of Congress and the White House, embedded in the laws and governmental processes of America are pathways for nonviolent moral, social, and political reform. But those processes must be learned and understood before they can be properly applied. Being passionate about an issue is fine, but real and lasting change requires a disciplined approach, using the systems that are already in place for us, by which we can make those changes take place.

If you don't like the votes your elected representatives are casting in Congress or the state legislature, then you have the power to remove them and elect others who will do the job better. If you don't like the idea of forced health care or of redistribution of wealth through excessive taxation, stop complaining and do something about it. The process for making changes—from the schoolhouse to the courthouse to the White House—is available to every citizen. So learn the process, and dig into your rights as a citizen. Learn the American process of government, and use it for the good.

FOURTH: WE MUST PARTICIPATE IN THE ARENA

Participating within the process for change is the ultimate key to success. It is futile to gripe and complain concerning what we consider wrong or unjust if we are not willing to participate in making changes for the better. Most Americans would be startled if they knew how many of their friends and fellow citizens never bother to vote. According to statistics compiled through Restore America's demographic study of voting, there are now fifty-two million evangelical Christians of voting age in this country. In the 2010 general election, however, only twenty-two million of them voted. Another twenty million who were registered chose not to vote. And at least ten million who were eligible to vote didn't even bother to register. The other side loves to see statistics like that, but we must not give them the pleasure of laughing at us next time.

Even if these numbers are disappointing, they nevertheless show the great potential for positive change if we can rally not just these uncommitted evangelicals but also the millions of patriotic Americans who love their country and who have every reason to participate in the process of government.

FIFTH: WE MUST PROCLAIM THE TRUTH

The Bible tells us, "you shall know the truth, and the truth shall make you free" (John 8:32 NKJV). But as Christians we also believe that when the truth is known, those who have found it have a duty to make it known to others. I often fear that many of the problems we have experienced in this country over the past half century are due in large part to the fact that the men and women in the pews and pulpits of America have not taken the challenge seriously. No other nation has as many churches and places of worship as we do in this country, yet the mighty roar of honor, virtue, and truth that arose from the churches in times past now seems to have been replaced with a pitiful whimper. Where there was once courage and conviction, too often today we find apathy and self-doubt. But we have no one to blame but ourselves.

It was the preaching of men such as Jonathan Edwards, Gilbert Tennent, and George Whitefield during the Great Awakening that forged upon the anvil of truth the foundational values so vividly inscribed in our founding documents. Throughout the revolutionary era, America's pastors preached with a fiery passion against the tyranny of the British monarchy—they cried out for revolutionary change.

They spoke the truth boldly, without fear of men or governments because they believed this nation had been given a special mission by God Himself. They were fully committed to the cause of liberty.

Thanks to the propaganda machine of groups such as the ACLU, People for the American Way, and the Freedom from Religion Foundation, along with secular liberals in the mainstream media, our pastors and teachers have been beaten into submission, silenced. They say nothing that would offend the dogma of political correctness. Hollow threats concerning the loss of their tax-exempt status, or violation of the policy of "separation of church and state," have turned the power of the pulpit into something far less than it is intended to be. What has happened to the backbones of our pastors? My prayer is that a new generation of pastors and teachers will arise who will preach with power and boldness, with the knowledge that they have no one to fear other than our eternal God Himself.

But none of this should suggest that it is only pastors, teachers, and other leaders who are called to speak up boldly about what is going on in America today. We all have our pulpits. They may be in our homes, our workplaces, our schools, or our neighborhoods; there are many places where we can speak up and express our views on the issues of the day, where we can take a stand for what is right and do whatever we can to help bring about a restoration of virtue and honor in this nation.

FINALLY: WE MUST PERSEVERE UNTIL WE PREVAIL

When fighting for the right, we must never cease until we prevail. The battle is not always won by the strongest, the smartest, or the most gifted, but ultimately the victory comes to those who persist and persevere to the end. When General and soon-to-be president George Washington led his troops into battle during the first six years of the American Revolution, he lost most of those battles. He and his troops endured tremendous challenges and suffered great hardships in taking on the most powerful army in the world, but through perseverance and faith in the nobility of their cause, they won the battles that really mattered, and ultimately they won the War of Independence. It is because of that fierce determination and perseverance that we are a free and independent nation today.

But here is the best news: All the resources we need to regain our freedom are available now. There really is no reason we cannot reclaim America now. The forces threatening our liberties today are small, compared to the obstacles Americans of previous generations have had to overcome. So instead of moaning and complaining, we need to get up, get out, gather with others who share our passion, and do it.

If we have the courage of our convictions, we are able to take this country back from those who are doing their best to destroy it from within. And when we make the decision to become engaged, we are not just doing it for ourselves but for all those who come after us. We are also doing it to honor the legacy that was given to us by all those brave men and women who came before us. What a tragedy it would be if, having been given so much, we should fail to pass on to future generations the blessings of liberty that have been entrusted into our hands.

THINGS YOU CAN DO TODAY

The renewal of a culture is not a job for any one individual, group, or political party; it is a challenge for every citizen. The motivation for this book is the hope that every American will think carefully about all the achievements the men and women of this nation have made over the past four hundred years, and will make a personal commitment to join the struggle for renewal—that would be the greatest Great Awakening I can imagine.

That process begins on a personal and private level, between you and God. Following that spirit of rededication, there needs to be evidence of renewed hope and resolve, and I would suggest that one of the ways all the various conservative groups can make a big difference is by making cultural renewal a part of the overall game plan.

Here are some things all of us can do today to get involved in this growing movement:

1. Pray for America, and pray that with God's help We the People will prevail in the struggle for the heart and soul of the nation.
2. Register to vote; then make sure you know the positions of the candidates on all the critical issues.
3. Let your national, state, and local representatives know how you feel by attending town hall meetings, writing letters, calling their offices, and writing letters to the editors of your local newspapers, magazines, and community websites.
4. Join a group in your area that is speaking up about these concerns, and if there isn't one already, start one yourself.
5. Help support organizations that are standing up for fiscal, social, and moral responsibility.
6. Subscribe to newsletters, blogs, Twitter feeds, and other media updates to help you stay informed.
7. Use the Internet to find out what the candidates and incumbents are saying on both sides of the issues.
8. Attend meetings of your local political organizations.
9. Attend meetings and scheduled events of the organizations you support, and offer to help with promotion, arrangements, and logistics or in any way you can.
10. Spread the word among your friends and neighbors, and help others in your community become active in the movement to restore the founding principles of this great nation.

All these things are in the best traditions of the revolutionary spirit. John Adams once wrote, "What do we mean by the American Revolution? Do we mean the American war? The revolution was effected before the war commenced. The revolution was in the minds and hearts of the people; a change in their religious sentiments, of their duties and obligations. . . . This radical change in the principles, opinions, sentiments, and affections of the people was the real American Revolution."[20] This is what I have been saying: the real revolution is always in the minds and hearts of the people.

Until recently I often sensed an attitude of hopelessness in this country, of which President Obama and company were the progenitors. I saw it in many settings, but I believe things are changing now. There are still many challenges and plenty of work yet to do, but I am seeing a new spirit of hope emerging. It is not just a slogan of Hope and Change but real hope, coming from a renewed sense of purpose.

All of this brings us back once again to the American Spirit, to our identity as citizens of this great nation, and to what we stand for as a people. It is about the American experience. Why are you here? What is your purpose as a man or woman, a member of a family, a citizen, an employee or employer, a taxpayer, a child of God? The way we answer such questions says a lot about what we believe and where we stand.

What I hope to see in coming weeks and months is a new level of optimism about America's future. We have every reason to be optimistic if we continue to walk in the footsteps of the Founders—politically, morally, and spiritually. Not every man or woman putting in eight or ten hours a day on the job can run out and join the march on city hall, and I don't expect every mother with three children at home to go out and join the Tea Party and carry banners on the Capitol steps. But there are things everyone who cares about the future of the republic can do.

Moms and dads can teach their children what it means to be an American; they can take time for family devotions, pausing to consider the important role faith played in the lives of the Founders. They can send e-mails, make phone calls, donate to good causes, and contribute to a blog or a social network. They can make a difference by speaking out about what they believe in. If all of us who care for this country would do just one or two of these things, we would be making as valuable a contribution as anyone. It doesn't have to be big, but it ought to be something. Each of us can do our part as a caring citizen and be a voice for righteousness in our national culture.

This is the Coming Revolution: this is a transformation we can all take part in, living up to the dream the Founders gave us all those years ago. The American Dream is not about government handouts or class warfare with one class of citizens fighting against another. It is about a way of life in a free society, where each man and woman has the right of self-determination. The fact that such a life is so incredibly rare is what has made this country the envy of the world.

Each facet of liberty that we now enjoy has been given to us by the sacrifices—and often the very blood—of those who have gone before us. Let every American go out into the public arena and speak proudly about those great freedoms that we cherish as Americans and refuse to surrender to the onslaught of the radical left-wing minority. But most importantly, we must flood America's voting booths in the coming elections and put into office those men and women who are willing to go to Washington for the distinct purpose of reinstating those rights and freedoms that are currently being stolen and reinstituting the values that once made our nation great.

If and when this happens, the feeble wall of ultra-liberalism and godless socialism will crumble beneath the force of the will of the people. Once again the economic might of our free enterprise system will strengthen us. The principles of common sense and decency will have their rightful place in our nation's capitol, and America will return to its place in the world as the "shining light upon a hill."

Best of all, a much-needed revival of patriotism and pride will fill our nation's heart. For we will have fought the noblest of battles and won our own revolution to return America to "the land of the free and the home of the brave" once again. We can. We must. And I truly believe we will!

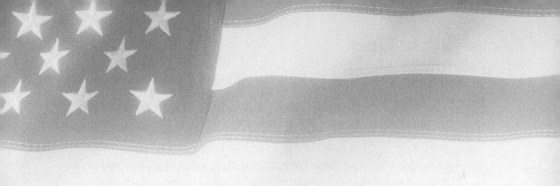

Notes

Introduction

1. Douglas Schoen, "Polling the Occupy Wall Street Crowd," *Wall Street Journal*, October 18, 2011, http://online.wsj.com/article/SB10001424052970447950457 6637082965745362.html.

Chapter One: Portrait of a Nation

1. Giving USA Foundation, Giving Report 2009 (Center on Philanthropy at Indiana University, June 9, 2010), http://www.givingusa.org/press_releases /gusa/gusa060910.pdf (accessed May 2, 2011).
2. Alexis de Tocqueville, *Democracy in America*, ed. J. P. Mayer, trans. George Lawrence (New York: Harper Perennial, 1988), 513.
3. Ibid., 554.
4. Ibid.
5. William Ewart Gladstone, "Kin Beyond Sea," *The North American Review*, September–October 1878, 185.
6. Russell Kirk, *The American Cause* (Wilmington, DE: ISI Books, 2002), 18–19.
7. Charles Colson with Ellen Santilli Vaughn, *Against the Night: Living in the New Dark Ages* (Ann Arbor, MI: Servant Publications, 1989), 67.
8. Kirk, *American Cause*, 19.
9. Mark Mather and Diana Lavery, "In U.S., Proportion Married at Lowest Recorded Levels," Report of the Population Reference Bureau, Sept. 2010, https://www.prb.org/Articles/2010/usmarriagedecline.aspx.
10. Centers for Disease Control and Prevention, "Births: Preliminary Data for 2008," *National Vital Statistics Report* 58, no. 16 (April 6, 2010): 13, table 7, http://www. cdc.gov/nchs/data/nvsr/nvsr58/nvsr58_16.pdf (accessed May 2, 2011).

11. Daniel Patrick Moynihan, *The Negro Family: The Case for National Action* 1, U.S. Department of Labor, Office of Policy Planning and Research, 1965, 44.

12. William J. Bennett, *The Broken Hearth: Reversing the Moral Collapse of the American Family* (New York: Doubleday, 2001), 178–79.

13. Ibid., 179–80.

14. Ibid.

15. Jon Kraushar, "We Need More 'Sullys,'" FoxNews.com, January 15, 2010, http://www.foxnews.com/opinion/2010/01/15/jon-kraushar-miracle-hudson -sully-sullenberger-usairways-hero#ixzz1PXqeYeW9 (accessed May 2, 2011).

16. Michael Phillips, interview by Dena Ross, "Beyond Fighting for the Flag," Beliefnet.com, http://www.beliefnet.com/Inspiration/2005/07/Beyond -Fighting-For-The-Flag.aspx (accessed May 2, 2011).

17. "Medal of Honor Nominee Celebrated," ABC News, May 27, 2005, http://abcnews.go.com/GMA/story?id=796298&page=1. See also: Michael M. Phillips, "In Combat, Marine Put Theory to Test, Comrades Believe," *The Wall Street Journal*, May 25, 2004.

18. *Northwest Ordinance*, art. III (1787).

19. Rush to the Citizens of Philadelphia, March 28, 1787, in *Letters of Benjamin Rush*, vol. 1, *1761–1792*, ed. L. H. Butterfield (Princeton, NJ: Princeton University Press, 1951).

20. Massachusetts Constitution of 1780, part 1, art. 2.

21. John Adams to Zabdiel Adams, June 21, 1776, in *Letters of Members of the Continental Congress*, vol. 1, *August 29, 1774, to July 4, 1776*, ed. Edmund Cody Burnett (Washington: Carnegie Institute, 1921), 501.

22. Elias Boudinot to Society of the Cincinnati, September 23, 1783, in *The Life, Public Services, Addresses and Letters of Elias Boudinot, LL. D.*, ed. Jane J. Boudinot (Cambridge, MA: Riverside Press, 1896), 365.

23. Paul Hollander, *Anti-Americanism: Rational and Irrational* (New Brunswick, NJ: Transaction Publishers, 1995). "Higher Education: Reservoir of the Adversary Culture" is a section included in Part I of this work.

24. "World population must be stabilized and to do that we must eliminate 350,000 people per day. This is so horrible to contemplate that we shouldn't even say it. But the general situation in which we are involved is lamentable." Jacques Cousteau, interview by Bahgat Elnadi and Adel Rifaat, *UNESCO Courier*, November 1991, 13.

25. Jim Nelson Black, *Freefall of the American University: How Our Colleges Are Corrupting the Minds and Morals of the Next Generation* (Nashville: Thomas Nelson, 2004), 4.

26. Wendy S. Grigg, Mary A. Lauko, and Debra M. Brockway, "The Nation's Report Card: Science 2005," U.S. Department of Education, National Center for Education Statistics, May 2006, http://nces.ed.gov/nationsreportcard/pubs /main2005/2006466.asp.

27. Dan Lips and Jena Baker McNeill, "A New Approach to Improving Science, Technology, Engineering, and Math Education," Heritage Foundation, April 15, 2009, http://www.heritage.org/Research/Reports/2009/04/A-New-Approach -to-Improving-Science-Technology-Engineering-and-Math-Education (accessed May 2, 2011).

28. "2009 Program for International Student Assessment Scores," *Wall Street Journal*, December 7, 2010, http://online.wsj.com/public/resources/documents /st_PISA1206_20101207.html (accessed May 2, 2011); Sam Dillon, "Top Test Scores from Shanghai Stun Educators," *New York Times*, December 7, 2010, http://www.nytimes.com/2010/12/07/education/07education.html ?_r=1andpagewanted=2 (accessed May 2, 2011).

29. Amanda Paulson, "'Report Card' on Science: Most U.S. Students Aren't 'Proficient,'" *Christian Science Monitor*, January 25, 2011, http://www.csmonitor.com/USA/Education/2011/0125 /Report-card-on-science-Most-US-students-aren-t-proficient.

30. Statement by U.S. Secretary of Education Arne Duncan on the release of the NAEP Science Report Card, U.S. Department of Education, January 25, 2011, http://www.ed.gov/news/press-releases/statement-us-secretary-education -arne-duncan-release-naep-science-report-card.

31. National Council on Excellence in Education, "A Nation at Risk," April 1983, http://www2.ed.gov/pubs/NatAtRisk/risk.html (accessed May 2, 2011); Dan Lips, "Still 'A Nation at Risk,'" Heritage Foundation, May 15, 2008, http://www .heritage.org/Research/Commentary/2008/05/Still-A-Nation-at-Risk (accessed May 2, 2011).

32. Charles J. Sykes, *Dumbing Down Our Kids: Why America's Children Feel Good about Themselves but Can't Read, Write, or Add* (New York: St. Martin's Press, 1995).

33. "Daily Presidential Tracking Poll," Rasmussen Reports, December 12, 2010, http://www.rasmussenreports.com/public_content/politics/obama _administration/daily_presidential_tracking_poll (see Daily Archives).

34. "Daily Presidential Tracking Poll," Rasmussen Reports, June 18, 2011, http://www.rasmussenreports.com/public_content/politics /obama_administration/daily_presidential_tracking_poll.

CHAPTER TWO: THE PROMISE OF AMERICA

1. Historical revisionists have taught our children that Columbus was motivated by greed and imperialism, but the explorer made his purposes perfectly clear in his journals. In his *Book of Prophecies*, he writes, "For more than forty years, I have sailed everywhere that people go. I prayed to the most merciful Lord about my heart's great desire, and He gave me the spirit and the intelligence for the task: seafaring, astronomy, geometry, arithmetic, skill in drafting spherical maps and placing correctly the cities, rivers, mountains, and ports. . . . It was the Lord who put into my mind (I would feel His hand upon me) to sail from here to the Indies." What motivated the great adventurer was his Christian faith. The idea of discovering new lands where the gospel could go forth was a mission placed in his mind, he says, by the Lord.

2. The Scrooby separatists left England in the same year that the first colony of the London Company was established at Jamestown under the leadership of Captain Christopher Newport, Captain John Smith, and the Reverend Robert Hunt. The Jamestown settlement suffered many losses but eventually became the first successful colony in Virginia.

3. King James I, Hampton Court Conference, January 16, 1604.

4. William Bradford, *Of Plymouth Plantation (1620–1647)*, ed. Charles Deane (Boston: Little, Brown, and Co., 1856), 78.

5. Ibid., 78.

6. Edwin Gaustad and Leigh Schmidt, *The Religious History of America: The Heart of the American Story from Colonial Times to Today* (New York: HarperOne, 2002), 52.

7. Rod Gragg, *Forged in Faith: How Faith Shaped the Birth of the Nation 1607–1776* (New York: Howard Books, 2010), 45–46.

8. John Winthrop, quoted in Gaustad and Schmidt, *Religious History of America*, 53.

9. John Winthrop, "A Modell of Christian Charity, written on board the Arbella, on the Atlantic Ocean, by the Hon. John Winthrop, Esq., in his passage from the Island of Great Brittaine to New-England in the North America, Anno 1630," in *Life and Letters of John Winthrop, Governor of Massachusetts*, ed. Robert C. Winthrop (Boston: Little, Brown, and Co., 1869), 2:18.

10. Winthrop in Gaustad and Schmidt, *Religious History of America*, 53.

11. Gaustad and Schmidt, *Religious History of America*, 54.

12. Ibid.

13. Daniel J. Boorstin, "The Puritan Tradition: Community Above Ideology," in Grady McWhiney and Robert Wiebe, *Historical Vistas: Readings in United States History*, vol. 1, *1607–1877* (Boston: Allyn and Bacon, 1963), 107.

14. William Perkins, "The Art of Prophesying," in Boorstin, "Puritan Tradition," 108.

15. Boorstin, "Puritan Tradition," 108 (emphasis added).

16. Ibid., 109.

17. Ibid.

18. New England Colonies, 1620–1636, in Robert Hall, Harriet Smither, and Clarence Ousley, *A History of the United States* (Dallas, TX: The Southern Publishing Company, 1920). Downloaded from *Maps ETC*, http://etc.usf.edu /maps (map #05273).

19. "Salem Church Covenant," quoted in Gaustad and Schmidt, *Religious History of America*, 54.

20. "Massachusetts Body of Liberties," quoted in Gragg, *Forged in Faith*, 56–57.

21. Boorstin, "Puritan Tradition," 109.

22. John Cotton, "Limitation of Government," in *The American Puritans, Their Poetry and Prose*, ed. Perry Miller (New York: Columbia University Press, 1956), 85.

23. Josiah H. Benton, Jr., *Early Census Making in Massachusetts, 1643–1765* (Boston: C. E. Goodspeed, 1905), 102.

24. The Glorious Revolution (1688–89) led to the overthrow of James II (who is believed to have converted to Catholicism in 1668) by Parliamentarian forces (who remained Protestant) and the ascension of the Protestant monarchs William of Orange (a Dutch Protestant) and Mary, his English Protestant queen. The restoration of the throne from Catholic to Protestant monarchs would have a major impact on the form and structure of British government ever after.

25. Daniel Webster, "A Discourse Delivered at Plymouth, on the 22d of December, 1820," in *Great Speeches of Daniel Webster* (Coln St. Aldwyns, UK: Echo Library, 2006), 38.

26. Samuel Eliot Morison, "The Pilgrim Fathers: Their Significance in History," in *By Land and by Sea: Essays and Addresses by Samuel Eliot Morison* (New York: Knopf, 1953), 235–36.

27. Noam Chomsky, interview by David Niose, "Noam Chomsky: On Humanism, the Vulnerability of Secular Nationalism, and the Mother of All Book Plugs," *The Humanist*, January 1, 2007, http://www.thefreelibrary.com/Noam+Chomsky%3a+on+humanism%2c+the+vulnerability+of +secular+nationalism%2c . . . -a0159178785 (accessed May 3, 2011).

28. Barack Obama, press conference with President Gul, Cankaya Palace, Ankara, Turkey, April 6, 2009, http://www.whitehouse.gov/the_press_office/Joint -Press-Availability-With-President-Obama-And-President-Gul-Of-Turkey (accessed May 3, 2011).

29. Gary Langer, "Poll: Most Americans Say They're Christian," ABC News, July 18, 2006, http://abcnews.go.com/US/Story?id=90356andpage=1 (accessed May 3, 2011).

30. Frank Newport, "Church Attendance Lowest in New England, Highest in South," Gallup News Service, April 27, 2006, http://www.gallup.com /poll/22579/Church-Attendance-Lowest-New-England-Highest-South.aspx (accessed May 3, 2011).

31. James Madison to the General Assembly of the Commonwealth of Virginia, 1778.

32. Patrick Henry to the Virginia House of Burgesses, May 1765.

33. Supreme Court of South Carolina, 1846. *City of Charleston v. S.A. Benjamin*; 2 Strob. 520 (1846).

34. *Church of the Holy Trinity v. U.S.*; 143 U.S. 457, 458 (1892).

35. *Zorach v. Clauson*; 343 U.S. 306 (1952).

CHAPTER THREE: WHAT THE FOUNDERS BELIEVED

1. William Byrd, *The Secret Diary of William Byrd of Westover, 1709–1712*, ed. Louis B. Wright and Marion Tinling (New York: Arno Press, 1972).

2. Rod Gragg, *Forged in Faith: How Faith Shaped the Birth of the Nation 1607–1776* (New York: Howard Books, 2010), 16.

3. The plaque inscription at the site of the Robert Hunt Memorial may be seen online at Historical Marker Database, http://www.hmdb.org/marker .asp?marker=17023.

4. Frank Lambert, *The Founding Fathers and the Place of Religion in America* (Princeton: Princeton University Press, 2003), 49.

5. The settlers' benefactor and new governor was Thomas West, the third Baron de La Warr, and the man for whom the Colony of Delaware would be named, as well as the Delaware River, Delaware Bay, Delaware Indian tribe, and eventually the state of Delaware.

6. Lambert, *Founding Fathers*, 48.

7. Ibid.

8. Crandall Shifflett, "The Powhatan Indian Attack of March 22, 1622," Virtual Jamestown, 1998, http://www.virtualjamestown.org/phatmass.html (accessed May 3, 2011).

9. Ibid.

10. James H. Hutson, *Religion and the Founding of the American Republic* (Washington, DC: Library of Congress, 1998), 18.

11. Edwin Gaustad and Leigh Schmidt, *The Religious History of America: The Heart of the American Story from Colonial Times to Today* (New York: HarperOne, 2002), 41.

12. Ibid.

13. Francis Parkman, "The American Colonies in the 1750s," in Wiebe and McWhiney, *Historical Vistas* (Boston: Allyn & Bacon, 1963), 147.

14. Ibid.

15. Frank E. Smitha, "From British Colony to Independence: The American Revolution, 1701–1791," Macrohistory and World Report, http://www.fsmitha.com/h3/h32-rv.htm (accessed May 3, 2011).

16. Ibid.

17. The British statesman, philosopher, and advocate of American independence Edmund Burke first used the term *salutary neglect* in remarks before the English House of Commons on March 22, 1775, in which he said: "[T]he colonies in general owe little or nothing to any care of ours, and that they are not squeezed into this happy form by the constraints of watchful and suspicious government, but that, through a wise and salutary neglect, a generous nature has been suffered to take her own way to perfection." Cited in Edmund Burke, *The Works of the Right Hon. Edmund Burke, with a Biographical and Critical Introduction* (London: Hodsworth and Ball, 1834), 186.

18. William G. McLoughlin, *Revivals, Awakenings, and Reform: An Essay on Religion and Social Change in America, 1607–1977* (Chicago: University of Chicago Press, 1978), 51.

19. Ibid.

20. Jonathan Edwards, quoted in Douglas A. Sweeney, *Jonathan Edwards and the Ministry of the Word* (Downers Grove, IL: Intervarsity Press Academic, 2009), 111.

21. Patricia Bonomi, *Under the Cope of Heaven: Religion, Society, and Politics in Colonial America* (New York: Oxford University Press, 1986), 105.

22. Ibid.

23. Hutson, *Religion and the Founding*, 22.

24. Ibid.

25. Ibid.

26. The journal of the Reverend Charles Woodmason, entry for Saturday, September 3, 1767: "Baptized negro man, 2 negro children, and 9 white infants and married 1 couple. The people thanked me in the most kind manner for my services. I had very pleasant riding but my horse suffered greatly. The mornings and evenings now begin to be somewhat cool, but the midday heat is almost intolerable. Many of these people walk 10 or 12 miles with their

children in the burning sun. Ought such to be without the word of God, when so earnest, so desirous of hearing it and becoming good Christians, and good subjects?!"

Charles Woodmason (1720–1776), *Journal: The Carolina Backcountry on the eve of the Revolution; the Journal and other writings of Charles Woodmason, Anglican itinerant*, ed. with an introd. by Richard J. Hooker (Chapel Hill, NC: Institute of Early American History and Culture, 1953).

27. Edwin S. Gaustad, *Historical Atlas of Religion in America* (New York: Harper and Row, 1962), 3.
28. Patricia Bonomi, *Under the Cope of Heaven*, 274.
29. Hutson, *Religion and the Founding*, 25.

CHAPTER FOUR: THE BIRTH OF THE AMERICAN SPIRIT

1. "Estimated Population of American Colonies, 1630–1780," *World Almanac and Book of Facts*, ed. Robert Famighetti (New York: St. Martin's, 1998), 378, http://merrill.olm.net/mdocs/pop/colonies/colonies.htm (accessed May 3, 2011).
2. Indentured servants, also referred to as "bound boys" or "bound girls," were generally British subjects under the age of twenty-one who were obligated to work for planters, farmers, merchants, or other affluent families for a specific period of time, usually three to seven years. They received no salary, but food, clothing, and lodging were normally provided. Redemptioners, who were mostly Germans, were given free passage to America under similar circumstances.
3. Alan Taylor, *American Colonies*, Penguin History of the United States, ed. Eric Foner (New York: Viking Penguin, 2001), 319.
4. John A. Garraty and Peter Gay, ed. *The Columbia History of the World* (New York: Harper and Row, 1972), 672–73.
5. Thomas Paine, *Common Sense (Addressed to the Inhabitants of America), and Other Political Writings* (New York: Bobbs-Merrill, 1953), 21.
6. Ibid., 19.
7. Ibid., 32.
8. Ellis Sandoz, from the foreword to Alan Heimert and Perry Miller, eds., *The Great Awakening: Documents Illustrating the Crisis and Its Consequences* (Indianapolis: Bobbs-Merrill, 1967), xiv.
9. Jonathan Edwards, "Sinners in the Hands of an Angry God," Life-Changing Pamphlet Series (Murfreesboro, TN: Sword of the Lord, 1741), 13.
10. Ibid., 19.
11. Jonathan Edwards, *Some Thoughts Concerning the Present Revival of Religion*, in *The Works of President Edwards* (London: James Black and Son, 1817), 6:87.
12. Edwards, "Sinners," 21.
13. Arnold A. Dallimore, *George Whitefield: God's Anointed Servant in the Great Revival of the Eighteenth Century* (Westchester, IL: Crossway, 2010), 83–86.
14. George Whitefield, quoted in Dallimore, *George Whitefield*, 91.
15. Benjamin Franklin, *Autobiography of Benjamin Franklin*, ed. John Bigelow (Philadelphia: J. B. Lippincot, 1869), 251.

16. Ibid., 253.

17. Ibid., 255.

18. From the journal of New England farmer Nathan Cole, in George Leon Walker, *Some Aspects of the Religious Life of New England* (New York: Silver, Burnett, and Company, 1897), 89–92.

19. James Downey, *The Eighteenth-Century Pulpit: A Study of the Sermons of Butler, Berkeley, Secker, Sterne, Whitefield and Wesley* (London: Oxford, 1969), 157.

20. Ellis Sandoz, ed., *Political Sermons of the American Founding Era: 1730–1805* (Indianapolis: Liberty Fund, 1998), 1:18.

21. Daniel J. Boorstin, "The Puritan Tradition: Community Above Ideology," in Grady McWhiney and Robert Wiebe, *Historical Vistas: Readings in United States History*, vol. 1, *1607–1877* (Boston: Allyn and Bacon, 1963), 108.

22. Perry Miller and Alan Heimert, ed., *The Great Awakening: Documents Illustrating the Crisis and Its Consequences* (Indianapolis: Bobbs-Merrill, 1967), 9.

23. Samuel Adams, from the essay "Loyalty and Sedition," published in *The Advertiser*, 1748.

24. McLoughlin, *Revivals, Awakenings, and Reform*, 96–97.

25. Thomas S. Kidd, *The Great Awakening: The Roots of Evangelical Christianity in Colonial America* (New Haven: Yale University Press, 2007), 323.

26. Frank Lambert, *Inventing the Great Awakening* (Princeton: Princeton University Press, 1999), 118.

27. John Adams to Dr. J. Morse, December 2, 1815, in *The Works of John Adams, Second President of the United States*, ed. Charles Francis Adams (Boston: Little, Brown, and Co, 1856), 10:185.

28. Ibid.

29. McLoughlin, *Revivals, Awakenings, and Reform*, 21.

30. Kidd, *The Great Awakening*, 289.

31. H. R. Niebuhr, *The Kingdom of God in America* (Middletown, CT: Wesleyan University Press, 1988), 126.

32. Benjamin Franklin, in *Farrand's Records of the Federal Convention of 1787*, ed. Max Farrand (Washington, DC, 1911): 1:451.

33. Ibid., 452.

34. Barbara W. Tuchman, *The March of Folly* (New York: Alfred A. Knopf, 1984), 381.

35. Federalist 51, http://www.constitution.org/fed/federa51.htm (accessed May 3, 2011).

36. George Washington, "Farewell Address," in *Independent Chronicle*, September 26, 1796, http://avalon.law.yale.edu/18th_century/washing.asp (accessed May 3, 2011).

37. Matthew Spalding, *We Still Hold These Truths* (Wilmington, DE: ISI Books, 2010), 221.

CHAPTER FIVE: FAITH IN THE TWENTY-FIRST CENTURY

1. Michael Lind, "America Is Not a Christian Nation," Salon.com, April 14, 2009, http://www.salon.com/news/opinion/feature/2009/04/14/christian_nation (accessed May 3, 2011).

2. Claire Berlinski, *Menace in Europe: Why the Continent's Crisis Is America's Too* (New York: Crown Forum, 2006), 8–9.

3. Don Feder, "Bill Maher: The Village Atheist Meets the Village Idiot," Coldsteel Caucus Report, http://www.donfeder.com/articles/0604maher.pdf (accessed May 3, 2011).

4. Russell Kirk, *The American Cause* (Wilmington, DE: ISI Books, 2002), 18.

5. Don Feder, "Atheists Write, Believers Yawn," Coldsteel Caucus Report, http://www.donfeder.com/articles/0703atheistBooks.pdf (accessed May 3, 2011).

6. John Jay to John Murray, October 12, 1816, in *The Life of John Jay: with Selections from His Correspondence and Miscellaneous Papers*, ed. William Jay, (Freeport, NY: Books for Libraries, 1972), 2:376.

7. R. J. Rummel, "How Many Did Communist Regimes Murder?" *Death by Government* (New Brunswick, NJ: Transaction Publishers, 1994), 4, table 2.1.

8. John Adams, letter to Zabdiel Adams, June 21, 1776.

9. Alan Heimert, *Religion and the American Mind: From the Great Awakening to the Revolution* (Eugene, OR: Wipf and Stock, 2006), 9.

10. Ibid.

11. Ibid.

12. John Cleaveland, in Thomas S. Kidd, *The Great Awakening: The Roots of Evangelical Christianity in Colonial America* (New Haven: Yale University Press, 2007), 294.

13. Ibid.

14. James H. Hutson, *Religion and the Founding of the American Republic* (Washington, DC: Library of Congress, 1998), 46.

15. Rod Gragg, *Forged in Faith: How Faith Shaped the Birth of the Nation 1607–1776* (New York: Howard Books, 2010), 173.

16. Declaration of Congress for a national day of prayer and fasting, March 16, 1776, from the Journals of the American Congress, 1774 to 1788 (Washington: Way and Gideon, 1823), vol. 1, 286–87.

17. Engrossing is the process of copying a document in a large and clearly legible hand.

18. Gragg, *Forged in Faith*, 175.

19. Ibid., 182.

20. Adams to Mercy Otis Warren, April 16, 1776, in *Warren-Adams Letters*, vol. 1, *1743–1777* (Boston: Massachusetts Historical Society, 1917), 221.

21. Franklin D. Roosevelt, radio address, June 6, 1944, *Congressional Record* 153 (June 6, 2007): S 14867.

CHAPTER SIX: THE COMING REVOLUTION

1. Malachi Martin, *The Keys of This Blood: The Struggle for World Dominion* (New York: Simon and Schuster, 1990), 209.

2. Dimitry V. Pospielovsky, *A History of Soviet Atheism in Theory, and Practice, and the Believer* (New York: St. Martin's Press, 1987), 1:34.

3. V. I. Lenin, "Program of the Communist International," in William Henry Chamberlin, ed., *Blueprint for World Conquest: The Official Communist Plan* (Washington, DC: Human Events, 1946), 187.

4. Ibid., 189.

5. Edvard Radzinsky, *The Last Tsar* (New York: Doubleday, 1992), 344–46; Mark Weber, "Assessing the Grim Legacy of Soviet Communism," Institute for Historical Review, http://www.ihr.org/jhr/v14/v14n1p-4_Weber.html (accessed May 3, 2011).

6. Richard N. Ostling, "Cross Meets Kremlin," *Time*, June 24, 2001, http://www.time.com/time/magazine/article/0,9171,150718,00.html (accessed May 3, 2011).

7. "Freedom in Decline Worldwide: U.S. Report," Freedom House, January 13, 2011, http://www.breitbart.com/article.php?id=CNG.b7ab9f89dccc945f6545ca445a6fac5a.4a1andshow_article=1 (accessed May 3, 2011).

8. For chilling evidence of the horrors of communism, visit the Victims of Communism Memorial Foundation at http://www.globalmuseumoncommunism.org.

9. James Burnham, *The Suicide of the West: An Essay on the Meaning and Destiny of Liberalism* (Washington, DC: Regnery Gateway, 1985), 59–60.

10. Mark Levin, *Liberty and Tyranny: A Conservative Manifesto* (New York: Simon and Schuster, 2009), 4.

11. Hubert H. Humphrey, "Six Liberals Define Liberalism," *New York Times Magazine*, April 19, 1959, 13.

12. Aleksandr Solzhenitsyn believed that Russian society fell victim to communism because, thanks to the atheist creed of Marxist-Leninism, it fell under the grip of atheistic totalitarianism. He recognized the truth in the words of an old peasant he overheard years earlier. "Men have forgotten God," the old man said. "That's why all this has happened to us." Of course, he was right, and that ought to be fair warning for America.

13. For more information, see Robert Kulak, "Abortions: Safe, Legal and Not So Rare," *Hartford Independent Examiner*, February 13, 2011, http://www.examiner.com/independent-in-hartford/is-abortion-as-rare-as-it-should-be-democrats-collectivist-or-indivualist#ixzz1RXOyKhEc.

14. James Capretta, "Obama's Plainly Unserious Budget," *National Review*, February 17, 2011, http://www.nationalreview.com/articles/259947/even-president-seems-oppose-his-budget-james-c-capretta (accessed May 3, 2011).

15. M. Coleman, et al., "Cancer Survival in Five Continents: A Worldwide Population-Based Study (CONCORD)," *The Lancet Oncology*, vol. 9, no. 8. (August 2008), 730–56.

16. Sally Pipes, "The Myth of Efficient Government Health Care," in *The Top Ten Myths of American Health Care: A Citizen's Guide* (San Francisco: Pacific Research Institute, 2008).

17. Ibid.

18. Ibid.

19. David Limbaugh, "Obama Can't Afford to Tell Truth on Health Care," *Human Events*, August 4, 2009, http://www.humanevents.com/article.php?id=32995. See also N. Gregory Mankiw, "Beyond Those Health Care Numbers," *New York Times*, Nov 4, 2007, http://www.nytimes.com/2007/11/04/business/04view.html?ex=1351828800&en=7ebf86b6773f35bd&ei=5090.

20. Michael Medved, "The Spending Sickness Makes for Unhealthy Reform," Creator's Syndicate, August 26, 2009.

21. Levin, *Liberty and Tyranny*, 113.

22. Tom Bethell, "Culture versus Economy," *American Spectator*, February 2011, http://spectator.org/archives/2011/02/22/culture-versus-economy (accessed May 3, 2011).

23. Joseph Story, *Commentaries on the Conflict of Laws* (Cambridge, MA: Charles Folsom, 1834), 100.

24. U.S. Census Bureau, "Annual Social and Economic Supplement, 2007," Current Population Survey, http://pubdb3.census.gov/macro/032008/pov/toc.htm (accessed May 3, 2011).

25. Jennifer Roback Morse, "The Limited-Government Case for Marriage," *Indivisible: Social and Economic Foundations of American Liberty* (Washington, DC: Heritage Foundation, 2009), 32–33.

26. Ibid.

27. Bob Unruh, "Lesbian Awarded Custody of Christian's Only Child," WorldNetDaily.com, December 5, 2009, http://www.wnd.com/?pageId=117969 #ixzz1EvhDuOZl (accessed May 3, 2011).

28. William J. Bennett, "A Nation Worth Defending," *USA Today Magazine*, Nov 1, 2002, also available at FindArticles.com, http://findarticles.com/p/articles /mi_m1272/is_2690_131/ai_94384312.

29. Paul Weyrich, "Western Civilization at Stake," Newsmax.com, March 24, 2006, http://archive.newsmax.com/archives/articles/2004/3/24/93948.shtml (accessed May 3, 2011).

30. Ibid.

31. Jim Nelson Black, *Freefall of the American University*, (Nashville: WND/ Nelson Current, 2004), 137–38.

32. Mona Charen, "Don't Know Much About History," Jewish World Review, July 15, 2003, http://jewishworldreview.com/cols/charen.html (accessed May 3, 2011).

33. "Losing America's Memory: Historical Illiteracy in the 21st Century," American Council of Trustees and Alumni, February 21, 2000, https://www .goacta.org/publications/downloads/LosingAmerica%27sMemory.pdf (accessed May 3, 2011).

34. Doug Bandow, "Religious Liberty Lost Worldwide," *American Spectator*, December 7, 2010, http://spectator.org/archives/2010/12/07/religious-liberty -lost-worldwi (accessed May 3, 2011).

CHAPTER SEVEN: WHAT YOU CAN DO

1. Samuel Adams, "The Rights of the Colonists: The Report of the Committee of Correspondence to the Boston Town Meeting, November 20, 1772," in *Old South Leaflets* no. 173 (Boston: Directors of the Old South Work, 1906), 7:417–428.

2. Thomas Jefferson to Richard Henry Lee, May 8, 1825, in *Thomas Jefferson's Writings* (New York: The Library of America, 1984), 1501.

3. Adams, "Rights of the Colonists," 7:417–428.

4. Glenn Beck, "Do You Recognize America?" *Glenn Beck Show*, December 3, 2009, http://www.glennbeck.com/content/articles/article/198/33794/ (accessed May 3, 2011).

5. Thomas Sowell, "Dismantling America," *National Review*, August 17, 2010, http://www.nationalreview.com/articles/243918/dismantling-america-thomas-sowell (accessed May 3, 2011).

6. Elizabeth Mendes, "U.S. Satisfaction Remains Near 12-Month Low," Gallup Poll, January 14, 2011, http://www.gallup.com/poll/145610/Satisfaction-Remains-Near-Month-Low.aspx (accessed May 3, 2011).

7. "Right Direction or Wrong Track," Rasmussen Reports, February 23, 2011, http://www.rasmussenreports.com/public_content/politics/mood_of_america/right_direction_or_wrong_track (accessed May 3, 2011).

8. "Voter Concern about Economy Hits Highest Level in Over Two Years," Rasmussen Reports, January 4, 2011, http://www.rasmussenreports.com/public_content/politics/mood_of_america/importance_of_issues (accessed May 3, 2011).

9. Raghavan Mayur, "Gov't That Governs the Least Is One Americans Want Most," *Investors Business Daily*, February 28, 2011, http://www.investors.com/NewsAndAnalysis/Article/564494/201102281859/Govt-that-Governs-the-Least-Is-One-Americans-Want-Most.htm (accessed May 3, 2011).

10. Ronald Reagan, "Farewell Address," January 11, 1989, http://www.americanrhetoric.com/speeches/ronaldreaganfarewelladdress.html (accessed May 3, 2011).

11. Ibid.

12. Jonathan Mayhew, "A Discourse Concerning Unlimited Submission and Non-Resistance to the Higher Power," delivered at Old West Church, Boston, Massachusetts, January 30, 1750. (Subsequently printed as a pamphlet and distributed throughout New England.)

13. Ibid.

14. Michael Novak, "God Bless the Tea Party," *National Review Online*, November 8, 2010, http://www.nationalreview.com/articles/252720/God-bless-tea-party-michael-novak (accessed May 4, 2010).

15. James Ceaser, "The 2010 Verdict," RealClearPolitics.com, November 10, 2010, http://www.realclearpolitics.com/articles/2010/11/10/the_2010_verdict_107908.html (accessed May 4, 2010).

16. Ibid, emphasis added.

17. Novak, "God Bless the Tea Party."

18. Ibid.

19. James McHenry in *The American Historical Review*, ed. George B. Adams (New York: Macmillan, 1906), 11:618; James McHenry in *Farrand's Records of the Federal Convention of 1787*, ed. Max Farrand (Washington, DC, 1911), 3:85.

20. John Adams to H. Niles, February 13, 1818, in *Works of John Adams*, 10:282.

TOPICAL INDEX

ABOUT THE AUTHOR

D R. RICHARD LEE is the founding pastor of First Redeemer Church in metropolitan Atlanta. He is also the speaker for the award-winning *There's Hope America* television series and is widely recognized as a popular spokesman on the influence of America's religious history and its impact upon today's culture.

Dr. Lee is a frequent speaker at national conventions and on university campuses and media outlets across the country, including FOX News, Fox Business News, CBS News, BBC, and CNN. His articles have appeared in publications such as *USA Today, London Times, L.A. Times, Essence*, and *Newsweek*.

He is the author of eighteen popular books; his more recent work, *The American Patriot's Bible*, reached the number five spot on Amazon .com's bestseller list.

Dr. Lee was educated at Mercer University and Luther Rice Seminary with postdoctoral studies at Oxford University. He also serves as a member of the prestigious Oxford Round Table, Oxford, England.